MOTIVATION AND LEARNING STRATEGIES FOR COLLEGE SUCCESS

A Self-Management Approach

MOTIVATION AND LEARNING STRATEGIES FOR COLLEGE SUCCESS

A Self-Management Approach

Myron H. Dembo
University of Southern California

LEA
LAWRENCE ERLBAUM ASSOCIATES, PUBLISHERS
2004   Mahwah, New Jersey   London

Senior Acquisitions Editor:	Naomi Silverman
Assistant Editor:	Erica Kica
Cover Design:	Kathryn Houghtaling Lacey
Textbook Production Manager:	Paul Smolenski
Full-Service Compositor:	TechBooks
Text and Cover Printer:	Hamilton Printing Company

Lawrence Erlbaum Associates, Inc., Publishers
10 Industrial Avenue
Mahwah, New Jersey 07430-2262
www.erlbaum.com

Library of Congress Cataloging-in-Publication Data

Dembo, Myron H.
    Motivation and learning strategies for college success: a
self-management approach / Myron H. Dembo.
        p. com.
    Includes bibliographical references.
    ISBN 0-8058-4648-4 (pbk. : alk. paper)
  1. College student orientation. 2. Achievement motivation.
  3. Learning strategies. I. Title.
LB2343.3.D46 2004
378.1'98—dc22   2004000639

Books published by Lawrence Erlbaum Associates are printed
on acid-free paper, and their bindings are chosen for strength
and durability.

Printed in the United States of America
10 9 8 7 6 5 4 3

To Nancy, Debbie, and Lisa

Brief Contents

Figure and Table Credits

Figure 1.1. Zimmerman, B. J., Bonner, S., & Kovich, R. (1996). *Developing self-regulated learners: Beyond achievement to self-efficacy*. Washington, DC: American Psychological Association. Copyright © 1996 by the American Psychological Association. Adapted with permission.

Figure 2.2. From Bower, G. H., Clark, M. C., Lesgold, A., & Winzenz, D. (1969). Hierarchical retrieval schemas in recall of categorized word lists. *Journal of Memory and Language (Journal of Verbal Learning and Verbal Behavior)*, 8, 323–343. Reprinted with permission from Elsevier.

Table 3.1. Ames, C., & Archer, J. (1988). Achievement goals in the classroom: Students' learning strategies and motivation processes. *Journal of Educational Psychology*, 80, 260–267. Copyright © 1988 by the American Psychological Association. Adapted with permission.

Figure 4.1. From *The 10 natural laws of successful time and life management* by Hyrum Smith. Copyright © 1994 by Hyrum Smith. By permission of Warner Books Inc., New York.

Table 8.1. From Kiewra, K. A., & Dubois, N. F. (1998). *Learning to learn*. Boston: Allyn & Bacon. Adapted with permission.

Table 10.1. From *College study skills: Becoming a strategic learner* (1st ed.), by D. Van Blerkom. Copyright © 1994. Reprinted with permission of Wadsworth, a division of Thomson Learning: www.thomsonrights.com, Fax 800 730–2215.

Contents

Preface

Many textbooks are available on how to become a more successful learner. As an instructor of a "learning to learn" course, I have been concerned that many students who take such a course to improve their learning and study skills fail to change their behavior during or after the course. I strongly believe that simply telling students how to learn and providing some practice does not necessarily change attitudes, beliefs, or behavior. Changing ineffective learning and study habits is a difficult process, as is losing weight or stopping smoking.

This textbook is the result of an instructional program I developed and evaluated with a wide range of college students identified "at risk" to those entering college with a B or higher grade-point average. I have used the approach presented in this text with students in high schools, community colleges, and 4-year colleges.

The primary purpose of the textbook is to help students change aspects of their motivation and learning strategies. I place the responsibility for determining what behaviors or beliefs need to be changed on them, not the instructor. The process of change begins by observing and reflecting on one's own behavior and then determining what needs to be changed and learning how to change. The features of this textbook are designed to identify the components of academic learning that contribute to high achievement, help students learn and practice effective learning and study strategies, and then complete self-management studies whereby they are taught a process for improving their academic behavior.

FEATURES OF THE TEXT

I attempt to accomplish my goals by incorporating the following features in the text.

First, I identify six components that students need to control to become successful learners—motivation, methods of learning, time management, physical and social environment, and performance. These components serve as the basis for organizing and integrating the content throughout the text. Further, this focus allows for the integration of both motivation and learning strategies. As students learn new learning strategies, they must develop the motivation to use them.

Second, the text begins with an overview of important research and theory to help students understand the reasons why they are asked to use different study and learning strategies in the text. Most study skill textbooks are atheoretical; that is, little, if any, research or theory is presented to students. I believe that learning how to learn is a specific academic specialization based on scientific knowledge, and students should learn this knowledge. Further, I find that students are more motivated to learn when the course is conducted like a "real" academic course and not as a remedial experience.

Third, various Exercises are included in each chapter to help students observe and evaluate their own learning and study skills. In addition, more detailed follow-up activities at the end of each chapter allow students to apply the content to their own academic learning. The primary purpose of these experiences is to encourage self-observation and evaluation.

Fourth, beginning with chapter 5, the first Follow-Up Activity identifies a topic to include in a self-management study. The appendixes provide information as to how to conduct a self-management study (Appendix A) and include three studies conducted by students (Appendix B) in a "learning to learn" course. Note the instructor's evaluation at the end of each self-management study. The appendixes should be read before students begin their own study.

Fifth, the Student Reflections sections allow students to read about the experiences of other students as they attempt to change their behavior and become more successful students.

Sixth, at the end of each chapter, a review of the specific procedures for using a learning strategy is provided. This section is particularly useful for students when they need a quick review of how to implement a given strategy.

Seventh, the Key Points at the end of each chapter highlight the important ideas presented in each chapter.

Eighth, a glossary is included, with important terms in bold in the text.

OVERVIEW OF THE CHAPTERS

Unit I of the text includes three chapters. Chapter 1—"Academic Self-Management"—identifies the academic components that students need to control to attain their academic goals. In addition, the chapter introduces a four-step process used to change behavior—self-observation and evaluation, goal setting and strategic planning, strategy implementation and monitoring, and strategic-outcome monitoring. This process is used as the basis for conducting a self-management study and is explained in depth in Appendix A. Chapter 2—"Understanding Learning and Memory"—introduces the information processing system and explains why students remember and forget information. This chapter emphasizes that the way students learn often determines what they remember. Chapter 3—"Understanding Motivation"—helps students understand how motivation can influence learning behavior. Important exercises are included to help the reader evaluate his or her own motivation.

Unit II of the text focuses on motivational strategies. Chapter 4—"Goal Setting"—instructs students how to write and implement specific goals. This chapter emphasizes that students cannot be motivated unless they have goals to attain in different areas of their life. Chapter 5—"Management of Emotion and Effort"—focuses on how to change negative emotions to more positive emotions, as well as managing self-talk and reducing anxiety.

Unit III of the text deals with various behavioral strategies related to academic success. Chapter 6—"Time Management—"explains how students can better manage their time rather than having time manage them. Chapter 7—"Management of Physical and Social Environment"—focuses on improving attention and concentration and structuring productive study environments. In addition, the chapter provides information on how to seek help from instructors and conduct effective group study sessions.

Unit IV of the text introduces important learning and study strategies: "Learning From Textbooks" (chapter 8), "Learning From Lectures" (chapter 9), "Preparing for Exams" (chapter 10), and "Taking Exams" (chapter 11). Excerpts are used from textbooks and lectures to help students practice the skills in chapters 8 and 9. Chapter 10 helps students develop a study plan for each exam, and chapter 11 provides information about specific strategies for taking objective and essay tests.

WHAT'S NEW IN THE SECOND EDITION?

- Discussion of flaws in human memory (chapter 2)
- Extended coverage of the factors that influence motivation and test anxiety, and discussion of why students have difficulty changing their academic behaviors (chapter 3)
- Discussion of identity development (chapter 4)
- Extended coverage of emotions and how to change them (chapter 5)
- Extended discussion of procrastination elimination strategies (chapter 6)
- Extended discussion of improving communication skills in the classroom (chapter 7)
- Added additional follow-up activities

An instructor's manual is available with the text. The manual provides helpful information for teaching the material and includes additional exercises and experiences for students. It also provides both objective and essay test questions. Finally, it includes information on how students can maintain a portfolio to demonstrate their acquisition of learning and study skills and guidelines for helping students complete a self-management study of their own academic behavior.

It is suggested that Unit I of the text be covered first to provide a framework for both the content and exercises in the remaining chapters. The remaining chapters can be covered in any order. One of the difficulties in teaching a "learning to learn" course is that one would like to cover many topics during the first 2 weeks, because everything is important. Unfortunately, all the chapters and topics cannot be taught in the first few weeks. This textbook allows the instructor to sequence the chapters as he or she sees fit.

Finally, I would appreciate reactions from students and instructors concerning the text. Please e-mail me at dembo@usc.edu. I welcome your praise and criticism.

ACKNOWLEDGMENTS

I would like to acknowledge a number of individuals who played an important role in the development of this textbook: Alonzo Anderson, who encouraged me to work in the area of learning strategies; Claire Ellen Weinstein and the late Paul Pintrich, who provided helpful insights as to how to teach learning strategies; Bill Webber at Lawrence Erlbaum Associates, who encouraged me to write a book in the area; Barry Zimmerman, whose work on self-regulation provided a framework for organizing the content in the book; Richard Clark, who offered many suggestions concerning the design of the text; Amy Gimino who wrote Appendix A, read drafts of the manuscript, and provided feedback on the effectiveness of the material as a teaching assistant in my course.

I also would like to thank the following reviewers who provided helpful feedback on the manuscript: Julia Beteler, the University of Akron–Wayne; Russ Hodges, Southwest Texas State University; Peggy Pritchard Kulesz, University of Texas–Arlington; Arnaldo Mejias, Jr., State University of New York–New Paltz.

Finally, I would like to acknowledge all my students, especially Kyle Williams, and my teaching assistants, who contributed a great deal regarding how to teach students to become more successful learners; and editor Naomi Silverman, who provided helpful assistance throughout the project; and Joanne Bowser, who was the project manager for the textbook.

—Myron H. Dembo

FOUNDATIONS OF LEARNING AND MOTIVATION

The purpose of this unit is to explain how you can become a more successful learner by taking charge and managing your own learning. To accomplish this goal, you need to understand how you learn and the factors that determine your motivation to learn. Learning and motivation are interrelated processes. Simply learning a new skill does not mean that you will use it unless you are motivated to do so. Therefore, my objectives are to teach you some new learning strategies and to convince you that there are payoffs for using them. These payoffs include the possibility of higher grades, more time to participate in enjoyable activities, and the confidence to become a successful learner in any course. The three chapters in this unit provide a framework for understanding why you need to use different strategies to manage the factors influencing your academic achievement. The remaining units teach you how and when to use these strategies.

Chapter 1 presents a model for academic self-management, identifying six components that you can control—motivation, methods of learning, use of time, physical and social environment, and performance (Zimmerman & Risemberg, 1997). These components are organized by categories—motivational, behavioral, and learning and study strategies. Finally, a four-step process is described to help you change aspects of your academic behavior.

Chapters 2 and 3 provide an overview of learning and motivation from a cognitive perspective. Cognitive psychologists believe that behavior is always based on cognition—an act of knowing or thinking about the situation in which the behavior occurs. As a result, they believe that learning can be explained by how knowledge is processed and organized. This means that the way one learns is an important factor in how much is remembered.

The cognitive view of motivation focuses on how an individual's internal state (i.e., his or her goals, beliefs, perceptions, and emotions) influences behavior. The guiding principle of motivational change can be described as follows: If an individual wants to change his or her motivation, beliefs and perceptions must be changed. However, before beliefs and perceptions can be changed, they first must be identified.

1

Academic Self-Management

As readers of this book, you are a diverse group with varied backgrounds and goals. Some of you are beginning your education at a college or university, whereas others of you have selected community colleges. Some of you may have taken college courses last term, whereas others are returning to school after an absence. Some of you are taking a learning and study skills course because it is required, whereas others are enrolled in the course as an elective. Some of you are looking forward to taking the course, whereas others may doubt its usefulness. Although I recognize the wide range of interests, motivation, and abilities of those of you reading this book, I have one goal: to help all those who read this volume become more successful learners. Once you learn how to learn, you can apply these skills to any academic or work setting in which you participate.

Who is a successful learner? Most of us know, read about, or have observed successful and expert individuals in some field or profession (e.g., a plumber, musician, athlete, teacher, or artist). These individuals have special knowledge and skills in a particular field. Similarly, successful learners

3

also possess special knowledge and skills that differentiate them from less successful learners.

Successful students are not simply individuals who know more than others. They also have more effective and efficient learning strategies for accessing and using their knowledge, can motivate themselves, and can monitor and change their behaviors when learning does not occur.

Just as individuals cannot learn to become expert musicians, dancers, or golfers without practice, learning to be a successful learner requires more than simply reading and listening to class lectures. For this reason, you will be asked throughout this book to respond to questions and exercises, and to actually practice some new ways of learning. The key to success is practicing the learning strategies taught here so they become automatic. As you practice, you will be able to learn more material in less time than prior to using these new strategies. Thus, you will learn to study "smarter," not necessarily harder.

Most of you have expertise in some activity or hobby. You have spent considerable effort and persistence in acquiring knowledge and developing your skills and probably feel competent and motivated to excel. You are now beginning the process of developing the necessary expertise to meet the academic demands of college learning. Much of the same self-discipline and self-motivation you apply to your present area(s) of expertise will be needed in your pursuit of academic excellence. After studying this chapter, you will be able to:

- Identify specific behaviors that influence the level of academic success.
- Use a process to self-manage your academic behavior.

WHAT IS ACADEMIC SELF-MANAGEMENT?

At one time, it was thought that intelligence was the main factor determining academic success. After years of research in learning and motivation, educators have found that students can learn how to become more successful learners by using appropriate strategies to manage their motivation, behavior, and learning.

The word *management* is a key term in understanding successful learners. They self-manage or control the factors influencing their learning. They establish optimum conditions for learning and remove obstacles that interfere with their learning. Educators use a variety of terms to describe these students (e.g., *self-regulated, self-directed, strategic,* and *active*). No matter what term is used, the important factor is that these students find a way to learn. It does not matter if the instructor is a poor lecturer, the textbook is confusing, the test is difficult, the room is noisy, or if multiple exams are scheduled for the same week, successful learners find a way to excel.

Let's look at an example of how one student managed his academic learning:

It was Thursday night and Robert was completing his final preparation for the following day's history exam. On the previous Sunday evening, he developed a plan for how he would prepare for the exam during the week. He identified what he had to learn, how he would study, and when he would accomplish each task. He began his study on Monday, attempting to gain a general understanding of the main ideas and recall the most important facts. He paraphrased each section of the readings, underlined the important information, and monitored his own progress during study by developing possible questions that might be asked on the exam. While studying Wednesday night, he realized that he had difficulty comparing and contrasting some of the battles discussed in class. Therefore, he decided to develop a chart listing the different battles on top and different characteristics down the side. When he filled in the information on the chart, he found he was better able to answer the questions that might be asked regarding the material.

Around 10 p.m., Thursday, Robert's roommate came home from the library with some friends and began discussing a concert they planned to attend over the weekend. They were finished studying for the night. Robert decided to go to the study lounge down the hall to complete his last hour of studying. He told his friends that he would return for pizza around 11 p.m. As he returned to his study, he noticed some information in his notes that he did not understand. He made a quick telephone call to a friend for clarification about the notes.

After another 20 minutes of studying, Robert got tired and started thinking of the double cheese and mushroom pizza he would be eating in a short time. He decided that he needed about 30 minutes to finish his studying for the evening. Therefore, he decided to take a 5-minute break and go for a walk. He came back and finished his study for the evening.

What actions did Robert take to ensure optimum learning? First, he established a goal and action plan for how he was going to prepare for the examination. The plan started 4 days before the exam. Second, he used a variety of learning strategies, such as underlining, developing and answering questions, and making a chart to better compare and contrast the relevant information. In other words, when he found that he was not learning, he did something about it by changing his learning strategy. Third, he monitored his understanding of the material as he studied. He changed learning strategies and asked for help when he failed to understand his notes. Fourth, when his friends returned from the library, he decided that he would not be able to study in his room, so he left for the lounge. Finally, when he began to get tired and became less motivated to complete his studying, he took a break and was then able to return to his work. All of Robert's decisions played a major role in his ability to do well on the history exam the following day.

Given the same situation, think about how another student with less knowledge about learning and study strategies, and less self-management skills might have behaved in the same situation. The example just presented came from a student's journal. The situation occurred exactly as stated, only "the name was changed to protect the innocent." Robert did not come to college as an A student. As a matter of fact, he struggled during the first few weeks of the first term. When he began to learn how to learn and to take responsibility for his own learning, his academic performance improved dramatically.

As you develop the personal qualities to manage your learning, you will find that you can apply the same skills to situations outside the classroom, even at work. It does not matter what course, seminar, lecture, or job you experience, once you manage the factors influencing your learning, you can be more successful in any task.

One of my students came to my office to discuss the amount of work she had to do in my learning course. She tended to turn in assignments late and, in general, appeared to have difficulty managing her time and motivation. During the conversation, she stated that she only wanted a C in the course. I stated that I had no problem giving her a C, but that many students who set this standard often underestimate their achievement and earn a D. I decided to pursue the issue further by asking the student the following question: "Are you also willing to find an average job and get an average salary?" "Oh No!" she stated, "I want a rewarding career and plan on making a great deal of money!"

Many individuals fail to realize that the self-management strategies used to become more successful learners often generalize to their personal and work lives. Who is more likely to be promoted in a job: an employee who can work independently and set and attain goals, or an employee who needs constant supervision and direction in his or her daily work? Educators who emphasize the importance of self-management take the position that students can do a great deal to promote their own learning through the use of different learning and motivational strategies. In other words, these learners "view academic learning as something they do for themselves rather than as something that is done to or for them" (Zimmerman, 1998b, p. 1).

Think about Zimmerman's quote and what it means to you as someone who is attempting to become a more successful learner. What are some of the changes you think you may have to make?

I have taught thousands of undergraduates and have come to the conclusion that I cannot make students learn if they do not want to. I can help them and guide them, but I cannot make them learn. Personally, it is a joy to work with students who take an active role in their own learning. However, some students say they want to learn but do not want to do the things that are necessary to manage their own learning. How many times have you observed parents and teachers prodding or almost begging students to learn? In many cases, these students really want to be successful, but they do not fully understand their responsibilities in the learning process.

WHAT IS THE DIFFERENCE BETWEEN HIGH SCHOOL AND COLLEGE?

One of the major differences in the transition from high school to college classrooms is the change from a teacher-directed to a student-directed environment. In high school, many teachers tend to guide students' learning by telling them what, when, and how to learn. For example, when assignments are given, high school teachers frequently help students manage the tasks necessary to complete the assignment, such as requiring outlines or drafts of papers. In college, students are on their own. They can ask questions and obtain more information about an assignment, but rarely does a college instructor monitor students' progress. In college, students are expected to manage their own learning.

Another difference between high school and college is that high school teachers often spend considerable time attempting to motivate students to learn, whereas college instructors generally expect students to be self-motivated. Although students are told about the demands of college, many freshmen experience culture shock when they enter learning environments that differ from their past experiences. The following are comments written in a journal by a student in her first term in college:

> My professor was completing his last lecture on the first unit of the course and asked if we had any questions. We had to read chapters in three different textbooks, and I had about 40 pages of notes. I simply asked: "Could you tell us what are some of the important ideas you might cover on the exam?" He looked at me and said: "That's for you to

determine!" Well, I felt like crawling under my desk. In high school, most of my teachers would summarize the key ideas that would direct our studying behavior. Here, I quickly learned that I have to do this work on my own!

This student had some difficulty in her first college term. She realized that she had to change some of her learning and study strategies. When she learned how to identify the main ideas in lectures and textbooks, she had little trouble predicting most of the test questions in her courses. Her ability to modify and manage her methods of learning were important factors in her improvement toward the end of the term.

WHY ARE SOME STUDENTS LESS SUCCESSFUL LEARNERS?

When I discuss reasons for low achievement, I am not including students who have serious learning disabilities, poor language skills, or who have experienced an inadequate education because of factors beyond their control. Instead, I am referring to students who should be achieving higher than their present performance. In many cases, more than one explanation may be appropriate for a given student.

They Hold Faulty Beliefs About Their Ability, Learning, and Motivation

Students' beliefs about learning and motivation influence their behaviors. The following beliefs can impact achievement: If students believe they are less capable than others, they may spend considerable time using failure-avoiding strategies in the classroom (e.g., trying not to be called on, copying material from friends, and appearing to be trying hard when they really are not). Other students who believe they can achieve are more likely to spend their time using effective learning and study strategies, and tend to persist longer on difficult tasks.

Some students believe that ability or intelligence is fixed. That is, people are born with a certain amount of ability, and there is not much that can be done about it. This misperception often causes some students to accept their low achievement or to become satisfied with a B or C average, thinking that only the brightest students obtain an A. Psychologists have found that intelligence is the result of how much information students know and the strategies they use to control their thinking and learning. In other words, "smart" students do not possess abilities that other students cannot learn. "Smart" students study more effectively than other students. If other students learn and use these same methods, they become "smart."

It is unfortunate that many students go through school thinking they are not good learners and that little can be done to improve their achievement. This faulty belief often remains with individuals throughout their lives and limits their goals and aspirations. The problem is not that these students are incapable of being successful learners, they simply have not been taught how to study and learn effectively.

They Are Unaware of Their Ineffective Learning Behavior

Many students believe that if they simply spend a good deal of time studying, they will be successful. Successful learners do work hard, but they realize that how they study is more important than how much time they spend studying. For example, many college students report that they spend considerable time reading a book many times before an examination. Some students are not aware that the practice of underlining (highlighting) words and phrases in textbooks and simply rereading are generally ineffective learning strategies, because they are relatively passive activities involving little thinking. It is possible to spend considerable time underlining or rereading a chapter and still not remember many of the important ideas presented. Reading and remembering are two different tasks. Unless students are actively involved in outlining, organizing, questioning themselves, and summarizing the material while they read, much of the time is wasted (Cortina, Elder, & Gonnet, 1992).

They Fail to Sustain Effective Learning and Motivational Strategies

Students usually take more exams and quizzes in high school. Therefore, if they score well on most of the evaluations but low on one or two, they can still maintain a high grade. In college, the situation is different. Fewer evaluations are given throughout the term. For example, a course may require a paper, two exams, and a final; each evaluation may involve 20% to 30% of the final grade. Students who want high grades cannot afford to let down during the semester.

Many students demonstrate the knowledge of how to learn and do well at times, but fail to attend class regularly, do not keep up with their assignments, and, in general, get behind in their work. Although these students have the potential for doing well, they cannot sustain their motivation and effort throughout the term. The end result is lower academic performance.

They Are Not Ready to Change Their Learning and Study Behavior

Some students are not convinced they need to change. After all, they got through high school and were able to get into college. These students often raise questions, publicly or privately: "Why do I need to change?" "I graduated from high school," or "I was accepted to this college." It is not until the first midterm exams that some students realize that many of the learning and study skills used in high school are insufficient for academic success in college. The earlier students become aware of this fact, the quicker they can begin to make the necessary changes.

Although many students realize they need to improve, they tend to stick with familiar strategies, even though they are not achieving the best results. They simply are not motivated to change. Some students believe that it takes too much effort and time to learn new methods of learning. Learning to play a new song on the guitar or a new dance routine takes effort. Yet, because individuals enjoy the activity and gain special satisfaction from excelling in an area, they do not consider it work. When students use their effort and time more wisely and use more effective methods of learning, they find that the amount of effort and time does pay off in terms of higher grades, greater knowledge and confidence, and more time for fun.

HOW CAN I MANAGE MY ACADEMIC BEHAVIOR?

The following are six major components of academic self-management or self-regulation. Learning the self-management skills related to each of these components can help you exert control over your own learning and promote your own academic achievement (Zimmerman & Risemberg, 1997):

- Motivation
- Methods of learning
- Use of time
- Physical environment
- Social environment
- Performance

 Motivation

> "Each semester I write down goals that I want to attain."

> "When I feel down, I talk to myself to motivate me to keep on task."

Although there are many different ways to define motivation, the approach taken in this book views motivation as the internal processes that give behavior its energy and direction. These internal processes include your goals, beliefs, perceptions, and expectations. For example, your persistence on a task is often related to how competent you believe you are to complete the task. Also, your beliefs about the causes of your successes and failures on present tasks influence your motivation and behavior on future tasks. For example, students who attribute failure to lack of ability behave differently from students who attribute failure to lack of effort.

In chapter 3, you will learn that when you change your beliefs and perceptions, you change your motivation. During a presentation on self-motivation at a high school, a student asked me: "You mean that if you are bored, you can do something about it?" It was obvious that the student had not thought about the extent to which she had the ability to control her own motivation.

Think about the pilot of a 747 who wakes up in the morning knowing that she must fly a few hundred people from Los Angeles to New York, or the surgeon who must perform a delicate heart operation. The public is fortunate that these individuals know how to motivate themselves even when they do not feel like doing something. It would be alarming to hear a pilot say: "I don't feel like flying today," or a surgeon say: "Not another operation, I'm not in the mood."

One of the major differences between successful and less successful individuals in any field or specialization is that successful individuals know how to motivate themselves even when they do not feel like performing a task, whereas less successful individuals have difficulty controlling their motivation. As a result, less successful individuals are less likely to complete a task, or more likely to quit or complete a task at a lower level of proficiency. Although successful learners may not feel like completing required tasks, they learn how to motivate themselves to completion to maintain progress toward achieving their goals.

Another issue is whether one has a problem in motivation or persistence. A student may be motivated to engage in a task but have difficulty persisting because he or she easily becomes distracted while engaging in the task (Kuhl & Beckman, 1985).

Think about your own behavior. Identify a situation in which follow-through, not motivation, was a problem. That is to say, you really wanted to complete a task, but you had difficulty persisting because you were easily distracted. Also, think about a situation in which you were successful in controlling your behavior in a potentially distracting situation. What self-management strategies do you use to maintain your persistence in a task?

To be a successful learner in college, students must be able to concentrate and deal with the many potential personal and environmental distractions that may interfere with learning and studying. Students use many different processes to control aspects of their behaviors. The following are examples of self-management processes:

- "When I am in the library and distracted by a conversation, I move to another table."

- "When I start worrying on an exam, I immediately begin con-
  vincing myself that I can do well if I take my time."
- "When I start thinking that I don't have the ability to achieve,
  I remind myself that more effort is needed."

Dealing with distracting factors in learning is an important aspect of
self-management, because it helps protect one's commitment to learn.

A number of important motivational self-management techniques
can be used to develop and maintain these important beliefs. The first
is goal setting. Educational research indicates that high achievers
report using goal setting more frequently and more consistently than
low achievers (Zimmerman & Martinez-Pons, 1986). When individuals establish and attempt to attain personal goals, they are more
attentive to instruction, expend greater effort, and increase their confidence when they see themselves making progress. It is difficult to be
motivated to achieve without having specific goals.

A second motivational self-management technique is *self-verbalization*,
or self-talk. This procedure takes many forms. For example, verbal
reinforcement or praise can be used following desired behavior. You
simply tell yourself things like: "Great! I did it!" or "I'm doing a great
job concentrating on my readings!" Reinforce yourself either covertly
(to yourself) or aloud. At first, you may think it sounds strange or
silly to use self-verbalization. Once you get familiar with it, you will
find that it works. Don't underestimate the power of language in self-
control of motivation. World-class athletes have been trained to use
verbal reinforcement for years.

More elaborate self-talk training programs are available to help
individuals control anxiety, mood, and other emotional responses
(e.g., Butler, 1981; Ottens, 1991). These programs are based on the
belief that what one says to oneself is an important factor in determining attitudes, feelings, emotions, and behaviors. This speech or
self-talk is the running dialogue inside our heads. Some of our speech
motivates us to try new tasks and persist in difficult situations; other
self-talk is unproductive and inhibits our motivation to succeed. The
goal of these programs is to change negative self-talk to positive self-
talk. Chapter 5 describes this process in more detail.

Another motivational self-management technique is arranging or
imagining rewards or punishments for success or failure at an academic task. Students who control their motivation by giving themselves rewards and punishments outperform students who do not use
this control technique (Zimmerman & Martinez-Pons, 1986). What
self-control strategies have you used in the past to control your motivation? The following are examples reported by my students: "If I
study for 50 minutes, I'll allow myself to speak on the phone for 10
minutes"; or "If I work on my term paper for an evening, I'll treat

myself to a pizza"; or "If I find that I'm keeping up with my work, I'll go to a movie on a weeknight."

In summary, to control your motivation, you need to set goals; develop positive beliefs about your ability to perform academic tasks; and maintain these beliefs while faced with the many disturbances, distractions, occasional failure experiences, and periodic interpersonal conflicts in your life. You will have difficulty managing your behavior if you do not have confidence in your ability to succeed. In turn, you develop confidence in your ability by learning how to use different learning and study strategies that lead to academic success.

Methods of Learning

"While reading my sociology textbook, I write important questions to answer after reading each main heading."

"I use a time line to recall the dates of major battles in my history course."

Another term for methods of learning is learning strategies. Learning strategies are the methods students use to acquire information. Higher achieving students use more learning strategies than do lower achieving students (Zimmerman & Martinez-Pons, 1988). Underlining, summarizing, and outlining are examples of learning strategies. You will learn in chapter 2 that different learning strategies serve different purposes.

Think about the large array of tools a plumber brings to each job. If he arrived at jobs with only a few wrenches or pliers, he would not be able to complete many jobs. Just as there are different tools for different jobs, there are different learning strategies for different academic tasks (Levin, 1986). Successful learners also need a large number of "tools" to make schoolwork easier and to increase the probability of their success. For example, knowing how to use maps or representations to organize information and generate and answer questions from notes and textbooks are important learning tools. Many students who have difficulty learning in school attribute their problem to a lack of ability when the problem actually may be that they have never been properly taught how to learn. Some students use one or two major learning strategies for all tasks in all courses. These students often do not have the necessary tools to learn the complex material they encounter in the courses they are required to take. For example, on exams, many instructors ask questions relating to topics that they did not directly discuss in lectures. Students must be able to organize and analyze notes so they are prepared to answer questions such as: "How does the government effect the allocation of resources through tax policy?" or "Why does the temperature of the water influence the velocity of sound?"

The plumbing example can be used to provide a practical example of understanding the relation between learning and motivation. I am going to admit something: I don't have confidence in my ability to do many household chores. Therefore, I procrastinate, fail to purchase tools that could help me complete tasks, and don't pay much attention when friends try to explain how I can be a successful handyman. When my wife tells me that a water faucet is leaking and asks me to fix it, I often tell her to wait a few days—perhaps the leaking will stop! Even if I had the tools, I still might not attempt to complete the job myself.

You cannot become a successful learner merely by acquiring new learning and study skills. You also must deal with your motivation (i.e., beliefs and perceptions) regarding a task. Even if you know how to use an effective strategy, you may not be motivated to use it. Some educators (e.g., Paris, 1988) describe these two important components of learning as the *skill* (i.e., learning strategies) and *will* (i.e., the motivation to use strategies).

Use of Time

"I keep a weekly calendar of my activities."

"I start studying at least 1 week before exams."

Educators have found a relation between time management and academic achievement. Students with better time-management skills tend to have a higher grade-point average (GPA) than students with poorer time-management skills. In fact, Britton and Tesser (1991) found that time management skills measured in the freshman year were more predictive of GPAs in the senior year than were SAT scores.

Why does time management appear to be so important in determining academic success? One explanation is that use of time impacts self-management. If a student has difficulty dealing with time, he or she ends up doing what is most urgent when deciding which task to do first. If a paper is the next task that needs to be done, one works on the paper; if an exam is the next challenge, one studies for the exam. Little time is spent on any long-term planning to consider the importance of different tasks and how they can best be completed (Zimmerman, Bonner, & Kovach, 1996).

How many times have you heard individuals state: "I don't have time." The problem for most individuals is not that there is not enough time to accomplish what needs to be done, but that they do not know how to manage the amount of time that is available each day. When students analyze their use of time, they find a great deal of it is wasted.

A close friend of mine is a manager at IBM. Each year he sends members of his sales force to time-management workshops. He explained that effective use of time by his total sales force can result in hundreds of thousands of dollars in increased sales. Many of his sales staff are experts in technology, have excellent interpersonal skills, and are highly motivated to succeed. The problem is that many of them do not know how to manage their time, and this deficiency prevents them from becoming more successful.

Physical and Social Environment

*"I turn off the TV or stereo so I can concentrate on what
I am doing."*

"I go to the library to study before exams."

*"When I find that I don't understand any material, I immediately
make an appointment with my instructor."*

"I organize a study group before an examination."

Another important aspect of self-management is the ability of learners to restructure their physical and social environments to meet their needs. Zimmerman and Martinez-Pons (1986) found that high achievers reported greater use of environmental restructuring and were more likely to seek help from others than were low-achieving students. For the most part, environmental restructuring refers to locating places to study that are quiet or not distracting. Although this task may not appear difficult to attain, it poses many problems for students who either select inappropriate environments initially or cannot control the distractions once they occur.

Self-management of the social environment relates to an individual's ability to determine when he or she needs to work alone or with others, or when it is time to seek help from instructors, tutors, peers, or nonsocial resources (such as reference books). Knowing how and when to work with others is an important skill often not taught in school.

Educational research indicates that high-achieving students are more likely than low-achieving students to seek help from instructors, just the opposite of what one might expect (Newman & Schwager, 1992). Newman (1991) stated: "Seeking help from a knowledgeable other person can be more beneficial than giving up prematurely, more appropriate than waiting passively, and more efficient than persisting unsuccessfully on one's own" (p. 154).

It would seem logical that everyone would want to use all available resources and seek assistance from teachers and peers. Unfortunately, this is not the case. Some students do not seek help because they do not want to appear "dumb" or incompetent in the eyes of their peers or instructors (Newman & Goldin, 1990). Other students fail to seek help because of the extra effort it may entail. For example, in a class discussion, one of my students mentioned that she did not do well on a biology exam because she did not understand the instructor's expectations of the response to the essay questions. I suggested that she meet with the instructor to discuss his expectations. She agreed that this would be a good strategy. However, when I saw her the following week and asked about the outcome of the meeting, she stated that too many students were waiting to talk to the instructor, so she got frustrated and left. My response was that meeting with her instructor was a task that she had to accomplish. It was her responsibility to call for an appointment, wait to meet him after class, or at the beginning or end of the school day. If her success in the course depended on learning how to prepare and take his exams, then her job was to get to the instructor, one way or another.

Here is another example of the need to seek assistance. A student approached me at the end of the second lecture in the term and stated: "You're not going to count my quiz today? I haven't had an opportunity to buy my textbook?" I stated that the quiz would count and that he had numerous opportunities to locate the required five pages of reading for the quiz. He could have read the material at the reserve section of the library, where I placed numerous copies of the reading. He could have borrowed the reading from another student in the class or asked me if I had a copy to loan him. In other words, it was his responsibility to get the material.

Both of these interactions with students provide excellent examples of the importance of managing one's learning. In both situations, the students failed to understand their responsibility in the learning process. Think about situations in your past where you would have benefitted from managing some aspect of your physical or social environment.

Performance

> *"I evaluate the results of each of my exams to determine how I can better prepare for future exams."*

> *"If I find that I don't understand what I'm reading, I slow down and reread the material."*

The final factor that you can manage is your academic performance. Whether writing a paper, completing a test, or reading a book, you can learn how to use self-management processes to influence the quality of your performance. One of the important functions of a goal is to provide an opportunity for you to detect a discrepancy between it and your present performance. This analysis enables you to make corrections in the learning process. When you learn to monitor your work under different learning conditions (e.g., test taking and studying), you are able to determine what changes are needed in your learning and studying behavior. It is interesting that successful students tend to be aware of how well they have done on a test even before getting it back from an instructor (Zimmerman & Martinez-Pons, 1988).

World-class athletes are good examples of individuals who learn how to self-manage their performance. For example, competitive skiers often imagine themselves going through each slalom gate before making an actual run and concentrate on remaining relaxed during their run (Garfield, 1984). After each run, they observe and assess their performance (both from their perceptions and on videotape) to determine what modifications are needed to reach greater accuracy on the next run. They often use subvocal speech or self-talk to guide their behaviors and maintain attention to avoid distractions that may interfere with their performance.

When you learn how to monitor and control your own performance, you become your own coach or mentor. You can practice skills on your own, critique your own performance, and make the necessary changes to meet your goals at a high level of success.

THE SIX COMPONENTS OF ACADEMIC SELF-MANAGEMENT

The following example is how one student, Josh, exhibited self-management behavior in each of the components just discussed: Josh's goal was to join the debate team during the second term of his freshman year. He believed he could attain his goal by expending effort (motivation) in preparing for the tryouts. He first decided to study the topics that would dominate the debate season by reading magazine and newspaper articles (methods of learning). He then decided to practice his arguments with another friend (social environment) who also was interested in joining the team. They decided to reserve space at the speech clinic two evenings each week (time management) and use the available recording equipment (physical environment) to videotape their presentations and spend time critiquing themselves (performance).

Would Josh and his friend be successful if they failed to manage one or more factors influencing learning? Perhaps so, but we really do not know. For example, could they have been as successful practicing their arguments in their dorm rooms or whenever they found some time to meet, or without the recording machine? Could Josh have been as successful preparing by himself?

Although it is possible to self-manage behavior in all six of the areas discussed, not all students do so. A reasonable goal is to manage as much of one's behavior and thoughts as possible. In the example discussed, Josh and his friend believed they would be better prepared to make the debate team following their plan of action. If you were in the same situation, you may have approached the task differently.

Remember the example I provided earlier in the chapter about Robert's study behavior for his history exam? Return to the description of his learning and studying behavior and identify how he managed each of the following factors: motivation, methods of learning, use of time, physical environment, social environment, and performance.

Throughout this book, you will be asked to set goals and develop a plan of action to attain them. During this process, you will learn how to manage different aspects of your academic learning that will affect your level of success. In each chapter, I provide examples of students' perceptions or beliefs about the learning strategies discussed in this textbook. These perceptions or student reflections, as I call them, are from students who have taken my course in learning strategies. As you read each reflection, think about your own perceptions, beliefs, or behavior related to the topic or issue. The following reflection illustrates how learning to manage one's academic behavior also can influence other aspects of one's life.

Student Reflections

I first thought that self-management was confined to academic learning. Now I see that it is also a great tool for life in general. As I learn more about self-management and practice the related skills, I find that I'm much more organized. Most important, I'm getting my work done instead of putting it off and procrastinating, as I have always done. As the class has progressed, it has affected my daily life. I'm starting to see that my life outside of school is starting to run more smoothly as well.

I was always an incredibly unorganized person. I would throw all my stuff (from mail, schoolwork, even clothes) everywhere. I always was looking for things, losing things, and making a mess. Now I'm much more organized. I put things back when I'm finished with them, I keep my mail and outside school material in certain areas where I can find things, and my roommate is especially pleased, because I keep the room clean now. I'm also more prepared for whatever I have to do. I stick to schedules and plan for the events in my life. Basically, my life is more enjoyable! I'm happy now because of my continuing success at school, and this success has translated to my day-to-day life.

EXERCISE 1.1: SELF-OBSERVATION: ASSESSING YOUR SELF-MANAGEMENT SKILLS

Directions: Rate the extent to which you *generally manage or control the factors influencing your learning* by checking Always, Sometimes, or Never in the corresponding box and be prepared to offer a short explanation of your ratings. What areas are you strengths and weakness? Explain why you rated each dimension as you did.

	Always	*Sometimes*	*Never*
Motivation (e.g., "I can self-motivate when I need to").			
Use of time (e.g., "I plan how I use my time").			
Methods of learning (e.g., "I use different study methods for different types of assignments and tests").			
Physical environment (e.g., "I modify or change my study environment so I can concentrate").			
Social environment (e.g., I seek help when I need it").			
Performance (e.g., "I evaluate my work to determine my progress toward meeting personal and academic goals").			

Comments:

_____

_____

_____

_____

Comments:

_____

_____

_____

_____

_____

HOW CAN I CHANGE MY BEHAVIOR?

Zimmerman et al. (1996) suggested a process that students can use to develop the self-management skills necessary for academic success (see Fig. 1.1). This process will help you develop control over the six components of motivation and behavior identified in the previous section. Self-management involves the four interrelated processes defined here:

> *Self-observation* and *evaluation* occur when students judge their personal effectiveness, often from observations and recordings of prior performances and outcomes.

Each semester, students come into my office to discuss a poor performance on an examination. They tell me they were prepared for the examination because they read each chapter two or three times. Obviously, these students have not learned to check their understanding. Baker (1989) referred to this situation as the *illusion of knowing*. Students often

FIG. 1.1. A process for self-management of academic behavior (adapted from Zimmerman et al., 1996).

think they understand but do not test themselves to confirm or deny their belief. This lack of understanding is one of the reasons why many students are so confident of their performance during the first few weeks of college. They do not know they are in trouble. They wait for an examination for feedback, and then learn they don't know the material.

Think about a science or mathematics examination you have taken. How often have you memorized formulas, but could not solve new problems because you did not understand the basic principles involved? You may have convinced yourself that you understood the material before the examination, but you really did not.

One problem is that some students study and prepare for examinations in the same way that they did in high school. They have yet to realize the differences in the two academic environments. In high school, teachers take most of the responsibility for their students' level of comprehension. High school teachers actively monitor the degree to which content is understood: They constantly quiz students, ask questions as they present new material, and place key ideas on the board. In contrast, college instructors expect students to do their own monitoring of their understanding. Therefore, problems arise early during the first college term if students do not know how to monitor their own understanding. An important part of becoming a more successful student is developing the ability to monitor one's knowledge and recognize when something is not understood.

Think about expert performers in a variety of fields. In sports, elite athletes begin observing their performances by viewing videotapes. After a short period of time, they are able to modify their performances from the feelings and feedback they obtain by viewing their own physical movements; dance studios place handrails next to mirrors to enable students to self-observe as they practice their routines; musicians learn to listen to their playing to critique their own performances (Glaser, 1996).

Behavior cannot be managed unless you are aware of it. Therefore, you will be asked throughout this book to observe and evaluate your current learning and study methods to determine those that are ineffective so they can be replaced by better methods. Most important, you need to become aware of when and how these new learning and study methods improve your learning.

Each semester I ask students to assess their use of time for a week. They usually are surprised to learn how much time they waste. They appear more motivated to change their time management after they have monitored and observed their use of time. Self-observation is an important first step in motivating students to consider changing their learning and study behaviors.

> *Goal setting and strategic planning* occur when students analyze the learning task, set specific goals, and plan or refine the strategy to attain the goal. (Zimmerman et al., 1996, p. 11)

This second step is important in all academic tasks, including writing a paper. When given the task of writing a paper, you should start by analyzing your strengths and weaknesses. Then analyze the assignment to determine the nature of the paper and what needs to be done. Next you should establish a goal for completion, with a number of intermediate or subgoals (e.g., locating necessary references and proofreading) for completing different sections of the paper. Finally, you should develop a strategy for completing each of the intermediate goals. I discuss this process in more detail in chapter 4.

The same procedure can be used in test preparation. After analyzing previous tests as well as your present knowledge of the content (using self-observation and evaluation), you should determine what course material will be examined, establish goals for preparing for the exam, determine how you will study (i.e., what strategies will be used), and, finally, plan a time-management program consistent with your goals.

After you better understand your current behavior (through self-observation and evaluation), you will be in a better position to determine what needs to be accomplished (goals) and to develop a strategy to do it. Much of the content in this book focuses on this step in the cycle.

> *Strategy-implementation and monitoring* occurs when students try to execute a strategy in structured contexts and to monitor their accuracy in implementing it. (p. 11)

The third step in the cycle focuses on the effectiveness of your learning strategy. Is the strategy working? Are you attaining each of your goals in completing your paper? Are you learning the necessary content for your exam? If your strategy is working, keep going. If not, you had better consider what needs to be done to change your behavior.

When you learn anything new, there is a tendency to revert back to familiar methods (even though they may be less successful). This happens to athletes, dancers, and students. Therefore, performers and learners need to monitor their behaviors closely to determine whether they are applying new strategies appropriately. The result of this monitoring may indicate a need to adjust the learning strategy to improve progress toward the attainment of your goal. You may even decide that it is time to seek help.

When an individual realizes that he or she does not understand a portion of the text, he or she rereads the difficult section, slows the reading pace through difficult or unfamiliar material, reviews course material that was not understood, or skips certain questions on an examination, returning to them after easier questions are answered. It is important that students learn how to modify their study behavior to improve their understanding.

All students need to learn "fix-up" strategies to remedy learning problems. That is, they need to learn what to do after they find that they do not understand certain content. Often, different methods or strategies for learning must be undertaken (e.g., asking and answering questions) instead of continuing with the same ineffective strategy (e.g., underlining the content in a textbook).

> *Strategic-outcome monitoring* occurs when students focus their attention on links between learning outcomes and strategic processes to determine effectiveness. (p. 11)

The final stage in the cycle involves expanding your monitoring to include performance outcomes. The following questions must be answered: "Did the learning plan or strategy help me attain my goal?" "Did I have to make changes in my learning and study methods?" For example, you may have developed a strategy for studying for an objective test for the first examination of the term. You used the same strategy for a second examination, an essay test. Was the study strategy effective for both tests?

The cycle keeps going as self-observation is used to evaluate your exam performance by determining what questions you missed and the location of the information (i.e., notes or readings). A self-directed learner is constantly monitoring learning outcomes to determine whether different strategies are needed to attain goals and maintain a high level of academic success.

When researchers study expert performance in such fields as music, sports, medicine, chess, and reading, they find a common element in their learning. Initially, experts depend on instruction from others, and with time, they increasingly rely on their self-observation and self-judgments about their behavior. The ability to self-manage enables experts to profit a great deal from practice and study by themselves without assistance from their coaches and teachers (Glaser, 1996).

Zimmerman et al. (1996) believe that one of the major advantages of using the self-management process is that it can improve not only one's learning, but it can enhance one's perception of self-confidence and control over the learning process. By learning to self-observe your current learning and study behavior, and by determining for yourself what methods are effective and ineffective, you can begin replacing ineffective methods with better ones and can become more aware of the improved effectiveness of these new strategies. This process helps you to become a more self-directed or self-regulated learner.

The first exercise in the Follow-up Activities section of this book, beginning with chapter 5, identifies a topic and questions related to each of the four processes just discussed to change or modify your behavior. These questions provide the structure for conducting your own self-management study. Take a moment to look at the self-man-agement study at the end of chapter 5, focusing on reducing anxiety.

Appendix A provides detailed procedures for how to conduct such a study. You will learn in Appendix A how to identify a problem, observe your behavior, and develop a plan to improve and evaluate your academic learning. Read Appendix A as soon as possible. Appendix B provides three examples of such studies. You will find an evaluation of each self-study at the end of each report. Your instructor will provide specific directions about conducting such a study.

You may want to conduct a self-management study to improve your time management, study environment, test preparation, motivation, or any other study-related skill. Read ahead in the textbook if you wish to conduct a study on a topic that will be discussed later in the term.

HOW DOES SELF-MANAGEMENT OCCUR IN AN ACADEMIC CONTEXT?

Figure 1.2 is useful for understanding the organization of the remaining chapters in this book. Although all the components of self-management interact, it is easier in a textbook to present content in a linear fashion. Therefore, I have grouped the components into three different units. The self-management cycle can help you gain compe-tence in each of the areas identified.

There are four key skills that must be mastered to perform success-fully in any academic setting: learning from text, learning from lectures, preparing for exams, and taking exams. Writing, another important skill, is discussed under learning how to respond to essay exams.

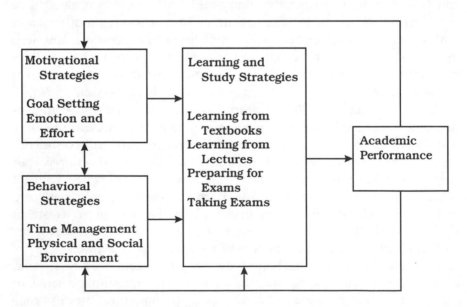

FIG. 1.2. Academic self-management.

The main factor influencing the effectiveness of your learning these skills is your ability to manage the various elements of your behavior. I group goal setting and management of emotion and effort under motivational strategies, and time management and management of physical and social environment under behavioral strategies. It is important to note that behavioral and motivational self-control are interrelated. The academic performance box in Fig. 1.2 represents the performance dimension aspect of self-management.

The process I described here places a great deal of responsibility on you, the learner. I wish there were an easy way to become a more successful learner. Unfortunately, I do not know any other way. Educational research clearly indicates that students who take charge of their own learning are more likely to achieve at a higher level than students who fail to take this responsibility (Schunk & Zimmerman, 1994).

In each chapter, you will acquire important strategies to assist in managing your learning behavior. For each strategy discussed, you will learn *why* it is important, *when* it can be used, and *how* it can be implemented. The key to success in this course is practicing the different strategies so they become automatic. As you practice, you will be able to learn more material in less time than you did prior to using these new strategies. In other words, you will learn to study smarter, not harder.

You are not alone on your journey to become a more successful student. Your instructor and peers will provide support and encouragement. You will be asked to complete various individual and group exercises and assignments as you read this book. You will find that working collaboratively with peers and giving and receiving feedback will be a valuable experience throughout the course.

Finally, you will only be taught strategies that thousands of students have found useful in learning academic material. After learning and practicing a strategy, only you will decide whether it is worth the effort and time to use it regularly in school. If the strategy proves useful, you will use it. Likewise, if you do not find the strategy helpful, you will modify it or disregard it. Try each new strategy before you reach any conclusions. Do not make the mistake of rejecting something new before you have the opportunity to see how it works.

Key Points

1. Successful learners use specific beliefs and processes to motivate and control their own behavior.
2. Some students fail to recognize the differences between high school and college learning during the first weeks in college.
3. Students can self-manage six key components of academic learning that can influence their achievement level: motivation,

methods of learning (i.e., learning strategies), use of time, physical environment, social environment, and performance.

4. The self-management cycle involves four interrelated processes: self-
   observation and evaluation, goal setting and strategic planning, strategy-implementation monitoring, and strategic-outcome monitoring.

5. An important part of becoming a more successful student is developing the ability to monitor knowledge, recognize when something is not understood, and do something about it.

Follow-up Activities

1. Analyze Your Beliefs About Learning and Motivation

Read each of the following statements and place the corresponding
letter or letters whether you agree (A), disagree (D), or are not sure
(NS) about the accuracy of each statement. After identifying your
beliefs, think about how they influence your motivation and learning.
Discuss your ratings with other students in your class.

___1. "I can't do well in a course if I'm not interested in the
       content."
___2. "I will not learn much if I am bored in class."
___3. "Competition is a great motivator."
___4. "Human intelligence is fixed by the time a student begins
       school."
___5. "Sometimes there is not enough time in the day to do
       everything that needs to be done."
___6. "If I simply listen in class and read my assignments, I
       should do well in college."
___7. "The most important aspect of studying is finding
       enough time."
___8. "The key to success in college is having good instructors."
___9. "Procrastination is a personality trait that can't be
       changed."

2. Analyze the Meaning of Two Statements

An educational researcher has stated that self-directed individuals
believe that "learning is not something that happens to students; it is
something that happens *by* students" (Zimmerman, 1989, p. 22).
What do you think this statement means? What implications does it
have for improving one's learning?

How does the following statement relate to your own learning
experiences?

Part of being a good student is learning to be aware of the state of one's own mind and the degree of one's own understanding. The good student may be one who often says that he does not understand, simply because he keeps a constant check on his understanding. The poor student, who does not, so to speak, watch himself trying to understand does not know most of the time whether he understands or not. Thus, the problem is not to get students to ask us what they don't know; the problem is to make them aware of the difference between what they know and what they don't. (Holt, 1982, p. 17)

3.   Analyze Course Demands

You learned in this chapter that a successful student takes charge of his or her own learning. Therefore, it is important to understand the demands of each of the courses you are taking this term. In this way, you can set goals and develop a plan for achieving them. Use the summary sheet provided to analyze the syllabus, textbooks, and professor in each course. Write comments in abbreviated form so you can discuss them in class.

- Review each syllabus and identify major assignments and demands during the semester (e.g., papers, projects, weekly papers, etc.).
- Analyze each textbook to determine what learning aides are included (i.e., glossary, questions, summaries, objectives, or test questions), that help you comprehend the material. Also, identify any other characteristics of the books that make them easy or hard to read (e.g., bold headings, graphics, small type).
- Analyze the instructor's teaching style to determine whether it will make it easy or hard to take good notes. What do you like most and least about his or her style? How does she or he let you know what is important? What note-taking problems do you encounter? Identify any of the following characteristics about your instructor: speaks rapidly, speaks slowly, speaks loudly, speaks softly, does or does not use board or overheads, is well organized or is disorganized, and so forth.

What are your general impressions of the instructor and course demands? Identify your interest level and expectancy for success in each course. Identify any concerns you may have about doing well in a course and the steps you can take to deal with your concerns.

Courses	Syllabus	Textbooks	Professor
General Comments			
1.			
2.			
3.			
4.			
5.			

2

Understanding Learning and Memory

You are reading this book because you want to become a more successful learner. Before I explain how to use effective learning strategies, it is important to understand how humans learn. It is difficult to understand why you should give up certain learning and study skills and replace them with new skills without the knowledge presented in this chapter. Also, once you acquire important knowledge concerning human learning, you can better evaluate your own learning processes. This chapter describes how information is received and processed in the mind and how memory and forgetting occur. After studying this chapter, you will be able to:

- Identify the flaws in human memory.
- Identify how the information-processing system (IPS) operates.
- Explain why it is important to use a variety of learning strategies to learn different material.
- Assess the effectiveness of your own learning and study strategies.

WHAT ARE THE FLAWS IN HUMAN MEMORY?

As we begin our study of learning and human memory, I think it would be helpful to discuss some of the flaws of human memory that all individuals experience. Many of my students think their memories are flawless and they can remember all, or at least most, of the essential information needed to function successfully in their lives. Unfortunately, no matter how young or old you are, they are certain memory flaws that can affect your behavior.

In his book *The Seven Sins of Memory,* Schacter (2001) explored the nature of memory's imperfections. We can all recall the problems we have in forgetting different types of information. For example, we often fail to recall information in a textbook, or forgot our bank passwords or PIN identifications for the many Web sites we use on the Internet. This type of forgetting, called *transience,* is only one of the seven flaws in our memory. Transience refers to the situation when individuals fail to remember a fact or idea. It is a weakening or loss of memory over time. We will emphasize this type of memory problem in this chapter.

A second flaw in our memory is called *absent-mindedness*. It involves the breakdown between attention and memory. It often occurs when we are preoccupied with distracting concerns like placing sunglasses down at a friend's home and forgetting to take them when you leave. Although this type of memory problem occurs more often in older adults, it is prevalent as well in individuals of all ages.

A third flaw is called *blocking*. It is the unsuccessful search for information that we may be desperately trying to retrieve, such as the name of an attractive woman or man we met at a party the previous night.

Have you ever been in a situation where you are with a friend and see another person who knows you and you are embarrassed because you can't think of the person's name, and thus can't introduce your friend to that individual? You start the conversation hoping that the individual will introduce himself or herself to your friend.

A fourth flaw is called *misattribution*. It involves assigning a memory to the wrong source or incorrectly remembering that someone told you something that you actually read about in a newspaper. You are sure that a friend told you something, but find that he or she never mentioned a thing about the topic. We often see this flaw on television programs in cases of mistaken eyewitness identification.

A fifth flaw is called *suggestibility*. It refers to memories that are implanted because of leading questions, comments, or suggestions. Numerous examples of this flaw are special concerns in legal situations where suggestive questioning by law enforcement officials can lead to errors in eyewitness identification. This flaw also has been identified in cases of child abuse where psychotherapists have elicited memories of traumatic events that never occurred.

A sixth flaw is called *bias*. It involves the editing or changing of previous experiences based on what we now feel rather than what happened in the past. Schacter (2001) pointed out that we think of memories as snapshots from family albums that are retrieved in the exact way they were stored. Unfortunately, our memories do not work in the same manner as a photo, because we recreate or reconstruct our experiences rather than retrieve exact copies of them. Sometimes, in the process of reconstructing memories, we add feelings, beliefs, or even new information we obtained after the experience. Barbara Streisand's song "The Way We Were" illustrates bias as it relates to recollections of close personal relationships. Do the lyrics remind you of any personal experiences where you might view the situation or relationship differently now than you did in the past?

> Memories
> May be beautiful, and yet
> What's too painful to remember
> We simply choose to forget;
> For it's the laughter
> We will remember
> Whenever we remember
> The way we were.

The last flaw in our memory is *persistence*. It refers to remembering what we would prefer to omit from our memory. Have you ever had problems sleeping because you can't stop thinking about a poor grade on an examination or bad interview you had? I bet you can still remember a certain negative experience in your life and how you recalled the experience repeatedly in the days and weeks after it occurred, even though you would have liked to forget it.

Can you think of situations where you experience one or more of these memory flaws? If so, share them with your classmates when you discuss this chapter in class or with your study group. Let us now turn to the major focus of this chapter, the memory problem of transience.

HOW DOES THE INFORMATION-PROCESSING SYSTEM EXPLAIN LEARNING?

Have you ever wondered why you remember certain information and why you cannot even remember the important ideas in a course you completed a few months or weeks ago? Many learning experts believe how individuals learn provides the answer to this question.

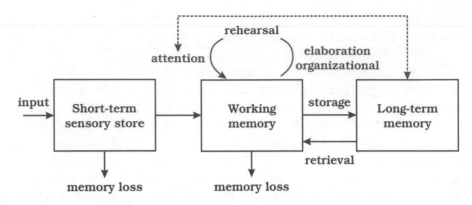

FIG. 2.1   A model of the information-processing system.

Psychologists provide many different theories and explanations of human learning. One way to understand how information may be acquired or lost is to understand the **information-processing system** (see Fig. 2.1). This model is used to identify how humans store, encode, and retrieve information. Storage is the process of placing information into memory. **Encoding** is the process used to change information in some way before it is stored, because information is not stored exactly as it is presented. For example, when an individual reads a textbook, he or she derives meaning from the words read and stores the meaning rather than the specific words on the page. Sometimes when a person reads, he or she remembers the information by changing the words to an image of the event. **Retrieval** refers to the process of remembering or finding previously stored information. Sometimes it is easy to recall information, other times, it takes considerable thought and effort to remember.

Three important points are emphasized in this chapter:

1. Learning involves getting information into long-term memory (LTM), a component of memory that holds knowledge and skills for long periods of time.
2. Much of what we think we have learned is soon forgotten or never really learned in the first place.
3. The specific strategies used to store information in LTM affect the likelihood that the information will be remembered. In other words, how we learn often determines what we remember.

Short-Term Sensory Store

As shown in Fig. 2.1, the flow of information begins with input from the environment, such as the visual perception of words in a text. This information enters the short-term sensory store (STSS). Information in the STSS is stored briefly until it can be attended to by the working memory (WM). Everything that can be seen, heard, or smelled is stored in the STSS, but it only lasts for a matter of seconds before it is forgotten.

Many of the stimuli humans experience never get into our WM because we do not attend to them. We are constantly barraged with stimuli from our environment. For example, by the time an individual wakes up, gets dressed, and walks or drives to class, he or she observes hundreds, or perhaps thousands of objects that cannot be recalled. If you drove to class today, do you remember the color or make of the car next to which you were parked? Do you remember the student who sat next to you in your first class? What did he or she wear? If you found the person attractive or interesting, you may be able to answer these questions, because you may have been attentive to such details. However, the fact is that we are not attentive to most of what we see or hear in our daily lives.

If you have not attended to information, there is little concern about retention or retrieval, because no information will have been acquired. When you attend a lecture and your attention fades in and out, you will fail to recall some of the important information presented by the professor. This is why it may be important for you to improve your attention.

Think about reading a textbook. As you read, you begin thinking about the party you are planning to attend next Saturday. When your mind goes back to the book you realize that you covered two pages but don't remember a thing. You read but you do not remember anything, because you were not paying attention to the words in the textbook. When students say that they can attend to many things at one time, they really mean that they can switch their attention from one task to another. It is difficult to read a textbook and watch a TV show simultaneously. Information is missed from both sources.

In summary, unless special attempts are made to attend to and record information, much of the material in lectures and textbooks is never stored in memory. Therefore, the information is never learned. A similar situation occurs when you are introduced to someone and 10 seconds later you cannot remember the person's name. The problem is not that you forgot the name but that you never learned it in the first place. When you mention to friends that you forgot important information during an exam, you need to consider whether the real problem was learning or forgetting.

Working Memory

Working memory is the active part of the memory system and has been described as the center of consciousness in the IPS. Whenever we are consciously thinking about something or actively trying to remember a forgotten fact, we are using our WM.

Working memory screens and decides how to handle different stimuli. Three events can happen when material gets into the WM (Eggen & Kauchak, 1997):

- It can be quickly lost or forgotten.
- The content can be retained in WM for a short period of time by repeating it over and over (i.e., rehearsing).
- The content can be transferred into long-term memory by using specific learning strategies.

The WM is limited in two ways—capacity and duration. At any one time, the WM of an adult can hold only five to nine chunks of information. This limitation is referred to as the "7 ± 2 Magic Number" (Miller, 1956). New information coming into WM will, if it catches the attention of the student, tend to crowd out old information already there. If information is believed to be important, it should not be left in WM, because it will be soon forgotten.

A number of control processes operate at the WM level and provide it with some flexibility in dealing with information. **Chunking**, or grouping information, is one way of keeping more than nine pieces (7 ± 2) of information in WM. For example, it is usually easier to remember a number such as 194781235 if the numbers are grouped in threes (194 781 235), because the original nine units are reduced to three chunks. When we read a word, we think of it as a single unit rather than as a collection of separate letters. For example, a sentence can be thought of as a single unit, or chunk, instead of a series of letters and words. By organizing information into larger chunks, the WM can handle more information, because the organization reduces memory load. Although our WM uses chunking strategies automatically and unconsciously, these strategies also can be learned.

EXERCISE 2.1: DEMONSTRATING THE CAPACITY OF WORKING MEMORY

Directions: Try this short memory experiment (Goetz, Alexander, & Ash, 1992, p. 323). Read the following list of letters once. Cover the page and attempt to recall them in order. Write your answers on a separate sheet of paper:

FB
IMT
VU
SAHB

OC
IA

Check to see how many letters you recalled in the right order.

Now, let's look at another list. Again, read the list once, and then cover the page and write all the letters you can remember in order:

FBI
MTV
USA
HBO
CIA

How many letters did you get right this time? I bet you did much better the second time. Notice that the same letters are presented in the same order in both lists. The only difference is that the second list is arranged in familiar patterns. Because the letters are familiar and meaningful, each set can serve as a single unit, or chunk, in WM. Instead of trying to remember 15 separate letters, as in the first list, you only have to recall five familiar chunks in the second list. The first list exceeds the 7 ± 2 guideline; the second list can be managed within your WM limits.

Because WM is characterized by a limited capacity, only a very small amount of information in the sensory store can ever be processed in WM. According to information-processing theory, information must be processed in WM before it can move on to LTM. This means the learner must do something active with the information to move it into LTM. However, because WM has a short duration (about 5 to 20 seconds), the processing must be completed fairly quickly, or at least rehearsed, until it can be processed.

Another common control process is **maintenance rehearsal.** This strategy helps keep information activated for more than 20 seconds in WM by rehearsing the information mentally. For example, if an individual gets out of the car to obtain directions to a location, the information could easily be forgotten by the time he or she gets back into the car. Therefore, after receiving directions, individuals often rehearse or repeat "left–left–right–left" while driving away to prevent forgetting.

Sometimes during a lecture, I will point out some information about the upcoming exam or make changes in reading assignments. Some students fail to enter the information in their notes because they mistakenly believe they will remember the information. Unfortunately, they probably forget the information as soon as they leave the lecture. Days or weeks later, some students will ask, "When did you tell us that?"

Gagné (1985) estimated that individuals are likely to learn only about one to six new ideas from each minute of a lecture, a small number of the ideas that are typically presented during that time. Therefore, students must constantly make important decisions about what information to attend to and what information to neglect. It is difficult enough to obtain important information from a lecture while trying to be attentive. Imagine how much information is lost in lectures when students are not attentive.

One of my favorite *I Love Lucy* reruns is when Lucy has a job where she must place chocolates into boxes moving on a conveyor belt. Initially, the conveyor belt moves slowly and she easily places each of the chocolates in the appropriate box. Soon the belt moves so rapidly that she cannot pick up the chocolates fast enough. Many of the chocolates move past her; some end up in her mouth, others in her blouse. It is really funny to see how Lucy deals with her problem.

This episode reminds me of the WM in the IPS. The conveyor belt represents information flowing into a human's mind. Consider a lecture at which the professor speaks rapidly and covers a great deal of information. As you listen to the presentation, you have to make quick decisions as to what content to process. When you decide something is important, you take notes on the information even if you do not completely understand it. Information that you do not write down is gone forever unless you read it in your textbook or get it from another student. In many ways, the limitation of one's WM is similar to the fast conveyor belt in the *I Love Lucy* episode.

One of the advantages of reading compared to note taking is that you do not have to make quick decisions about what is important, because you can read the material at your own pace and reread it as many times as necessary. Strategies to help you remember more information from lectures and textbooks are presented later.

Long-Term Memory

Long-term memory stores all the information we possess but are not immediately using. It is generally assumed that storage of information in the LTM is permanent. That is, the information does not fade from LTM, nor is it ever lost except perhaps as a result of senility or some other physical malfunction. Learning experts view the problem of forgetting as the inability to retrieve or locate information from memory rather than the loss of information.

Information enters the LTM through the WM. Although information must be repeated or rehearsed to stay in working memory, it must be classified, organized, connected, and stored with information already in LTM if it is to be easily retrieved at a later time. It takes time and effort to move information into long-term storage.

LTM can be compared to an office with filing cabinets. Each cabinet is labeled, and there are dividers within each drawer. Memories are placed in specific folders, in specific sections, and in specific drawers. Unless the material is carefully classified and placed in the correct file, it can easily be misfiled. Once material is misfiled, or poorly classified and filed, it is difficult to retrieve. It is believed that the human mind stores information in a similar manner. Therefore, the better we classify and organize information when we learn it, the better able we are to retrieve it when it is needed (Ormrod, 1998). Here is how one student made the connection between how information is stored in LTM and retrieval:

> I view long-term memory like a well-organized closet where there is a place for shirts, sweaters, jackets, pants, and so on. When I need something, my categorization and organization help me to find it quickly. If I just threw clothes into my closet, I would spend more time trying to recall what items I had and spend more time locating them. When I fail to organize and make sense of content in a course, I always have difficulty retrieving the information on exams.

You now have some idea as to how information flows in the IPS. Beginning with the environment, information flows to the STSS. The information that is attended to proceeds to the WM, where it may be modified and stored permanently in the LTM. Information then flows back from the LTM to the WM to direct behavior.

In some courses, students bring a great deal of prior knowledge to class because they may have already taken a course in the subject or have done some reading in the area. In other courses, students may have little or no prior knowledge of the subject matter. As might be expected, prior knowledge plays an important role in learning. For example, compare the ease or difficulty of taking lecture notes when you read prior to the lecture with another time when you did not read the material prior to the lecture. The more information you know before you attend a lecture, the easier it is to take notes and understand the material. This is why instructors ask you to complete reading assignments before lectures.

I can read textbooks in education and psychology with a great deal of understanding because I have a good background in the content presented in these texts. Yet, I know junior high students who can read an article in *Car Audio & Electronics* more rapidly and with greater understanding than me. I know the techniques and strategies for how to read, but I don't know much about the topics discussed in *Car Audio & Electronics.*

WHAT IS THE DIFFERENCE BETWEEN ROTE AND MEANINGFUL LEARNING?

The process of acquiring knowledge can be viewed on a continuum from basic to complex. Basic learning involves such things as recalling names and dates, associating a word in English to its equivalent in Spanish, and chronologically listing the events leading up to the Civil War. More complex learning involves understanding the main ideas in a story, solving verbal problems in algebra, or comparing and contrasting the poems of two different authors.

Many students do not realize that some of the strategies effective for learning basic knowledge may not be useful for learning more complex knowledge. Learning experts often make the distinction between rote and meaningful learning. In rote learning, the student learns through repetition without trying to make any sense of the material. In meaningful learning, the student attempts to make sense of the information so that it will be stored in LTM and retrieved when it is needed. One of the major problems in cramming for examinations is that students do not learn the material in a way that makes sense to them by relating the information to what they already know. The end result is that 24 hours after the exams, nothing, or very little information, is retained.

EXERCISE 2.2: UNDERSTANDING THE IMPORTANCE OF PRIOR KNOWLEDGE

Directions: Two learning experts (Bransford & Johnson, 1972) presented college students with the following passage to read. Read it for yourself and then see how much you can remember:

> The procedure is actually quite simple. First you arrange things into different groups depending on their makeup. Of course, one pile may be sufficient, depending on how much there is to do. If you have to go somewhere else due to lack of facilities that is the next step, otherwise you are pretty well set. It is important not to overdo any particular endeavor. That is, it is better to do too few things at once than too many. In the short run this may not seem important, but complications from doing too many can easily arise. A mistake can be expensive as well. The manipulation of the appropriate mechanisms should be self-explanatory, and we

need not dwell on it here. At first the whole procedure will seem complicated. Soon, however, it will become just another facet of life. It is difficult to foresee any end to the necessity for this task in the immediate future, but then one never can tell. (p. 722)

I am sure you recognized all the words in the paragraph. Yet, you probably still had difficulty understanding what you were reading. Don't be disappointed if you did not understand the passage or remember much of the content. I didn't remember one thing the first time I read it.

Now, read the passage again, but this time keep the title "Washing Clothes" in mind. You should be able to make more sense of the passage because the title provides a meaningful context or framework for understanding the text.

What does this simple experiment reveal? Anytime readers gain information about a reading passage or section in a textbook and relate the information to something they already know, they are better able to understand the incoming information. This is why certain authors provide outlines or questions before chapters or questions imbedded in the text. These components help readers think about the topics in the chapter they are about to read. When readers read outlines or think about the questions before they begin reading, they take advantage of important aides to facilitate comprehension and memory (Halpern, 1996). The effect is the same when students read assigned material before taking lecture notes. Note taking is easier when students know something about the material being presented.

WHAT LEARNING STRATEGIES PROMOTE LEARNING AND RETENTION?

Before you begin reading this section, think about some content you remember from a course that you took some time ago. Why do you remember this information when so much other information in the same course was lost? I will share some examples of my own learning here. I have been waiting for years for someone to ask me to name the planets from the sun, in order: Mercury, Venus, Earth, Mars, Jupiter, Saturn, Uranus, Neptune, and Pluto. I remember this information from elementary school, because the teacher taught us a **mnemonic**: "*M*y *v*ery *e*ager *m*other *j*ust *s*erved *u*s *n*ine *p*izzas." The beginning letter of each word corresponds to the first letter of each planet. I also can identify the components and functions of the human digestive tract many years after taking biology. My instructor taught the class to first draw an outline of the human body and place the

TABLE 2.1
EXAMPLES OF LEARNING STRATEGIES

Learning Strategies	Example	Learning Behaviors
Rehearsal	"I use note cards to learn definitions of terms."	Copying material Note taking Underlining text
Elaboration	"I try to relate new concepts to things I already know."	Summarizing Note making Answering questions
Organizational	"I try to separate main points from examples and explanations when I read a textbook.	Selecting main idea Outlining Representation (mapping)

name of each component near its location. Finally, we were told to write a short sentence describing the function of each organ below its name. I can still visualize each organ and function in the digestive tract.

Think about some content that you learned in a course and still remember. What factors contributed to your retention of the content?

Earlier in the chapter, we discussed encoding—the process of putting new information into the IPS and preparing it for storage in LTM. The best way to prepare information for storage is to make it meaningful and to integrate it with known information already in your LTM. Some learning strategies are better than others for getting information into your LTM.

Table 2.1 identifies a number of important learning strategies to help you understand, learn, and remember course material. As you review the table, place a check next to the strategies you have used most often and circle the strategies you have used least often in school. If you are not familiar with one or more of the terms, complete this task after you read more of the chapter.

Rehearsal Strategies

When we think of basic learning, we often imagine having information drilled into us through endless repetition. Whether memorizing a song or learning the capitals of each state in the United States, we have been told by our instructors that we must practice, practice, practice. But does it matter how we practice? Learning experts offer some advice as to how practice can be made more effective. Research has shown that **distributed practice** among frequent and short periods is more effective than a smaller number of sessions of **massed practice** (Underwood, 1961). If you want to remember the presidents of the United States without error, you should practice for many short sessions, chunking the list and repeatedly saying the names. The classic all-nighter, of which I must admit I experienced a few during my undergraduate days, is the best example of massed practice. Although this practice method may be effective in learning a large amount of basic information in a short time, it is a poor method of learning and remembering complex information.

Think about the examinations on which you used massed practice. How much of the content did you remember a few days after the examination?

Rehearsal strategies can be very effective in some types of learning. Copying material, taking verbatim notes, reciting words or definitions, and underlining material in handouts or textbooks are all examples of rehearsal strategies. However, the limitation in the use of rehearsal strategies is that they make few connections between the new information and the knowledge we already have in LTM. Therefore, if the information is not connected to anything when it is stored in LTM, it is difficult to retrieve. Your goal as a learner is to try to make the information meaningful if you want to increase the probability that you will remember it. For the most part, underlining is one of the least effective learning strategies used by college students.

Let's now turn to the two major learning strategies that will help you learn more information—elaboration and organization.

Elaboration Strategies

Elaboration strategies help retention by linking new information to information already in your LTM. These strategies can be very useful for improving the recall of names, categories, sequences, or groups of items. For basic learning, two popular mnemonics include **acronyms** and the **key-word method**. Acronyms use the first letter in each word to form a mnemonic. My earlier example about the order of the planets is an acronym. Here are some other popular acronyms:

HOMES

The five Great Lakes: Huron, Ontario, Michigan, Erie, Superior (geography)

Roy G. Biv

The colors of the spectrum: red, orange, yellow, green, blue, indigo, violet (physics)

King Phillip came over from Greece singing

The classification of organisms: kingdom, phylum, class, order, family, genus, species (biology)

A useful mnemonic for learning foreign language vocabulary is the key-word method, which involves the creation of an image that relates the English to the foreign word. For example, the Spanish word for *postal letter* is *carta*. An appropriate image might involve a huge postal letter being transported to the post office in a shopping cart. Thus, the word *carta* would be encoded both as an idea and as an image. The student's subsequent attempts to recall the Spanish word for *postal letter* will stimulate the image of the letter in the cart, providing a concrete cue to the correct word. This method has been shown to have significant success in teaching foreign vocabulary.

Elaboration strategies for more complex learning from texts include paraphrasing, summarizing, creating analogies, writing notes in one's own words, and asking and answering questions. When someone asks us to elaborate on an idea we have expressed in discussion, he or she wants us to add more information to what we have said to provide detail, give examples, make connections to other issues, or draw inferences from the data. The additional information makes our point more meaningful to the listener and also is likely to make the point easier to remember.

Table 2.1 lists two terms—*note taking* and *note making* (i.e., developing questions from notes). Writing notes directly from a lecture is a rehearsal strategy, but asking questions and underlining the answers in the notes (note making) is an elaboration strategy. Chapter 9 discusses that what is done with notes after a lecture is just as important as taking the notes in the first place. In that chapter, you will learn how to develop questions from your notes so you can check your understanding of lecture material.

We can elaborate when learning more complex information. As information enters WM, the successful learner thinks about the information: What does this new information mean? How does it relate to other ideas in the text and other information already learned? What type of analogies or examples can I generate?

A student learning that ancient Egyptian society depended on slavery may elaborate on this fact by adding details, making connections with other information, or drawing inferences. By way of providing detail, the student may notice that Egyptian slaves were largely prisoners of war. The student may connect the concept of Egyptian slavery with what is known of antebellum U.S. slavery, noting similarities and differences. The student may infer that life for an Egyptian slave was hard and held cheaply by Egyptian society at large. In this way, the learner integrates the new ideas into LTM by associating the new data with the old knowledge (Bransford, 1979). This procedure leads to improved understanding of the material and to an increased probability that the information will be remembered at a later time.

The following are other examples of analogies that promote connections between new ideas and existing student knowledge (cited in Ormrod, 1995):

- The growth of a glacier is like *pancake batter being poured into a frying pan.* As more and more substance is added to the middle, the edges spread farther and farther out. (p. 298)
- The human circulatory system is similar to a *parcel delivery system.* "Red blood cells work like trucks, carrying needed materials from a central distribution point for delivery throughout the body. Arteries and veins are like roads, acting as access routes through which the various points of delivery are reached. The heart is like the warehouse or the central point in which vehicles are loaded and dispatched, and to which empty vehicles are returned to be reloaded" (Stepich & Newby, 1988, p. 136).
- A dual-store model of memory is like the *information selection and storage system you use at home.* Some things (e.g., junk mail) are discarded as soon as they arrive, others (e.g., bills) are only briefly dealt with, and still others (e.g., driver's license) are used regularly and saved for a long period of time. (p. 298)

Have you ever used analogies in learning? If so, how did they help you recall information?

An important advantage of elaboration strategies is that they provide additional retrieval routes for remembering information. When you elaborate, you create additional ways of recalling the information. Therefore, if you cannot remember the original connection, you may be able to use other connections to retrieve the needed information.

Here is an example of elaboration in action (Gagné, Yekovich, & Yekovich, 1993): A student reads in her political science textbook: "Political action committees (PACs) influence Congress with money." She already read that a PAC is a group whose purpose is to influence policy. Another student who came to the same section of the textbook about PACs goes one step further. She elaborates on the new information by thinking that the National Rifle Association has a PAC.

Suppose the following day the instructor asks the class what political action committees do. Both students may recall that they are groups whose goal is to influence policy. But suppose they cannot recall the purpose of a PAC. The student who thinks of the National Rifle Association may be able to infer what a PAC does from her elaboration that the National Rifle Association has a PAC. The organization tries to influence policy in Congress. This could lead her to conclude that PACs try to influence votes, thus answering the instructor's question correctly. This example illustrates the importance of providing additional retrieval routes for remembering information.

Organizational Strategies

Psychologists have found that it is difficult, and sometimes impossible, for humans to learn unorganized bits and pieces of information (e.g., definitions, dates, names, ideas) without imposing patterns of organization on the information (Gaskins & Elliot, 1991). By organizing information, connections and interrelationships are made within a body of new information. Learning is facilitated when a learner becomes aware of the inherent organizational structure of new material or imposes an organizational structure on material when no such structure initially exists. A body of new information to be learned is stored more effectively and remembered more completely when it is organized (Ormrod, 1998).

EXERCISE 2.3: DEMONSTRATING THE IMPORTANCE OF CATEGORIZING KNOWLEDGE

Directions: Try the following experiment (Halpern, 1996, pp. 489–490). The following are two lists of words. Read the first list at a rate of approximately one word per second, cover the list, and write down as many of the words as you can remember, then repeat this process with the second list:

Girl
Heart
Robin
Purple
Finger
Flute
Blue
Organ
Man
Hawk
Green
Lung
Eagle
Child
Piano

Now, cover the list and write down as many words from this list as you can remember. Don't look!

Now read the next list, cover it, and then write down as many of the words that you can remember from this list:

Green
Blue

Purple
Man
Girl
Child
Piano
Flute
Organ
Heart
Lung
Finger
Eagle
Hawk
Robin

Stop now, cover the preceding list, and write down as many words from this list as you can remember.

Each semester my students report that they remembered more from the second list. The two lists include the same words, but the second list is organized by category. Obviously, you did benefit from seeing the list a second time, but most of the improvement on the second list came from the organization provided by presenting the words in categories.

Internal organization of material helps learning and retention. An investigation by Bower, Clark, Lesgold, and Winzenz (1969) illustrated this finding in an investigation in which college students were given four study sessions to learn 112 words that were classified into four categories (e.g., minerals, plants, etc.). Some students had words arranged randomly, whereas others had words arranged in four different hierarchies (see Fig. 2.2 for the

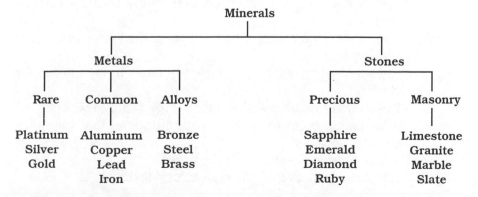

FIG. 2.2. Example of a hierarchy (Bower et al., 1969).

minerals hierarchy). After one study session, students who had studied the organized words could remember more than three times as many words as those who had studied the randomized words. After four study trials, the students in the organized group remembered all 112, whereas the students in the random group remembered only 70.

Categories can provide useful retrieval cues in many situations. For example, if you go to the supermarket with a shopping list, you can recall the items you need by checking different categories, such as dairy, meats, vegetables, drinks, and so forth (Loftus, 1980). Think about courses like biology, astronomy, or anthropology, where learning classification lists are essential to success in the course. The research is clear: If you learn ways to organize material, you will be able to learn and retrieve the information more effectively.

Organizational strategies are as useful in remembering prose passages as they are in recalling lists. Outlines and representations (or maps) can be useful organizational strategies. These techniques enable better understanding of text material by helping the learner analyze the text structure. Outlining is a strategy where major and minor ideas are written in abbreviated form using important words and phrases. Representation is a process of drawing a diagram to picture how ideas are connected (see Figs. 2.1 and 2.2).

EXERCISE 2.4: IDENTIFYING LEARNING STRATEGIES

Directions: The following behaviors represent different learning strategies used by students. Identify each type of strategy by placing the letter (R) for rehearsal, (E) for elaboration, and (O) for organizational in the space provided. Answers are on p. 49.

_R_ 1. "In preparing for a chemistry test, I keep writing down major formulae until I remember them."

_E_ 2. "I write a summary of each chapter in my political science book."

_E_ 3. "I think of a computer when studying the information processing system."

_O_ 4. "I use a chart to compare different theories in my philosophy class."

_E_ 5. "I ask myself questions after reading my history textbook."

_E_ 6. "After taking notes in class, I write questions that the notes answer."

_R_ 7. "I underline my textbook while I read."

_O_ 8. "I outline each chapter in my geology textbook."

One of the main points in this chapter is that there are different ways to learn and that some ways lead to greater information retention and retrieval. In Unit 4 you will learn how to use more elaboration and organization strategies in your learning and studying behavior.

Key Points

1. There are seven flaws in human memory: transience, absent-mindedness, blocking, misattribution, suggestibility, bias, and persistence.
2. The information processing system is a model that is used to identify how individuals obtain, transform, store, and apply information. It comprises the short-term sensory store, working memory, and the long-term memory.
3. Learning involves getting information into long-term memory.
4. There can be no learning without attention.
5. Memory is enhanced when the content is meaningful. When you learn something, try to relate it to something you already know.
6. Meaningful learning facilitates both organized storage and retrieval of information.
7. Many students use only rehearsal strategies in learning. As a result, they have difficulty understanding and recalling complex information.
8. Elaboration increases learning by linking new content to existing knowledge. It provides additional ways of remembering information.
9. Elaboration strategies include mnemonic devices, paraphrasing, summarizing, creating analogies and examples, writing notes in one's own words, explaining, and asking questions.
10. It is difficult to learn unorganized definitions, dates, names, and ideas without organizing the information.
11. Organizational learning strategies promote learning by imposing order on new content. Classifying, outlining, and representations or mapping are examples of such strategies.
12. How information is organized and elaborated influences one's ability to retrieve it when needed.

Follow–up Activities

1. **Analyze a Student's Behavior**

   Carla visited her biology professor to discuss her poor performance on the midterm exam. She was disappointed because she studied "very hard" for the exam. When the professor asked her to explain how she studied, she opened her book bag and produced more than 100 index cards with terms on one side and definitions on the other. She explained how she spent hours memorizing all the terms in the required textbook chapters. She did well on the multiple-choice questions, but poorly on the essay questions.

If you were the professor, what advice would you give her to prepare for the next examination?

2. Analyze a Student's Behavior

Read the following information concerning Ruben. Discuss the strengths and weaknesses of his motivation and learning strategies. What suggestions do you have for helping him become more successful?

Ruben is studying a chapter in his biology textbook for a quiz the next day. His experience taking biology in high school was mostly negative because his instructors focused on facts and definitions. As a result, he never developed much interest in the subject. He has been told that he will be asked to answer one essay question to test his knowledge of the material. He is not sure exactly what content will be tested but decides to develop a study plan to gain a general understanding of the main ideas and to recall the most important facts. He paraphrases each section of the chapter and underlines the important information. He realizes that he has difficulty comparing and contrasting some of the concepts discussed in class. Therefore, he decides to develop and write responses to short-answer essay questions he thinks may be on the test. He develops so many possible questions that he quickly becomes frustrated and only answers two essay questions. He then reads the chapter summary. Finally, he reviews the underlining in his textbook and decides it is time to move on to another subject.

_____

_____

_____

_____

_____

_____

3. Evaluate Your Learning Strategies

Think about the learning strategies you used in high school or in your last educational environment. How did you memorize basic material? How did you learn concepts in history, chemistry, and mathematics? If you had to do it over again, how would you improve your learning strategies in high school? Are you using the same strategies in college? What changes in your learning and study strategies do you think you have to make this year?

4. Prepare Study Materials

This chapter presented a number of strategies that promote learning. Identify a student in your class to review the content in this chapter and together develop a plan for studying the material in the chapter. Identify each study strategy you will use and discuss how you will apply the strategy.

Answers to Exercise 2.4

1. R   2. E   3. E   4. O   5. E   6. E   7. R   8. O

3

Understanding Motivation

As you consider the various components of academic self-management, you may find that you have no difficulty managing your motivation. You may exhibit a great deal of effort on tasks, persist even under difficult situations, and maintain positive beliefs about your academic abilities. If this is the case, this chapter will simply help you understand why you are motivated to succeed. However, if you have some difficulty managing your motivation, this chapter provides important background information to help you change.

MOTIVATIONAL PROBLEMS

Many of my students frequently state in class or in written assignments: "I have no motivation" or "I need to get motivated." Unfortunately, I find that many students do not understand the meaning of these statements. Actually, everyone is motivated. Educational researchers have found that many different patterns of beliefs and behaviors can limit academic success. Therefore, many different types of motivational problems can be identified in any group of students. Let's look at five students who have diverse motivational problems (adapted from Stipek, 1998): Defensive Dimitri, Safe Susan, Hopeless Henry, Satisfied Sheila, and Anxious Alberto.

Defensive Dimitri

Dimitri is having difficulty in his first term in college and is beginning to doubt his ability to compete with other students in his classes. As a result, he puts his energy into preventing anyone from interpreting his poor performance as evidence of lack of ability. Basically, he appears to be more motivated to avoid failure than to succeed. Dimitri uses a number of failure-avoiding strategies, such as asking instructors several questions to give the impression that he is interested in the material, telling friends that he does not spend much time studying for exams when he really does, and spending time trying to find out what information appeared on tests in other sections of the same course. Unfortunately, the strategies he uses to avoid looking like a poor student prevent him from developing his academic abilities.

Safe Susan

Susan is a bright student with high SAT scores. However, she can be classified as an underachiever. Her primary goal is to attain high grades and recognition from her instructors. She is upset if she obtains any grade less than an A. She takes courses that offer little challenge and overstudies for every test. Susan rarely reads anything that is not required in a course and does not allow herself to be challenged. She learns only what she is told to learn.

Hopeless Henry

Henry has a very negative opinion of his ability to do college work. He realized early in the term that he was having trouble understanding college textbooks and taking lecture notes. In fact, he has no study skills of which to speak. Henry does not attempt to seek help because he believes it is useless to try because nothing seems to work. When talking to friends, he constantly puts himself down. He sleeps late and misses many classes and finds himself falling further and further behind in his course work.

Satisfied Sheila

Sheila is a likable student who enjoys college life. She joined a number of social organizations the first term in college and is a C-average student who could easily attain A grades. Sheila does not want to push herself and let course work get in the way of having a good time. She is not worried about getting C grades and is especially satisfied with any grade that does not require much effort. Sheila enjoys reading novels and writes very well. In fact, she has submitted some of her poetry to her college literary magazine. Unfortunately, she does not apply her intellectual interests and abilities to her schoolwork.

Anxious Alberto

Alberto lacks self-confidence and is very anxious about academic tasks. He constantly worries about his performance on every test or assignment. His anxiety is so great that he forgets material on tests even though he prepares well. Alberto has trouble sleeping, constantly has stomachaches, and does not enjoy college.

Each of these students has a different set of beliefs and perceptions that limit his or her present and possibly future academic success. All of these students have motivational problems. Defensive Dimitri doubts his ability and is concerned that others will not see him as capable. Safe Susan does not want to take any risks or challenge herself. She just cares about doing well. Hopeless Henry does not believe anything he does will make a difference in succeeding in college. He has learned to be helpless. Satisfied Sheila does not value her academic accomplishments. As a result, she chooses to spend her time and effort in nonacademic areas. Anxious Alberto wants to be a successful student. However, his constant worry causes considerable anxiety that interferes with his academic success.

Do any of these students resemble anyone you know? As you read this chapter, think about how the content can help you better understand each of these students. After studying this chapter, you will be able to:

- Identify the factors that influence motivation.
- Assess your beliefs and perceptions to account for your own motivation.

WHAT IS MOTIVATION AND WHAT FACTORS INFLUENCE IT?

Student motivation in the college classroom involves three interactive components (adapted from Pintrich, 1994). The first component is the personal and sociocultural factors that include individual characteristics, such as the attitudes and values students bring to college based on prior personal, family, and cultural experiences. The second component is the classroom environment factors that pertain to instructional experiences in different courses. The third component is internal factors or students' beliefs and perceptions. Internal factors are influenced by both personal and sociocultural factors and classroom environmental experiences. Current research on motivation indicates that internal factors (i.e, students' beliefs and perceptions) are key factors in understanding behavior. Most of the attention in the chapter is given to the internal factors of motivation. I begin this section with a discussion of what behaviors determine students' motivation and then discuss how personal and sociocultural, classroom environmental, and internal factors influence motivated behavior.

Motivated Behavior

If you want to understand your own motivation, you might begin by evaluating your behavior in the following three areas:

- Choice of behavior
- Level of activity and involvement
- Persistence and management of effort

Students make choices everyday about activities and tasks in which to engage. Many students choose to learn more about a subject or topic outside of class, whereas others limit their involvement to class assignments. As an undergraduate, I had a roommate who slept until noon each day. This behavior would not have been problematic if his classes were in the afternoon. Unfortunately, all his classes were in the morning. Another student I knew could not say no when someone asked if she wanted to go to a movie or have pizza, even though she had to study for an exam or write a paper. Students do not have to be productive every moment. Having fun or wasting time is a part of life. However, the choices they make play important roles in determining the number of personal goals they will attain throughout life.

A second aspect of motivated behavior is level of activity, or involvement in a task. Some students are very involved in their courses. They spend considerable effort after class refining notes, outlining readings, and, in general, using different learning strategies to make sense of what they are learning. Other students are less engaged in their courses and do the minimal amount required to get by.

The third aspect of motivated behavior is persistence. The willingness of students to persist when tasks are difficult, boring, or unchallenging is an important factor in motivation and academic success. In many cases, students have to learn how to control their efforts and persistence in the variety of academic tasks they experience. Let's now examine the factors that influence motivated behavior.

Personal and Sociocultural Factors

The attitudes, beliefs, and experiences students bring to college based on their personal and sociocultural experiences influence their motivation and behavior, and even their persistence or departure from college. When you walk into your first college class, you bring all your precollege experiences with you, such as your study and learning strategies, attitudes and beliefs about your ability to succeed in college, your coping strategies, and the level of commitment to meet personal goals. All of these attributes will influence the way you interact with the college environment. If you receive a low grade on a paper or exam, will you remind yourself of your ability to succeed, or will you say something like: "Here we go, just like high school. I don't know if I can do well in this course?" All your past experiences with stressful situations and the way you handled them will influence your ability to deal with new stressful situations in your college environment. You are going to learn new copying strategies in this course (see chapter 5) that should result in a reduction of stress and increase confidence in your ability to succeed in college.

You also are influenced by your family and cultural experiences. Family characteristics such as socioeconomic levels, parental educational levels, and parental expectations can influence motivation and behavior. For example, first-generation and ethnic minority students have a more difficult time adjusting to college than do second- or third-generation college students (Ratcliff, 1995). Transition to college can be difficult for any student, but when an individual has family members who have experienced this transition, he or she is less likely to feel lost in a new or unfamiliar environment or unsure about what questions to ask. Also, Reglin and Adams (1990) reported that Asian American students are more influenced by their parents' desire for success than are their non–Asian American peers. They pointed out that the desire by Asian American students to meet their parents' academic expectations creates the need to spend more time on academic tasks and less time on nonacademic activities. In what ways has your family influenced your goals, motivation, and behavior?

Here is a list of some other student characteristics that can influence adjustment and involvement in college (adapted from Jalomo, 1995):

- Married students with family obligations
- Single parents
- Students who never liked high school or who were rebellious in high school
- Students who were not involved in academic activities or student groups during high school

- Students who are afraid or feel out of place in the mainstream college culture
- Students who have a hard time adjusting to the fast pace of college
- Students who lack the financial resources to take additional courses or participate in campus-based academic and social activities in college

Stereotype Threat. A distressing research finding is that African American and Latino students from elementary school through college tend to have lower test scores and grades, and tend to drop out of school more often than White students (National Center for Education Statistics, 1998). In addition, regardless of income level, they score lower than White and Asian students on the Scholastic Achievement Test (SAT). For years, educators have been concerned with these statistics, especially when capable minority students fail to perform as well as their White counterparts.

Professor Claude Steele (1999) and his colleague (Aronson, 2002) believe they have identified a possible explanation for this dilemma. They think the difference in academic performance has less to do with preparation or ability and more to do with the threat of stereotypes about the students' ability to succeed. They coined the term **stereotype threat** to mean the fear of doing something that would inadvertently confirm a stereotype. The following is an explanation of this phenomenon.

Stereotypes can influence an individual's motivation and achievement by suggesting to the target of the stereotype that a negative label could apply to one's self or group. For example, the commonly held stereotype that women are less capable in mathematics than men has been shown to affect the performance of women on standardized math tests. When females students were told beforehand of this negative stereotype, scores were significantly lower compared to a group of women who were led to believe the tests did not reflect these stereotypes (Spencer, Steele, & Quinn, 1999). In another investigation (Levy, 1996), half of a group of older adults were reminded of the stereotype regarding old age and memory loss while the other half were reminded of the more positive stereotype that old people are wise. The older adults performed worse on a test of short-term memory when they were presented with the negative stereotype than when they were reminded of the more positive stereotype. Why do you think the women and older adults scored lower under the stereotype threat condition?

Now let's review the research as to how stereotype threat may help to explain the low achievement of certain minority group members. There exists a stereotype that many African American and Latino students may not have the academic ability to succeed in college. As a result, many minority students may feel at risk of confirming this stereotype and wonder if they can compete successfully at the college level. Thus, just the awareness of the stereotype can affect a student's motivation and behavior. Steele and Aronson (1995) asked African American and White college students to take a difficult standardized test (verbal portion of the Graduate Record Examination). In one condition, the experimenters presented the test as a measure of intellectual ability and preparation. In the second condition, the experimenters reduced the stereotype threat by telling the students that they were not interested in measuring their ability with the test, but were interested in the students' verbal problem solving. The only difference between the two conditions of the experiment was what the researchers told the students: the test was the same; the students were equally talented and were given the same amount of time to complete the exam.

The results of the experiment indicated a major difference for the African American students. When the test was presented in the nonevaluative way, they solved about twice as many problems on the test as when it was presented in the standard way. Moreover, there was no difference between the performance of African American and White test takers under the no-stereotype threat condition. For the White students, the way the test was presented had no effect on their performance. The researchers believed that by reducing the evaluative condition, they were able to reduce the African American students' anxiety, and, as a result, they performed better on the exam.

Aronson (2002) pointed out that in numerous investigations, researchers have found that the stereotype threat condition doesn't reduce effort, but makes individuals try harder on tests because they want to invalidate the stereotype. Not all individuals are equally vulnerable by stereotype threat. Individuals who are more vulnerable include those who care most about doing well, people who feel a deep sense of attachment to their ethnic or gender group, and individuals who have higher expectations for discrimination in their environment. Students under the stereotype threat condition appear more anxious while taking a test. In addition, they also reread questions and recheck their answers more often than when they are not under stereotype threat. As a result, students placed in a stereotype threat condition become poor test takers!

Are you vulnerable to stereotype threat as a member of a minority group, a woman, an older student who has come back to college a number of years after graduating from high school? Can student-athletes experience stereotype threat? Could the stereotype threat "absent-minded professor" influence your instructor's behavior? Has stereotype threat influenced your motivation or behavior in any way? Are you aware of such influence?

What can educators do about reducing the influence of stereotype threat? Aronson (2002) pointed out that stereotype threat appears to be especially disruptive to individuals who believe that intelligence is fixed rather than changeable. In this course, you are learning that academic performance can be improved through the use of different learning and motivational strategies. Do you believe that you can become a more successful student and compete with other students at your college or university? There also is some evidence that stereotype threat may be reduced through cooperative learning and other forms of direct contact with other students.

In a successful program that improved the academic achievement of a group of African American freshman at the University of Michigan (Steele et al., 1997), students lived in a racially integrated "living and learning" community in a part of a large dormitory. The students were recognized for their accomplishment of gaining admission to the university and participated in weekly rap groups to discuss common problems they all faced. In addition, they participated in advanced workshops in one of their courses that went beyond the material in the course. All of these activities were useful; however, the weekly rap sessions appeared to be the most critical part of program. The researchers believed that when students of different racial groups hear the same concerns expressed, the concerns appear to be less racial. The students also may learn that racial and gender stereotypes play a smaller role in academic success than they may have originally expected.

It is important to realize that the researchers exploring the impact of stereotype threat are not saying that this phenomenon is the sole reason for underachievement by certain minority students. We have already discussed a number of other important academic and motivational factors that can make a difference between a successful and unsuccessful college experience. Nevertheless, stereotype threat must be considered an important factor in understanding underachievement of certain minority students.

EXERCISE 3.1: SELF-OBSERVATION: ANALYZING MY PERSONAL AND SOCIOCULTURAL BACKGROUND

Directions: What attitudes and beliefs have you brought to college that could influence your motivation and academic behavior? Check either Yes or No for each of the questions on p. 59 and then write a summary statement about how your personal, social, and cultural experiences influence your present motivation. What do you see as your areas of greatest strengths in meeting your goals? What areas do you need to work on to ensure your success in college?

	Yes	No
1. Did you like high school?		
2. Were you active in social activities in high school?		
3. Are you a member of a minority group with a small enrollment in your college?		
4. Do you have parents and/or siblings who have attended college?		
5. Do your parents want you to major in a specific area?		
6. Are your aspirations the same as your parents or other family members?		
7. Are you paying for your own education?		
8. Do you have responsibility for caring for children while in college?		
9. Are you older than most of the students in your classes?		
10. Have you met students with common interests?		
11. Have you been able to cope with the stressors of college life?		
12. Have your expectations about college life been fulfilled to date?		

Summary Statement:

_____

_____

_____

_____

_____

Classroom Environmental Factors

Many classroom environmental factors influence student motivation. These include types of assignments given, instructor behavior, and instructional methods. Ratcliff (1995) reported that a successful transition to college is related to the quality of classroom life. In particular, student motivation and achievement is greater when instructors communicate high expectations for success, allow students to take greater responsibility for their learning, and encourage various forms of collaborative learning (i.e., peer learning or group learning).

In an interesting book, *Making the Most of College,* Light (2001) interviewed hundreds of college seniors to identify factors that made college an outstanding experience. Here are some findings about college instruction that appeared to motivate students: First, the students reported that they learned significantly more when instructors structured their courses with many quizzes and short assignments. They liked immediate feedback and the opportunity to revise and make changes in their work. They did not like courses when the only feedback came late or at the end of the semester.

Second, the students reported that they liked classes where the instructors encouraged students to work together on homework assignments. They mentioned that some of their instructors created small study groups in their courses to encourage students to work together outside of class. This activity helped students become more engaged in their courses.

Third, many students found that small-group tutorials, small seminars, and one-to-one supervision were the highlights of their college careers. They highly recommended that undergraduate students find internships and other experiences where they can be mentored by faculty members.

Fourth, students reported the beneficial impact of racial and ethnic diversity on their college experiences. They reported how much they learned from other students who came from different backgrounds—ethnic, political, religious, or economic.

Fifth, students who get the most out of college and who are happiest organize their time to include activities with faculty members or with other students (see chapter 7 regarding seeking help and meeting with your professors). Most students need recommendations from faculty members for graduate study or jobs. Yet, they often fail to meet with their instructors to get a letter of recommendation. Light (2001) pointed out the advice he gives all his advisees: "Your job is to get to know one faculty member reasonably well this semester. And also to have that faculty member get to know you reasonably well" (p. 86). He reported that as his first-year advisees approach graduation, they tell him that this advice was the most helpful suggestion they received during their freshman year.

Professors differ as much as any other group of individuals; some are easy to approach, whereas others make it appear that they are trying to avoid students. In fact, in many large universities, a student has to work hard to make contact with some professors. Nevertheless, think about the challenge of getting to know at least one instructor or professor well each semester. Not only will you find that the experience will motivate you to achieve in his or her class, but when the time comes for letters of recommendation, you will have a list of professors to ask. So, try not to be intimidated by your instructors: go to office hours, sign up for study sessions, and get a few students together and invite the instructor to lunch if you don't want to do it by yourself.

EXERCISE 3.2: SELF-OBSERVATION: ANALYZING CLASSROOM EXPERIENCES

Directions: The following are some questions to consider about college courses. Select one of the courses you are taking this term and check either Yes or No for each of the questions listed. Think about how your responses could influence your academic motivation and behavior. Compare your responses to other students in your class who are taking the same or different courses. How can you be more active in making the most of your college experience?

	Yes	No
1. Are you given freedom to select your own topics for papers and assignments?		
2. Does the instructor offer an opportunity for discussion in class?		
3. Is there an opportunity to work with other students?		
4. Is the grading competitive (i.e., grading on a curve)?		
5. Does your instructor or teaching assistant appear willing to meet with you?		
6. Have you had a personal meeting with your instructor?		
7. Does the instructor provide clear guidelines as to what is expected in the course?		

continued

	Yes	*No*
8. Does this class have more than 50 students in it?		
9. Does your instructor provide timely feedback on assignments?		
10. Are you participating in group study sessions?		

Although it is important for students to understand that the class-room environment can influence their motivation, they need to take responsibility for their own behavior. My daughter came home one day during her freshman year and told me that she received a low C on a midterm exam. In the same breath, she reported that she did not like the instructor, implying a relationship between the low grade and her dislike of the instructor. I responded that my expectations for her academic performance were not based on her like or dislike of courses or professors, and told her she had to learn to do well in all types of situations.

In chapter 1 you learned that self-directed students learn how to overcome obstacles to increase the probability of their academic success. Think about some of the actions you can take to improve your academic learning when you don't like your instructor, find the course boring, or when the instructor spends all his or her time lecturing and doesn't encourage student interaction or small-group work.

Internal Factors

Students' goals, beliefs, feelings, and perceptions determine their motivated behavior and, in turn, academic performance. For example, if students value a task and believe they can master it, they are more likely to use different learning strategies, try hard, and persist until completion of the task. If students believe that intelligence changes over time, they are more likely to exhibit effort in difficult courses than students who believe intelligence is fixed. In this section of the chapter, I'm going to explain why the answers to the following questions can provide insight to your own motivation:

- How do I value different academic courses and tasks?
- What are my goals?
- What is my goal orientation?
- Do I believe I can do well on different academic tasks?

- What are the causes of my successes and failures?
- How do I feel about my academic challenges?

Notice that all of the questions deal with beliefs and perceptions. Students can learn a great deal about their motivation by examining how their beliefs and perceptions influence them.

How Do I Value Different Academic Courses or Tasks?   Values and interests play an important role in academic behavior. They affect students' choices of activities, as well as the level of effort and persistence they put forth on a task or assignment. For example, Satisfied Sheila enjoys intellectual challenges, as demonstrated by her interest in poetry. Unfortunately, she fails to incorporate her interests in her school courses and assignments.

Students in a given course may have different reasons for enrolling. Let's consider three students in a chemistry course. The first student decides to take the course because it fulfills a general education requirement. She has very little interest in the subject. The second student is enrolled in the course because she enjoys learning about science and would like to pursue a career in the health sciences. The third student wants to learn chemistry because doing well can help her get on the dean's list and feeling competent is an important value in her life.

All three of these students want to succeed but may behave differently during the term. At times, their different value orientations may influence them to make different decisions regarding their effort and persistence in the course. For example, during final exams, students often have to make decisions concerning where to place their greatest effort. Students who are taking a course just to complete an elective may decide to spend more time during finals on a course where higher achievement is more important.

Students who limit their involvement or effort in a particular class are not necessarily lazy or unmotivated. Instead, they are motivated to participate in different things such as athletics, social organizations, family activities, or relationships rather than academics (Stipek, 1998). College students do not develop a personal interest in or high value for all their courses. Some required or elective courses are more interesting than others. The task, however, is to manage motivation to successfully complete courses, even when there is little interest in them.

What Are My Goals?   I begin my "learning to learn" course by asking students about their goals. Each year I find many differences in the abilities of students to articulate their goals. Some students have clear and well-defined goals. They know why they are in college and what they are attempting to attain. At the other end of the spectrum, some students have not even defined their personal goals and are not sure why they are in college. Some of my students who are raising families or who have returned to college after some absence appear to have more specific goals than do some students who come directly from high school. How would you explain this difference?

Think about a musician, athlete, or businessperson who wants to excel in his or her area of expertise but has no specific goals to direct his or her behavior. It is very difficult to be motivated without personal goals. It is important to set goals in different life areas because such goals serve to motivate behavior. Goals enhance performance in five major ways (Locke & Latham, 1990):

- Effort: The goals you set for yourself influence what you attend to and how hard you try to maximize your performance. The more difficult the goal, the harder you are likely to work to attain it.
- Duration or persistence: When you work on a task without a goal, you are likely to allow your attention to drift, become more easily interrupted, and even stop working without completing the task. When you have a goal in mind, you have a more clearly defined point in the performance that defines when it is time to quit or withdraw from the task (i.e., when the goal is attained).
- Direction of attention: Goals direct your performance toward the task at hand and away from unrelated or irrelevant tasks.
- Strategic planning: To accomplish a goal, you need to develop an action plan or strategy. Goal setting encourages strategic planning, because the presence of a goal encourages you to decide how to proceed.
- Reference point: When you identify where it is you are headed (i.e., have a goal) and receive feedback on where you are, you can evaluate your performance and determine what further actions need to be taken (if any). In fact, it is your satisfaction or dissatisfaction with this evaluation that may have the greatest impact on your motivation.

Have you identified some goals you would like to attain this term or year? If so, do you have goals in any of the following areas: academic, social, occupational, or personal? How has your success or failure in attaining previous goals influenced your motivation in different areas of your life?

What Is My Goal Orientation?   Educators have determined that students have different reasons or purposes for achieving in different courses. Dweck and Leggett (1988) believe that the achievement goals students pursue "create the framework within which they interpret and react to events" (p. 256). They have identified two types of achievement goals: **mastery** and **performance**. A mastery goal is oriented toward learning as much as possible in a course for the purpose of self-improvement, irrespective of the performance of others. A performance goal focuses on social comparison and competition, with the main purpose of outperforming others on the task.

Think about how you approach different classes. Are you interested in learning as much as you can in a class, or is your major goal simply doing better than the majority of students so you can attain a satisfactory grade? Of course, in some classes you may value both learning and getting good grades because you can have multiple goals in school. It is not uncommon for students to have a mastery goal orientation in one class and a performance goal orientation in another. It is also possible to have a performance and mastery goal orientation in the same class.

An analysis of the distinction between mastery and performance goals in Table 3.1 shows how students define schooling and learning in different ways. The goal orientation that students adopt in a course influences the effort they exhibit in learning tasks and the type of learning strategies they use. Thus, when students adopt a mastery goal orientation, they are more likely to have a positive attitude toward the task (even outside the classroom), monitor their own comprehension, use more complex learning strategies, and relate newly learned material with previously learned material. In contrast, students who adopt a performance orientation tend to focus on memorization and other rote learning strategies and often do not engage in problem solv-

TABLE 3.1
TWO DEFINITIONS OF SCHOOLING

	Mastery	*Performance*
Success defined as . . .	improvement, progress, mastery, innovation, creativity	high grades, high performance compared with others, relative achievement on standardized measures
Value placed on . . .	effort, academic venturesomeness	demonstrating high performance relative to effort
Basis for satisfaction . . .	progress, challenge, mastery	doing better than others, success relative to effort
Error viewed as . . .	part of the learning process, informational	failure, evidence of lack of ability
Ability viewed as . . .	developing through effort	fixed

Adapted from Ames and Archer (1988).

ing and critical thinking. In general, they do not think about what they learn, but rather look for shortcuts and quick payoffs. Students with performance goals want to look competent (e.g., Safe Susan) or avoid looking incompetent (e.g., Defensive Dimitri).

In general, the research suggests that adopting a mastery goal orientation has positive academic outcomes (Ames, 1992). However, it has been found that performance goals, but not mastery goals, were related to academic performance in introductory college classes (Harackiewicz, Barron, Carter, Lehto, & Elliot, 1997). The researchers argued that in large lecture classes where instructors' grade on a curve and success is defined as outperforming others, performance goals can lead to academic success. Another important issue to consider is that multiple-choice tests often are used in such settings and may assess more factual rather than deeper understanding of the material. Thus, the grading method and/or type of tests used may create a performance-oriented classroom environment. In the same investigation, the researchers found that mastery goals predicted interest in the introductory class, whereas performance goals did not. We have an interesting dilemma: each goal was related to one indicator of success (academic performance or interest) but not the other. In this situation, it appears that students who endorsed both goals were most likely to like the course and achieve well.

EXERCISE 3.3: IDENTIFYING MASTERY AND PERFORMANCE GOAL ORIENTATIONS

Directions: Based on the information in Table 3.1, classify the following statements as either mastery (M) or performance (P) goal oriented by writing an M or a P in the space provided:

<u>M</u>1. "I enjoy finding extra material to read in this course."
<u>P</u>2. "It is important to me to do better than my friends."
<u>P</u>3. "If you don't have the ability to do well, more effort is a waste of time."
<u>M</u>4. "I'm not doing as well as I can, but I will improve."
<u>P</u>5. "My adviser thinks I should take another advanced math course, but I don't want to because it may lower my average."

In the following section, two students present different views on goal orientation. The first student admits that his primary goal orientation is to meet requirements, not learn. The second student reports that his goal orientation is influenced by the value he placed on different courses. What factors influence your goal orientations?

Student Reflections

For years, my goal in all my classes has been to achieve a certain grade. The grade differed from class to class depending on my confidence for success in the course. This strategy has been my plan of attack since elementary school. Unfortunately, my goals have never changed, and I rarely participate in class just for the simple pleasure of learning. I enjoy a class once a discussion begins, but I usually prefer to be somewhere else. I am performance rather than mastery driven. I do not care to learn anything for the sake of learning. Schoolwork is just a means to an end: graduation and a degree.

#   #   #   #

Learning how to understand my own motivation has helped my self-management in school. Every class is different, and I have learned to take its importance into consideration. Some classes are simply for utility purposes—a means to an end. In these classes, I set goals for myself based on performing at a level equal to or better than my peers. However, in my major courses, I am concerned with learning all that I possibly can. These classes are exciting, and I am strictly mastery oriented. By seeing my classes for what they are, I can set goals suitable for their purpose. Each one is different, and as I achieve in each class, my confidence is maintained because of the goals I set. Whenever I begin to feel discouraged with a low grade on an exam or paper in a class that I don't value, I remind myself of my goal for the course. In this way, I don't get down on myself.

Your goal orientation in a particular course can greatly impact your motivation, even before you ever open a textbook or take your first lecture notes. Analyze your goal orientation in each of the classes you are currently taking. Do you have the same goal orientation in all of your classes? Do you think you exhibit both orientations in some classes? Do you find that your learning behavior differs depending on your goal orientation? Also, think about a hobby or particular interest you have. How long can you persist on the task before getting tired or bored? How is your behavior related to your goal orientation?

Do I Believe I Can Do Well on Different Academic Tasks?   Values and goals determine students' reasons for engaging in different tasks. Another important belief is **self-efficacy**, which refers to the evaluation students have about their abilities or skills to successfully complete a task (Bandura, 1982). The key question that determines self-efficacy is: "Am I capable of succeeding at this task?"

Educational researchers have found that efficacy beliefs are important predictors of student motivation and self-managed behaviors (Schunk, 1991). Students with high efficacy are more likely than their low-efficacy counterparts to choose difficult tasks, expend greater effort, persist longer, use more complex learning strategies, and experience less fear and anxiety regarding academic tasks.

Self-efficacy is situation specific. A student may have a high self-efficacy for completing a term paper in a psychology course but a low sense of efficacy regarding his or her performance on multiple-choice questions that test knowledge of different learning theories. A student may judge him or herself to be very competent at basketball but not at tennis. We have efficacy beliefs about each task we undertake.

I mentioned in the first chapter that my primary goal is to help you become a more successful learner. An important step is to help you feel more competent to excel in the different academic tasks you experience. Setting goals is one way to enhance your sense of efficacy. As you work on academic tasks, you should determine your progress by analyzing your performance according to your goals. Recognizing that you are making progress toward your goals can validate your initial sense of self-efficacy and maintain your behavior as you move toward goal attainment. Learning how to use different learning strategies is another way to enhance your sense of efficacy.

Monitoring your self-efficacy on tasks can focus attention on your beliefs about the effectiveness of your study methods. Zimmerman, Bonner, and Kovach (1996) suggested a procedure that can be used for quizzes or homework assignments. Before taking your next quiz or exam, read all of the questions and estimate your ability to answer the questions on a 10-point scale. The lower the score, the less competent you feel; the higher the score, the more competent you feel. Compare your actual score on the quizzes or exams with your efficacy scores. Your self-efficacy ratings can operate like a thermostat, providing information you can use to modify or change your learning and study behavior. For example, how would you explain a situation in which your efficacy ratings are always higher than your actual test scores, or where your efficacy ratings are always lower than your actual test scores?

Self-efficacy monitoring helps you gain accuracy in predicting your learning. If you misjudge your self-efficacy, you might attempt to adjust your future standards. If quizzes or exams are more demanding than you expect, you may need to study harder to succeed. Rating your efficacy too low or being overly optimistic about your performance can be detrimental to your academic success. The more accurate your perceptions of competence or efficacy, the more likely you will be to use the information to make appropriate changes in your learning and study strategies.

What Are the Causes of My Successes and Failures?   When an event occurs, individuals can interpret it in different ways. Consider two college students of equal ability in the same class who just received a C on a term paper. The first student is very upset because he does not think the instructor's grading was fair. He decides that there is not much he can do to obtain a high grade in the course. The second student determines that the grade reflected the amount of time he spent completing the task and decides that he needs to work harder in the future.

Why did the two students of equal ability interpret their experiences differently? One explanation is that the two students made different attributions about their performances on the term papers. An attribution is an individual's perception of the causes of his or her success or failure. Attribution theory helps explain why individuals respond differently to the same outcomes.

The most common attributions for academic performance are ability ("I did well because I am smart" or "I did poorly because I am not capable") and effort ("I studied hard for the test" or "I did not study hard enough"). However, students often make other attributions, such as "I was lucky or unlucky," "The task was easy or hard," "I was tired," "I did not feel well," or "The instructor was unfair."

Weiner (1986), a leading motivational researcher, believes that how students perceive the causes of their prior successes and failures is the most important factor determining how they will approach a particular task and how long they will persist at it. For example, students who attribute their past successful performances to their ability are more likely to welcome similar challenges in the future because they anticipate doing well again. However, students are less likely to be optimistic about future tasks if they attribute their prior successes to luck or the generosity of the instructor.

Students who believe their failures are because of their own lack of effort are likely to try harder in future situations and persist on difficult tasks. Also, students who believe that success is a result of their own doing (i.e., controllable) are more likely to do the things that are necessary to attain success. These students are more likely to seek assistance from their instructor if they do not understand the material and will attend extra-help sessions when necessary. In contrast, students who believe their successes and failures are uncontrollable (e.g., because of luck or the generosity of the teacher) are less likely to seek the help they need.

Let's return to the example at the beginning of this section. Suppose the instructor was not biased in his or her grading of the first student's paper, but that the C grade was really because of the student's poor effort and planning. By attributing failure to teacher bias, an external and uncontrollable cause, the student is likely to be angry and unlikely to improve his behavior on future written assignments. In contrast, the student who attributed the cause of his grade to lack of effort, an internal and controllable cause, is more likely to be motivated to improve his performance in future assignments.

Now that you know that attributions can have a powerful impact on your success and failure, I will discuss how you can use this information. One implication of this theory is to understand the role of attributions in your own learning. Remember that the fact that you attribute a cause to some factor does not mean that your attribution reflects reality. Think about a friend who has the tendency to attribute a low test grade on "tricky" questions or an unfair instructor when the grade was really because of poor preparation.

It is important to consider how you interpret your own behavior. Educational research indicates that self-directed learners tend to attribute failure to corrective causes and attribute successes to their own personal abilities (Zimmerman, 1998b). Ask yourself the following questions:

- "What role do attributions play in my understanding of my achievement and motivation?"
- "When I perform poorly, do I attribute my performance to uncontrollable factors? Are there alternative explanations for the causes of my academic performances?"
- "Could I benefit from attributing a poor performance to lack of effort or failure to use appropriate learning strategies rather than to lack of ability?"

Many students have difficulty in courses because they lack prior knowledge, use inappropriate learning strategies, or fail to monitor their comprehension—all factors that are controllable or changeable. When students recognize that their behavior is modifiable, instead of thinking they lack ability and feeling poorly about themselves, they will more likely feel motivated to achieve.

As the semester progresses, it is not uncommon for students to feel "up and down" at different times. Attribution theory can help students to better understand their own feelings. Attributions are related to different emotional responses. For example, whether individuals attribute failure to ability or effort influences how they will feel about themselves. Attributing failure to lack of ability elicits feelings of shame and humiliation; attributing failure to lack of effort leads to embarrassment, which often leads to an increase of effort the next time. Emotions or feelings will change if attributions are changed. Therefore, individuals should carefully consider all the possible reasons for their performance before they draw any conclusions, especially when they do not perform as well as they expected. Most important, they should consider other causes besides lack of ability, especially effort.

How Do I Feel About Academic Demands?   Anxiety can negatively impact academic performance in many ways. Ottens (1991) identified four interrelated characteristics of academically anxious students:

- Disruption in mental activity
- Psychological distress
- Misdirected attention
- Inappropriate behaviors, of which procrastination is most common

Recent research has focused on the relative independence of two dimensions of test anxiety: worry versus emotionality. Worry is the major factor in the disruption of mental activity, whereas emotionality is more related to physiological distress. Worry reflects the cognitive aspects of anxiety—the negative beliefs, troubling thoughts, and poor decisions. Emotionality refers to the unpleasant affective reactions, such as tension and nervousness. Each of these dimensions can have differential effects on students. Although both dimensions can have a debilitating effect, the worry dimension has a stronger negative relation to academic performance than the emotional dimension. One reason for this finding is that emotionality tends to decrease once test taking begins, whereas worrisome thoughts often continue throughout the test and may be experienced for a period of time in advance of the examination. Also, achievement suffers because attention is affected during test taking, when the task requires remembering or retrieving what was learned.

   Covington (1992) has proposed a useful interaction model of test anxiety, where he shows the effects of anxiety at three stages—appraisal, preparation, and test taking. Students' motivation to succeed or avoid failure is determined in the test appraisal stage by whether they judge the upcoming test to be a challenge or a threat. In the test preparation stage, students begin studying while thinking about such things as their ability, expectations, and the futility and effectiveness of their study. They start thinking such thoughts as: "Will I do well on the exam?" or "Will it be worthwhile to spend a great deal of time studying?" Students threatened by failure may become involved in avoidance behaviors such as irrational goal setting (e.g., attempting to review the five most difficult chapters in one night, or procrastination that will further erode their study effectiveness. Finally, in the test-taking stage, students attempt to retrieve what they have learned, often faced with great physical tension and worry. Anxiety, at this stage, interferes with the retrieval of information. As the semester progresses, the processes repeats itself every time there is an examination. More specifically, the type of attribution to the feedback on the first test—either success or failure—influences how one will achieve on the next test. For example, if a poor performance is attributed to low ability, then shame is likely to occur and the effectiveness of study preparation is likely to be seen. This process can vary in duration from a few hours to weeks or even months.

Let's look at a specific example of how the process may operate. Phil arrives at college wanting to be a pharmacist, a career choice that pleased his parents and impressed his friends. Unfortunately, Phil didn't take all the science courses in high school that would have better prepared him for this major. As a result, he starts his freshman year taking three science courses. To make matters worse, Phil is a chronic procrastinator who put off tasks until the last minute because he relies on his superior intellect to get him through difficult tasks. Phil learned early in the semester that he couldn't wait until the last minute to study for exams like he did in high school. He received two Cs and a D in his first-semester grades. He decided not to be discouraged and that he would show his parents and friends that he could succeed by working very hard the second semester.

Now, let's see how anxiety influences his behavior during the three stages—appraisal, preparation, and test taking.

Appraisal Stage.   As he sits in the first session of his psychology course in the second semester of his freshman year, he listens to the instructor review the course requirements. Suddenly, he feels very uncomfortable and starts thinking whether he will flunk out of school. He becomes preoccupied with the thought that he will be found out as incompetent.

Preparation Stage.   The first exam is approaching, and Phil needs to start studying. The problem is that he again has procrastinated and knows that he will have difficulty reviewing all the material. Most important, however, he begins to doubt whether he can succeed and is preoccupied with worry. He has difficulty concentrating on reading his textbook; he starts thinking that perhaps he is not smart enough to become a pharmacist; he wonders if he would do better if he had a more interesting teacher. As a result of his negative perceptions, he spends little time studying and more time watching television and playing video games. The result is that he is unprepared for his examination.

Test-Taking Stage. As he is taking the examination, he notices that many students are completing their exams early and wonders if the test is easier than he thinks. He begins to question his ability and his worry begins to interfere with his ability to recall the little information he studied. He becomes frustrated because he is unable to think about the possible answers to the questions.

A different approach needs to be taken with anxious students who have good study skills but cannot handle evaluative pressure, and with anxious students who have difficulty learning the content (whose anxiety interferes in the appraisal and preparation stage; Naveh-Benjamin, McKeachie, & Lin, 1987). In chapter 5, I discuss relaxation techniques and cognitive therapies designed to reduce the worry components of test anxiety. You will be asked to think about and analyze your anxiety-provoking thoughts and develop new coping strategies, such as using positive self-talk before a test and instruct yourself to attend to the task while studying or taking tests. These strategies will help students who have difficulty with evaluative pressure. Researchers have found that high-anxiety students use poorer study strategies than students lower in anxiety and are more prone to use avoidance to cope with their academic problems (Zeidner, 1995). Thus, the learning strategies that you are acquiring in this course can help in reducing anxiety.

Another characteristic of anxiety is misdirected attention. Here the problem is with concentration or attention. No matter what the academic activity—taking notes, reading a textbook, studying, or taking an exam—anxious students easily lose their attention. This behavior handicaps students by not allowing them to complete their work efficiently, and can cause emotional upset. Anxious Alberto's motivational problem is that he constantly encounters distractions when he begins studying for an exam. He constantly thinks about the possibility of failure and forgets information. Safe Susan also has anxiety problems, but in her case, the anxiety leads to obsessive studying and preparation.

The final characteristic of anxious students is the tendency to act inappropriately. Procrastination is very common, as is quitting tasks before they are completed, conversing with a friend when time is running out to complete an assignment, or answering test questions in a rush to get out of the examination room as soon as possible. Test anxiety is a specific form of anxiety related to evaluation of academic ability. Educators are especially concerned about this type of anxiety, because it increases through the elementary grades to high school and becomes more strongly (i.e., negatively) related to indexes of intellectual and academic performance (Hembree, 1988). As students proceed through school, the higher their anxiety, the more likely they will experience lower achievement.

Covington's Self-Worth Theory. Self-worth is an individual's evaluative appraisal of him- or herself. It is similar to such terms as self-esteem or self-respect. According to self-worth theory (Covington, 1992), individuals learn that society values people because of their accomplishments. If a person fails at a task, the feedback evokes the possibility of a lack of ability and creates feelings of unworthiness and self-rejection. As a result, when individuals are faced with the possibility of failure, they will avoid the situation or develop strategies to protect any inferences to a lack of their ability. Covington (1992) identified a number of these strategies:

- Procrastination: If an individual studies at the last minute and does not have enough time to properly prepare for an exam, failure cannot be attributed to lack of ability.
- Unattainable goals: If an individual selects very difficult goals, failure is often assured. However, failure in such tasks reveals little about one's ability because most individuals would fail.
- Underachievers: If an individual avoids any test of his or her ability by just doing the minimum to get by, he or she can maintain an inflated opinion of ability: "I could do it if I really tried."
- Anxiety: If an individual argues that one's poor performance is the result of test-taking anxiety, then one can't blame the performance as the result of low ability. In other words, "It's better to appear anxious than stupid" (p. 88).

Examination of the role of effort from both the instructors' and students' perspectives reveals that, in some cases, both instructors and students operate at cross purposes. Although instructors highly value achievement, they often reward (or criticize) some students more than others for exactly the same level of performance. Students who are perceived as having expended effort (regardless of their ability) tend to be rewarded more and criticized less than students who do not try (Wiener & Kukla, 1970).

Instructors like students who try. Do you feel worse about a grade on a test or paper when you have worked hard or when you exhibited little effort? Educational research indicates that students experienced greatest shame with a combination of high effort and failure and least shame with a combination of low effort and failure (Covington & Omelich, 1979). This research helps explain why failure-avoiding students often do not try. Expending effort and still failing poses a serious threat to one's self-esteem. The student who does not try but fails can always rationalize that success could have been achieved through proper effort, thus maintaining a reasonable level of self-esteem. Instructors, however, tend to reinforce students who demonstrate effort and are more critical of those who do not. Understanding the perspectives of both the instructor and the student helps reveal how effort can become a "double-edged sword" for many students. They must walk the tightrope between the threatening extremes of high effort and no effort at all. They must demonstrate some effort to avoid negative sanctions from their instructors, but not enough to risk shame should they try hard and fail. Some students use excuses to maintain a balance between these extremes. A popular tactic is to try hard but to use excuses to explain why trying did not help. Such behavior avoids any inference to low ability.

Hopeless Henry believes that his failures are because of a lack of ability. As a result, he does not believe that hard work will pay off. The problem with this belief is that he is likely to exert little effort even in situations in which effort would lead to success.

What is interesting about self-worth theory is that it offers a different explanation of failure. Many students are motivated, but for the wrong reasons—they are more motivated to avoid failure than motivated to succeed. They are driven by circumstances to protect their self-esteem.

A college friend of mine was a bright but anxious student. He always told everyone that he never had enough time to study before an exam. Everyone was impressed by the success he achieved with little apparent effort. However, in situations where his achievement was unsatisfactory, he would also remind us that he did not spend much time studying. It was not until years later that I learned he had always found time to study regularly during the term. His strategy was to protect his self-worth. The moral of this story is not to gauge the amount of time and effort you need to prepare by listening to the comments of others.

What strategies have you used to protect yourself from the possibilities of failure? Have you ever raised your hand early in a class period to answer a question, knowing that the instructor might not call on you later? Have you remained silent when asked a question by an instructor, hoping that if you paused long enough, the instructor would rephrase the question once or twice until either the answer was given to you or someone else was called on?

I can identify with the following situation, and it may be uncomfortably familiar to you, too: A common practice in language classes is to require students to take turns translating sentences into English. As the instructor moves down the row asking one student after another to translate, anxious students are not paying attention to each translation. Instead, they are counting down the row to locate the sentence they will have to translate and begin practicing the sentence. During this time, they have missed the translations of all the previous sentences. Learning the sentences is vital to the content of the particular lesson, but some students are more motivated to avoid failure than to master the content of the lesson.

What is your experience with ability and self-worth? Do you think society communicates to children early in their lives that unless they achieve, they are unworthy? In what ways do school experiences threaten students' beliefs in their own ability? Does self-worth theory help you understand the behavior of anyone you know?

AM I MOTIVATED TO CHANGE MY ACADEMIC BEHAVIOR?

In the first three chapters you learned what it takes to be a self-directed learner. In addition, you learned why you need to acquire certain learning strategies and how certain motivational variables influence your behavior. The major issue that you now face is whether you are actually motivated to change your academic behavior. No one, not your parents, friends, or college instructors, can make you change. You need to decide whether you want to learn and study differently in college than you did in high school. Of course, if you were an A student in high school, I would recommend that you not change many things. However, if you think there is some room for improvement, then you should consider what aspects of your academic behavior in college you want to change.

The next student reflection was written by a student in my learning strategies course about six weeks into the semester:

Student Reflection

Last week I took my first political science midterm of this semester. Despite all the discussion in my learning and study strategies course, I basically studied the same way I have always been studying most of my life. I read over the material a few times, underlined some key points, and woke up early to review the material. It is not that I thought the new learning strategies would not be helpful, but it seemed to me that they took more time then it was worth. When I received a lower grade than I expected, I decided to try some of the new strategies. I now realize that I can cover the same amount of material in the same time or even shorter. Most important, instead of simply reading the material over and over again, I now understand the material much more because I am generating questions while I read and attempting to answer them. My mind does not wander as much as it did before because I have a purpose to my reading. I find that I can remember much more material after each study session.

Wouldn't it be nice if all students were influenced in the same manner? Unfortunately, students react differently to change. Prochaska and Prochaska (1999) suggested four reasons why individuals have difficulty changing their behavior: they can't, they don't want to, they don't know what to change, or they do not know how to change. If you would like to change but have difficulties, think about how these reasons might apply to you. I'll discuss each of these reasons to help you analyze your own behavior by using the motivational topics I discussed in the chapter. You might want to review self-efficacy, attribution and self-worth theory, and goal orientation and task value before you read this final section.

I Can't Change

Prochaska and Prochaska (1999) pointed out that people can't change aspects of themselves that are not conscious. Studies in psychology (e.g., Bargh & Chartrand, 1999; Wegner & Wheatley, 1999) indicate that some behavior is so automated (i.e., nonconscious, unintentional) that we have difficulty being aware when we engage in them and explaining how we do certain things. Try explaining how you bowl or how you hit a baseball or how you learn certain material for an exam. It is not as easy as you think. Without realizing it, you probably have automated your study habits through their repeated use during the 12 years of schooling prior to college. Changing such automated behaviors requires considerable commitment, effort, and time, leading some students to conclude that they lack the willpower and inner strength, and therefore cannot change. For example, when I teach a system of note taking in chapter 9, some students report that they can't learn the new system because their old methods, though ineffective, are automated to the point where they function in a nonconscious way. What makes matters worse is that when students are under pressure, such as preparing for an important midterm exam, they often resort to their existing automated skills even when they know that these skills are not as useful or effective as the new skills they have learned or practiced. In summary, expect changing your academic behavior to not be an easy process, but know that you can change if you are willing to put in the effort and time to practice a new skill. Remember that you didn't become good at playing basketball, the piano, chess, or whatever interests you in just a few sessions of effortless practice.

Another factor to consider when you believe that you can't change is your level of self-efficacy (or self-confidence) regarding a specific task. Remember that researchers have found that your level of self-efficacy can predict behaviors, such as choosing to engage in tasks and persisting at them in the face of difficulty (Bandura, 1982). Therefore, if you hold a low sense of efficacy for a particular task such as improving your note taking, you may avoid learning a new skill, give up easily when things get tough, and conclude that you cannot change that particular aspect of your academic behavior. However, if you put in the effort and experience success, your perception about your ability to master the skill will change.

I Don't Want to Change

I have found that most students identify this category for why they don't change their academic behavior. Let's look at some of the factors that contribute to this belief (Isaacson, 2002). First, students may have a high sense of self-efficacy in their abilities and the effectiveness of their existing study strategies. They tell themselves, "After all, I got through high school and was accepted into college!" This response is a reasonable approach to one's academic work and can lead to success for some students. There are, however, students who do not understand the difference in the required study skills between high school and college, and fail to realize what awaits them down the road. In fact, many of these students have such high self-efficacy that they are overconfident in their abilities. These students demonstrate displeasure when faced with a requirement to take a learning strategies course because it conflicts with their perception of the level of skills they possess for academic studies: Did you take this class as an elective or were you required to take it?

Students can demonstrate passive or active resistance in class. How would you analyze the behavior of the following student?

> I dislike this learning strategies class and I know that this
> is no reason for me to do poorly in the course. However, I
> still think my study strategies are as good as the ones that
> are discussed in class. Therefore, I do not see any reason for
> me to change.

Why does this student behave the way she does, considering the fact that she is not doing well in class? Why do some students persist in the same behavior in college even though they know their strategies don't work for them? Is this a way to protect their self-worth ? Are they concerned that they may not be able to learn or apply the new study and learning strategies?

Many students have experienced an academic background consisting of teacher-controlled learning (i.e., the instructor tells one what to learn, how to learn, and when to learn) and lower-level learning (i.e., studying factual learning—who, what, when, and where) with limited exposure to the academic demands that require persistence in the face of difficulty and failure. Thus, students are not accustomed to directing their own learning when the tasks are demanding and when their initial efforts do not result in success. These challenges often lead to early failure in college. The problem, however, is that early failure often doesn't shock the college students into realizing that they must do something to change their behavior. Instead, they resist changing their learning and study strategies (Hattie, Bioss, & Purdue, 1996).

Freshmen often fail to recognize that success in many college courses requires critical thinking skills: the ability to organize arguments and evidence from many sources that often disagree with one another. In his interview with college students, Light (2001) found that students who had academic difficulty pointed out that their high school courses did not demand much critical thinking, but in college courses it is an important skill for success. When students have difficulty in courses that require critical thinking skills, they often blame or attribute their poor results to the instructor, such as expressed in the following statement: "I always did well in high school. I can't believe these tests; they are so unfair." What often occurs are explanations for failure that can be categorized as external attributions—usually the teacher or the test—not oneself. In high school, if failure occurred, it was the teacher who was asked to change. Common requests include: "Slow down," "Explain it again," "Be more concise," "Give me examples," and "Make the test easier." Isaacson (2002) stated that blaming others by attributing the responsibility for lower academic success or failure on others influences the student not to take personal responsibility and take charge of his or her own learning. Thus, when an opportunity presents itself, like taking a learning strategies course in college, the students fail to recognize how it can help because they may not recognize that they are responsible for their own academic outcomes: What was your attitude when you registered for this course? Do you think you need to change any aspect of your learning and study behavior? Do any of the beliefs described in this section relate to your thinking? If not, explain why your attitudes or beliefs are different and what factors influenced your openness for the possibility of changing some of your own study behaviors?

In this chapter, I identified two major goal orientations–mastery and performance. In a mastery orientation, a person wants to learn as much as possible and improve one's academic performance. In a performance orientation, a person wants to perform better than others, or as one student put it: "I simply want to get through this course." Adopting a performance orientation and simply wanting to "get through courses" may cause students to lower their value for a study skills course, resulting in disinterest and an unwillingness to acquire and practice self-directed learning skills. A person with a mastery orientation is more likely to use advanced rather then simple rehearsal strategies in their courses. Therefore, your goal orientation may be a factor in your perceptions regarding the desire or need to change academic behavior.

The last point I would like to identify regarding the issue of not wanting to change is the ability of students' to observe, monitor, and direct their own learning. The key here is the ability during study to predict how well they will do on exams. Research has indicated that the ability to judge or estimate how well you know the material is an important indicator of future success on exams (Tobias & Everson, 2000). This finding makes sense, because the ability to estimate one's understanding of academic content helps in making decisions about the effectiveness of one's present learning strategies, as well as the need to change. Developing this skill is an important part of becoming a more successful learner.

I Don't Know What to Change

Often students come to class believing that they can and want to change their academic behavior but are not sure what they have to do to change. The purpose of the self-observation assessments at the beginning of each chapter is to provide information about your behavior.

Your instructor may ask you to take different study skill assessments to help you identify the areas that need change. Knowing what to change requires an understanding of your learning and study strategies. The more you understand your strengths and weaknesses, the better you will be able to develop a plan for changing your behavior. One of the instruments I use is the Learning and Study Skills Inventory (LASSI; Weinstein, Schulte, & Palmer, 1987). This instrument helps students compare their skills with other college students in such areas as: attitude and interest, motivation, time management, anxiety, concentration, information processing, selecting main ideas, self-testing, and preparing for and taking tests. Which of these areas do you think are your strengths and weaknesses?

I Don't Know How to Change

Even though this course teaches learning strategies to bring about change in your academic behavior, you may not know how to change. There are many possible reasons for this problem. First, you may experience difficulty in transferring your newly learned strategies to other courses you are taking because you are not practicing these strategies in other courses. If you learn strategies but don't practice them in other courses, it is unlikely that you will become a more successful learner. Once you practice the learning strategies in different contexts, you can then make changes in how you apply the strategies in different courses and become a more successful learner.

Second, problems in knowing how to change can also stem from a lack of self-control. Examples of self-control in the academic context are self-instruction and attention focusing. Self-instruction or self-talk, an important aspect of self-control, is an important strategy that can help you guide your behavior. Research has shown that verbalizations, such as how to apply a mathematical formula, can improve students' learning (Schunk, 1982). We shall discuss the importance of self-instruction or self-talk in chapter 5.

Attention focusing as another example of how academic self-control helps to eliminate distractions and competing intentions, such as recurring thoughts about past mistakes. Before you begin using a new learning strategy, identify the specific behaviors you have to perform and evaluate your performance as you proceed. For example, beginning in chapter 4, you will find special "procedures" sections to help you review the specific behaviors necessary for implementing a new strategy. These strategies provide the specific behaviors needed to change your behavior.

Finally, in the discussion of self-worth in this chapter, I mentioned that some students are uncertain that they possess adequate ability to succeed. As a result, they may actually handicap themselves by not studying and using other self-defeating strategies to have an excuse for failing that does not reflect poorly on their ability. Failing for a reason such as not adequately preparing for an exam is less likely to threaten self-worth than failing because of low perceived ability. Garcia (1995) found that college students who used self-handicapping strategies employed little practice and time-management strategies. Self-handicapping provides a significant obstacle to the intention of changing one's academic behavior. Even though a student may believe he or she can and wants to change, engaging in self-handicapping behavior instead of using effective learning strategies can lead to less successful academic outcomes. It is possible that through self-handicapping, students who do not know how to change may actually start to believe that they cannot change. Here is a statement from a student who is afraid to change:

> The only reason that I think I have not changed is because I don't know how to change my ways. I feel that I have been studying and preparing for my tests and quizzes the same way for so long that I am afraid that it will be too hard to change, and if I try to change I might do worse with the new way rather than the old way.

In summary, there are many motivational factors that influence your beliefs about changing academic behavior. The more you understand the dynamics of change, the more you can learn to control your behavior and, ultimately, make the necessary changes to attain your personal and academic goals.

You have now completed the first three chapters that provide a foundation for you to understand what academic and motivational strategies are necessary for successful learning. Now you are ready to learn the specific motivational, behavioral, and learning and study strategies that can allow you to attain higher levels of academic success. If you have any doubts about your motivation to change, now is a good time to discuss your concerns with your instructor or teaching assistant. Your perceptions and beliefs play a major role in determining how much you will learn in this course. Deal directly with these beliefs, and you are more likely to be a more satisfied student.

Key Points

1. Beliefs, perceptions, and emotions influence motivation and behavior.
2. Motivated behaviors are determined by choice of behavior, level of activity and involvement, and persistence and management of effort.
3. Motivation is influenced by personal and sociocultural factors, classroom contextual factors, and internal factors.
4. The answers to the following questions can provide important insights into one's motivation:
   • "What are my goals?"
   • "How interested am I in my courses?"
   • "Do I believe I can do well on different academic tasks?"
   • "What are the causes of my successes and failures?"
   • "How do I feel about my academic challenges?"
5. Achievement goals determine patterns of motivation that determine how learners think about and engage in different academic activities.
6. Goals enhance performance in five major ways: effort, duration or persistence, direction of attention, strategic planning, and as a reference point for evaluating performance.
7. It is difficult to be motivated to achieve in any area without goals.
8. A mastery goal orientation is more likely to lead to the use of more learning strategies than a performance goal orientation.
9. There is evidence that a performance goal orientation in introductory college classes leads to high achievement and low interests in course content.
10. Self-efficacy influences individuals' effort, persistence, and use of learning strategies.
11. Students should constantly monitor their attributional messages.

12. Self-efficacy and attributions have important influence on self-directed behavior.

13. Anxiety has two dimensions: worry and emotionality. Each dimension can have different effects on students. Worry has the strongest negative relation with achievement because it interferes with storage and retrieval of information.

14. Test anxiety can affect behavior in three stages: appraisal, preparation, and test taking

15. Anxiety can influence behavior by disrupting mental processes, producing psychological distress, misdirecting attention, and causing inappropriate behaviors such as procrastination.

16. Many students are motivated for the wrong reason—to avoid failure rather than to attain success.

17. There are four reasons why students have difficulty changing their academic behavior: they can't; they don't want to change; they don't know what to change; or they don't know how to change.

Follow-up Activities

1. Use the Self-Managment Process to Manage Your Motivation

The Follow-Up Activities section in each of the remaining chapters in this book identify a topic for self-study. The process for your self-study was identified in chapter 1 and is explained in depth in Appendix A, with examples provided in Appendix B. This study focuses on motivation. Complete the following self-study during a period of 2 to 3 weeks. Your report should include each of the processes below and should be approximately five to eight typed pages in length.

> **Self-observation and evaluation.** Am I satisfied with my academic motivation? Do I need to change my motivation? If yes, what problem(s) do I encounter? What are the symptoms of my problem (i.e., when, where, and how often does my problem occur)? How much of an impact does this problem have on my academic performance? What factors (e.g., beliefs, perceptions, feelings, physiological responses, or behaviors) contribute to this problem? What do I need to change to reduce or eliminate my problem?

> **Goal setting and strategic planning.** What are my goals? What strategies will I implement to improve my academic motivation? When will I use these strategies? How will I record my progress?

Strategy implementation and monitoring. What strategies did I use to improve my academic motivation? When did I use these strategies? What method(s) did I use to record my progress (e.g., documents, charts, logs, tally sheets, checklists, or recordings)? When did I use these methods? How and when did I monitor my progress to determine if my new strategies were working? What changes, if any, did I make along the way?

Strategic outcome monitoring. Did I attain the goal(s) I set for myself? Have the modifications in my motivation improved my academic performance or personal life? What strategies were the most and least effective? What changes, if any, do I need to make in the future?

2. Identify Factors That Influence Motivation

Select two different courses you are currently taking—one difficult and one less challenging, or one that you like and one that you don't like. Analyze your motivation in the two classes by discussing each of the following factors that determine students' motivated behavior:

	Class 1	*Class 2*
Goals		
Interests and values		
Self-efficacy beliefs		
Test anxiety		
Mastery vs. performance goal orientation		
Attributions for academic performance		

3. Analyze Efficacy Scores

Students in a learning course are given 10-point quizzes each week before the class lecture. Before they begin writing their responses, they are asked to rate how well they think they will do on the quiz on a scale from 1 (*low*) to 10 (*high*). The following scores represent the quiz scores and efficacy ratings for four different students for the first three quizzes of the term. Review these scores and describe each of the students' motivation and behavior as best you can. In what ways could these scores influence the students' motivation and study behaviors for future quizzes?

Student 1

Quiz Score	7	9	9
Efficacy Rating	4	7	6

Student 2

Quiz Score	2	5	4
Efficacy Rating	4	5	7

Student 3

Quiz Score	8	9	8
Efficacy Rating	9	9	8

Student 4

Quiz Score	3	5	4
Efficacy Rating	7	8	8

_____

_____

_____

_____

_____

_____

4. Discuss the Motivation Behavior of Different Students

In the beginning of the chapter, you were introduced to five types of students who had different motivational problems. Suppose you were an adviser at the college or university they attend. Each student has made an appointment to see you. How would you explain their own motivation and behavior to them?

Defensive Dimitri

_____

_____

_____

_____

_____

_____

Safe Susan

_____

_____

_____

_____

_____

_____

Hopeless Henry

_____

_____

_____

_____

_____

_____

Satisfied Sheila

_____

_____

_____

_____

_____

Anxious Alberto

_____

_____

_____

_____

_____

5. Help Students Deal With Different Attributions for Their Behavior

Suppose you took a part-time job as a peer counselor and were asked to meet with students who had academic problems. How would you respond to students who attribute poor test performance to the statements in the lefthand column? In the righthand column, write a response to each of the students.

Attribution	Suggested Responses
I lack ability.	
I didn't feel well.	
I wasn't in the mood.	
I'm not interested in the task.	
I don't do well on tests.	
The material was boring.	
The test was unfair.	
I didn't have enough time to study.	

6. Use Motivation Strategies

Here are some strategies that college students use to monitor and regulate their motivation (Wolters, 1998, pp. 228–229). The strategies are organized by categories. Place a check in the box near each category to indicate that you have used a strategy in the category, and in the space provided write the specific strategy you have used if it is different from the strategies listed. Identify one of the strategies listed that you don't use but could incorporate in your repertoire of motivation strategies.

☐Performance Goals
"I would think about how I wanted a good grade."
"I would remind myself about how important it is to get good grades in college."

☐**External Rewards**
"Give myself rewards when I finish studying."
"Each time I successfully know a topic, I might give myself a break and do something relaxing like watch TV or nap?"
"Tell myself that if I finish the next five pages of reading I can go and talk to a friend."

_____

_____

☐**Task Value**
"I would find ways that it relates to my life."
"I would try to relate it to my experiences or how I would feel in certain situations."

_____

_____

☐**Interest**
"Make studying into a game."
"Try to make it more interesting."

_____

_____

☐**Help Seeking**
"Ask to study with a friend."
"Talk to the (teaching assistant) or professor."

_____

_____

☐**Environment Structuring**
"Sit with the book in a quiet room with a soft drink."
"Take little breaks so I don't burn out."
"I'd take a break, completely forget the subject matter, and then return, hopefully refreshed."

_____

_____

□**Attention**
"Study at a time when my mind is more focused."

_____

_____

Answers to Exercise 3.3
1. M   2. P   3. P   4. M   5. P

MOTIVATIONAL STRATEGIES

Chapter 4: Goal Setting
Chapter 5: Management of Emotion and Effort

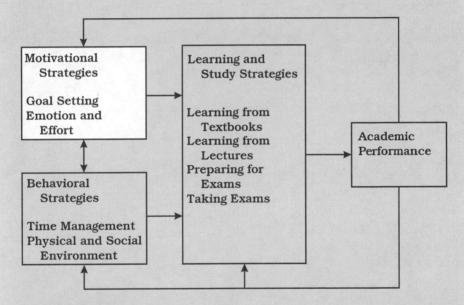

The purpose of this unit is to present strategies that can be used to manage motivation. Chapter 4 deals with goals and goal setting. The use of goal setting as a self–management strategy is widely used in business, academic, and sports settings. Goals serve as the basis of motivation. Without goals it is difficult to be motivated to achieve. More specifically, you learned in the previous chapter that goals influence how we allocate our attention, how hard we work, and how long we persist at a task.

Many individuals have experienced goal setting in areas that are challenging and interesting to them (i.e., a favorite subject, an athletic contest, or an artistic endeavor). However, goal setting also can be especially useful in uninteresting or unchallenging tasks. In these situations, goals can be used to counteract boredom and apathy by providing a sense of challenge and purpose (i.e., accomplishing the goal) that would otherwise be lacking. Hence, goal attainment can generate feelings of pride, satisfaction, or competence that may not be experienced by simply completing assignments or tasks (Reeve, 1996).

Chapter 5 covers additional motivational strategies that can be used to manage your emotion and effort. Often high–pressure situations cause individuals to experience irrational and self–defeating beliefs, and anxiety (e.g., "I can't do it" or "I'm not good enough to compete with the students in my class"). These conditions interfere with the motivation to learn. Fortunately, these negative beliefs can be handled by changing the way individuals talk to themselves. The emotional dimension of anxiety also can be reduced using relaxation strategies.

4

Goal Setting

One of the major goals of the college experience is for students to develop a coherent sense of identity. This development begins in adolescence and usually ends by the time an individual graduates from college (around 21 years of age). According to Erikson (1968), identity involves the search for a consistent image of who one is and what one wants to become.

Marcia (1980) has provided information about the development of identity by distinguishing four different patterns and common issues that college students experience. According to Marcia, the criteria for the attainment of a mature identity are based on two factors: crisis and commitment. "Crisis refers to times during adolescence when the individual seems to be actively involved in choosing among alternative occupations and beliefs. Commitment refers to the degree of personal investment the individual expresses in an occupation or belief" (Marcia, 1967, p. 119).

The following is a brief discussion of the four identity statuses (see Fig. 4.1). Adolescents begin in a state of *identity diffusion* (or confusion)—a situation in which the individual has not made any firm commitments to any ideology, occupation, or interpersonal

Crisis

	Yes	No
Yes	Achieved (crisis resolved)	Foreclosed
No	Moratorium (crisis in progress)	Diffusion

(Commitment — Yes / No)

FIG. 4.1. Criteria for Marcia's identity status.

relationship and is not currently thinking about such commitments (no crises, no commitment). As they develop and have greater interpersonal, work, and educational experiences, they may begin to reflect on the kinds of long-term commitments that could be made. This status is called *identity moratorium*—a situation in which alternative choices are considered and different roles are experienced, but final decisions are deferred during a period of uncertainty (crisis, no commitment).

Sometimes, the uncertainty of thinking about one's future can produce a great deal of anxiety, especially when one doesn't have the answers to the questions from parents and friends about future careers and educational options. For this reason, some young adults choose to remain in a state of identity diffusion, during which they stop thinking about choices and commitments, or opt for *identity foreclosure*. In his status condition, the individual selects some convenient set of beliefs or goals without carefully considering the alternatives. The best example of this status is the high school student whose mother is a doctor or lawyer and who answers the typical question, "What do you want to study in college?" by stating, "Pre-law" or "Pre-med" when he or she really hasn't considered the implications of the career in detail. Such a response gets people to stop asking further questions about life goals and is satisfying to the individual (for the time being), because he or she can stop worrying about what course of study to pursue (no crisis or commitment).

Additional experiences help clarify attitudes, values, and self-evaluations, so that the young adult resolves the identity crises and settles on the relatively stable commitments that constitute *identity achievement*.

These four identity statuses may be perceived as a developmental transition. But one stage is not a prerequisite for another. Only the moratorium status appears to be necessary for identity achievement, since one can't develop a mature identity without considering alternative options. Waterman (1982) has identified possible patterns in identity formation. For example, one model may be diffusion to moratorium or identity achievement; another model may begin with foreclosure, moving to moratorium and then toward identity achievement. The latter model often occurs when individuals find out in college that they really don't have the interest or aptitude for a particular goal. Still another model may be identity diffusion, to moratorium, to identity achievement, to identity diffusion. In this situation, the individual may lose a sense of purpose as a result of some life experiences and fail to seek new commitments. Can you be classified in one of the four identity statuses? If so, use the criteria for the identity statuses and explain why you think you would be classified in your selected status. Are you involved in any activities that might help you move closer to an identity-achieved status? What type of goals could lead to an identity-achieved status?

This chapter helps you understand the purpose of setting goals and developing plans for attaining them. Goal attainment plays an important role in developing your identity and influences the nature of your adult lifestyle.

The pyramid in Fig. 4.2 identifies the steps that lead from identifying values to accomplishing daily tasks (Smith, 1994). Everything starts with values, which are sometimes called principles or beliefs. Long-term goals are developed by translating principles and beliefs into long-term achievements. Long-term goals, in turn, are attained through a series of intermediate goals. Finally, the intermediate goals are attained through a series of specific, goal-oriented daily tasks.

Suppose an individual values education and sets a goal to earn a college degree. To accomplish this long-term goal, the student needs to

FIG. 4.2. The productivity pyramid (from Smith, 1994).

establish some intermediate goals. These intermediate goals often involve year-long goals (e.g., declaring a major and taking and passing a minimum number of classes), semester goals (e.g., exploring career possibilities and attending class regularly), monthly goals (e.g., meeting with an academic adviser and long-range planning for the completing of papers and other assignments), weekly goals (e.g., short-term planning for the completion of papers, assignments, preparation for examinations, and using effective learning and study strategies).

Smith (1994) stated that: "Values explain *why* you want to accomplish certain things in life. Long-range goals describe *what* you want to accomplish. Intermediate goals and daily tasks show *how* to do it" (p. 83). For example, a person may value health and fitness (the why). For this reason, he or she establishes a long-range goal of losing 20 pounds (the what), and an intermediate goal of losing 5 pounds by the end of the semester by developing a specific exercise program for 1 hour each day (the how). Each component—values, long-range goals, intermediate goals, and daily tasks—needs to be linked to one another.

If an individual's goals are not aligned with his or her values, the individual may never be satisfied with his or her accomplishments because he or she will be neglecting the things that matter most. Also, if the individual completes daily tasks that do not reflect long-range and intermediate goals, he or she will be busy doing things, but will not be productive.

The keys to goal setting and time management are governing values. Smith (1994) believes that one of the reasons many people are frustrated or stressed in their lives is because they ignore the first three levels of the pyramid. They complete many tasks, but do not base them on anything but urgency. As a result, they fail to get around to doing the things that are really important to them.

Have you thought about your own governing values? What is important in your life? Following are some values that people have identified as of greatest importance in their lives (Smith, 1994):

- Financial security
- Personal health and fitness
- Family
- Religion
- Integrity
- Honesty
- Service
- Self-respect
- Education and learning
- Happiness
- Pleasure
- Friendship
- Courage

Circle the values that are most important to you and be prepared to discuss your personal selection with other students in your class.

After studying this chapter, you will be able to:

- Establish personal goals.
- Develop and implement effective plans for attaining goals.

EXERCISE 4.1: SELF-OBSERVATION: IDENTIFYING YOUR VALUES

Directions: The purpose of this exercise is to help identify the activities you enjoy and determine whether you are finding time to participate in them. This exercise is part of a program called *values clarification* (Simon, Howe, & Kirschenbaum, 1972), and is based on the premise that many people do not know clearly what their values are:

- Make a list of 7 to 10 things that give you great pleasure or joy.
- After the name of each activity, write the date you last experienced it.
- Place a dollar sign after each activity that costs more than $10.
- Now go through the list again, and place a P after those activities that usually require considerable *planning*.
- Review your list, and place an S after activities that you share with others.
- Finally, place an A after those activities that you do *alone.*

What does this exercise tell you about yourself? What are the activities valued by the students in your class? Why is it that some people find time to do the things they enjoy, whereas others do not? How do values influence goals?

My Activities List

_____

_____

_____

_____

_____

_____

WHY IS GOAL SETTING IMPORTANT?

Goals have been defined as "what the individual is consciously trying to do" (Locke, 1968, p. 159), and goal setting refers to the process of establishing a standard for performance. Most of us have goals in many domains: academic, social, occupational, and personal. Some goals are short-term (e.g., earning an A on your sociology exam on Friday); others are long-term (e.g., raising your grade-point average (GPA) to 3.0 this semester); and still others are very long-term (e.g., becoming an attorney).

As mentioned in the introduction, long-term goals are accompanied by related intermediate goals. For example, a freshman student might set his or her sights on becoming editor of the college newspaper during his or her senior year. The goal is 4 years away and represents a major achievement, so, the student decides what needs to be done to work toward this long-range goal. If the student is interested in journalism, he or she may decide to major in this field and begin taking some English and journalism courses. Another goal would be to join the paper as a staff writer. An intermediate goal would be to become a section editor by his or her junior year. By setting intermediate goals that relate to the long-term goal, the student identifies a plan of action or path to follow to attain his or her ultimate goal. This path provides rewards as the student moves closer toward the long-range goal.

A similar process is needed to obtain the goal of becoming an elected official or to run a marathon. It is not likely that an individual could be nominated for an office without any experience or past involvement in community activities. It also is doubtful someone could run 26 miles the first time he or she decides to run a marathon without first setting short-term training goals.

Goal setting is a planning process and is an important aspect of self-management. This process puts meaning in people's lives, helps them achieve their dreams and ambitions, and sets up positive expectations for achievements. Students who set goals and develop plans to achieve them take responsibility for their own lives. They do not wait for parents or teachers to instruct them as to what they should be doing with their lives.

Unfortunately, many students fail to take responsibility for personal goal setting. For example, last semester one of my students complained he had difficulty attaining a goal set for him by his father for a 3.5 GPA. I asked him what his goal was. He stated that he did not have one. One of his peers commented that the student needed to achieve in college for himself, not for his parents. After all, parents are not going to be around all the time to set goals and direct their adult children.

Think about your own behavior. Are you in charge of your own behavior, or do you prefer that other individuals set goals and make important decisions for you? It is difficult to be a highly motivated individual without setting personal goals. While watching the last Olympics, I could not help but notice how often the topic of goals was discussed during interviews with athletes. Many athletes even mentioned that their coaches suggested they carry with them a list of their goals.

In team sports, coaches often meet with individuals to set both individual and team goals. In the business world, corporations set goals for sales and product development. In fact, the stock market is very sensitive to a company's performance goals. When a company announces its quarterly profits or losses, the investment world compares the performance to expected goals. The result often is immediate price fluctuation in the stock market.

The following news item was reported in the September 18, 1996, edition of *The Los Angeles Times:*

MONDESI LIVES UP TO STRETCH GOALS

The Dodgers had just lost three consecutive games, dropping 2½ games behind the San Diego Padres on August 21, and it was time for action.

Right fielder Raul Mondesi sat down with coach Manny Mota and decided to set goals for the final 36 games: 50 hits, 40 runs, 12 homers, and 40 RBIs.

The goals may have appeared unrealistic, but ever since that day, Mondesi has been on a torrid hitting streak, and the Dodgers have played their best baseball. The Dodgers have since won 19 of 24 games to vault into first place, and Mondesi is batting .361 with 14 runs, five homers and 24 RBIs.

Although goals help motivate our behavior, they cannot accomplish the whole job, because the quality of performance also is related to nonmotivational factors such as ability, training, and resources (Reeve, 1996). Life would be easy if the only thing we had to do was set goals and sit back and wait for them to be fulfilled. Setting goals, although important, is only the first step in a process to becoming a more successful individual. For goals to enhance performance, it is essential to make a commitment to attempt to attain them. In this chapter, I encourage you to set your own goals.

Goals help us become aware of our values and help us determine what we are willing to do. As a result, they influence our attitudes, motivation, and learning. Think about your goals. Do your goals motivate you in a positive way to be a successful learner, or do your goals motivate you to get by doing as little work as possible? Are your experiences with goals similar or different from the student who reported the following:

Student Reflections

I never really gave much thought to developing personal goals. My dad always told me to set my standards high, and that if I put my mind to something, I could do anything. I never used to believe this statement, but I do now. Setting goals is something that I need to do so that I know where I want to go and develop a plan to get there. I have a friend who has a poster on his wall with five goals that he would like to accomplish this semester. I remember walking into his room and thinking to myself: "Wow, this guy has got it together. He knows what he wants to accomplish." I know that I want to do well in college, but I do not have any specific goals. I want to set goals for the present and future so I have a way of showing myself that I have accomplished something. I feel better about myself when I accomplish something that I set out to achieve.

WHAT PROPERTIES OF GOALS ENHANCE MOTIVATION?

Schunk (1991) pointed out that the effects of goals on behavior depend on three properties: specificity, proximity, and difficulty. Goals that set specific performance standards are more likely to increase motivation than general goals such as "Do your best." Specific goals help the learner determine the amount of effort required for success and lead to feelings of satisfaction when the goal is attained. As a result, learners come to believe they have greater ability to complete the task.

Goals also can be identified by the extent to which they extend into the future. Proximal goals are close at hand and result in greater motivation directed toward attainment than more distant goals. Pursuing proximal goals conveys reliable information about one's capabilities. When students perceive they are making progress toward a proximal goal, they are apt to feel more confident and maintain their motivation. Because it is harder to evaluate progress toward distant goals, learners have more difficulty judging their capabilities, even if they perform well.

Student perceptions of the difficulty of a task influence the amount of effort they believe is necessary to attain the task. If they believe they have the ability and knowledge, learners will work harder to attain difficult goals than when standards are lower. As they work and attain difficult goals, they develop beliefs in their competence. However, if they do not believe they have the ability to attain a goal, they are likely to have low expectations for success and not become involved in the task.

Think about how the specificity, proximity, and difficulty level in goal setting in each class might impact your motivation and perceptions of ability.

WHAT ARE THE STEPS IN THE GOAL-SETTING PROCESS?

The first learning strategy you will learn in this text is goal setting. Five important steps comprise this strategy (adapted in part from McCombs & Encinias, 1987). Begin this term by setting a few major goals in different areas of your life and developing an action plan to implement them.

Step 1: Identifying and Defining the Goal

Think about all the things you would like to accomplish in the different aspects of your life (e.g., academic, personal, social, and career). Do you want to make the dean's list? Pass a difficult course? Date that girl or guy you have been talking to for weeks? Get a summer internship? Lose a few pounds? Learn to play the guitar? Ask yourself: "What areas of my life would I like to improve?" "What areas need to be worked on?"

Individuals set goals throughout their lives. As they attain one goal, they often identify another. In fact, one of the major ways individuals seek happiness is through goal attainment. When some students are asked what goal they would like to attain, they often mention being happy. Keep in mind that happiness is not a goal, it is a feeling or state of mind that occurs as the result of goal attainment.

Recently, I met a man in his 50s who always wanted to be a singer. He played some tapes of his songs at a party. His voice was outstanding! His problem was that he had a dream or wish, not a goal. He spent his adult life wishing he could work as an entertainer, but failed to set goals and develop any plans to attain them. As you set each of your goals, you want to make sure they are **SMART goals** (Smith, 1994): Specific, Measurable, Action-Oriented, Realistic, and Timely:

- *Specific—describes what you want to accomplish with as much detail as possible.* If you establish vague goals, you lessen the possibility of attaining them. Describe the context (i.e., course, situation, or setting), as well as the specific outcome. Avoid general terms like "good," "well," "happy," "understand," and "know."

  Poor: "I want to do well in English."
  Better: "I want an A on my next essay in English."

- *Measurable—describes your goal in terms that can be clearly evaluated.* If you fail to determine how a goal is measured, you will never know if you attained it. Be sure to include a statement of the minimal level of performance that will be accepted as evidence that you have achieved the goal.

Poor: "I want to study my biology textbook."
Better: "I want to read chapter 7 in my biology textbook and answer all the discussion questions."

* *Action-Oriented—identifies a goal that focuses on actions rather than personal qualities.* Be sure to identify your goal so that it includes an action to be completed, otherwise you will not know how to accomplish it.

Poor: "I want to *develop a better attitude about studying.*"
Better: "I want to *complete all my assignments before class and answer questions.*"

* *Realistic—identifies a goal you know you are actually capable of attaining.* Goals can be challenging but unrealistic. Therefore, you must carefully analyze your goals to determine that you can reasonably expect to reach them.

Poor: "I want to *read five chapters in my history textbook this evening and answer all the discussion questions.*"
Better: "I want to *read two chapters in my history textbook this evening and answer all the discussion questions.*"

* *Timely*—identifies a goal that breaks a longer term goal into a shorter term goal(s) and clearly specifies a completion date.

Poor: "I want to *graduate at the head of my class.*"
Better: "I want to *make the honor roll this semester.*"

An important task in goal setting is to determine how much time each long-term goal will take and to establish some smaller steps, or intermediate goals that will help you reach your final goal. One way to accomplish this step is to use a timeline. Write your final goal on the righthand side and identify the smaller goals that will help you reach this major goal. Estimate how long it will take to attain each intermediate goal.

Examples of SMART Goals. Following are examples of academic, social, occupational, and personal goals. Notice that each one of these goals is specific, measurable, action-oriented, realistic, and timely.

Academic

* "I want to take an advanced mathematics course next semester."
* "I want to attain a 3.0 GPA this semester."
* "I want to complete my research papers 1 week before handing them in so I have time to edit them."

Social

- "I want to join a square dancing class this semester."
- "I want to limit my partying to weekends."
- "I want to spend at least 1 hour during the week with my boyfriend/girlfriend."

Occupational

- "I want to work at least 10 hours per week this semester"
- "I want to obtain an internship this summer."
- "I want to complete all my general education requirements by my sophomore year."

Personal

- "I want to work out four times a week for 40 minutes."
- "I want to lose 5 pounds in 1 month."
- "I want to save $500 this semester."

Table 4.1 is a review of the procedures for writing SMART goals.

TABLE 4.1

Procedures for Writing SMART Goals	
Procedures	Examples
1. Identify the area in which you wish to write a goal.	"I want to write a goal for my next composition paper."
2. Evaluate your past and present achievement, interest, or performance in the area to consider the extent to which your goal is action-oriented and realistic.	"I have been having some difficulty in the course and would like to demonstrate some improvement in the next paper."
3. State what you want to accomplish. Begin with the words, "I want to..." and include a specific behavior; describe the goal so that it can be measured and include a specific completion date (timely).	"I want to obtain a grade of 'A' on the composition paper that is due on October 15."
4. Evaluate your goal statement. Is it a SMART goal (i.e., specific, measurable, action-oriented, realistic, and timely)?	"Because my grades have been low on other composition papers, it may not be realistic for me to move to an 'A' on the next paper. I will set my goal for a 'B' and then move to an 'A'."
5. If necessary, make modifications in your goal statement.	"I want to obtain a grade of 'B' on the composition paper that is due on October 15."

EXERCISE 4.2: WRITING PERSONAL GOALS

Think about the things you would like to achieve, obtain, or experience in life. Using the criteria and procedure for writing SMART goals, write at least four goals (include at least two major academic goals).

1.

2.

3.

4.

Step 2: Generating and Evaluating Alternative Plans

Now that you know how to write a goal, let's move on to the second step in the process—determining *how* you are going to attain your goal. The answers to the following questions can be very helpful:

- How would other people achieve this goal?
- Who can help me achieve this goal?
- How have I achieved similar goals in the past?

Let's consider a student whose goal is to attain a B on an English paper. Suppose the student has already written a few papers and is aware of his or her strengths and weaknesses. As part of developing an effective plan for the next paper, the student might ask him- or herself the following questions: Did I give myself enough time to complete the last paper? Do I understand the criteria for grading? Do I understand why my last paper was graded lower than expected? Do I understand my strengths and weaknesses? Would I benefit from having someone read the paper before I turn it in?

By asking these questions, the student begins to think about alternative ways to attain the goal and the advantages and disadvantages of each strategy. For example, the student might initially include in the plan time for two rewrites, but realizes he or she has an exam in another subject the same week. As a result, no matter how effective the plan might be for writing a better paper, the student probably will not do as well on the exam if he or she spends more time on the paper. Thus, the student needs to decide how best to spend his or her time. My point is that one constantly has to weigh the advantages and disadvantages of one strategy over another.

Step 3: Making Implementation Plans

In Step 1, you learned why it is necessary to be specific in writing a goal. It also is important for your plan to be specific so you know exactly what needs to be done to achieve your goal. One way to develop a plan is to identify each of the necessary tasks that must be completed and the date by which the tasks will be accomplished. Setting deadlines for each task is helpful in determining that you continue to make progress toward your goal.

Table 4.2 presents an example of a checklist for identifying intermediate goals and tasks for writing a research paper. Research (Schunk, 1989) indicates that as you attain each of the intermediate goals, you will become more confident in your abilities to complete the task. Thus, anytime you can break a major goal into several intermediate goals, you will be more motivated to move toward your major goal. Remember this finding whenever you get discouraged while thinking about completing a major task.

Step 4: Implementing the Plan

The first three steps in the goal-setting process are planning steps. Step 4 requires you to put the plan into operation by completing each of the planned activities. Check your progress as you implement each task. Do not hesitate to make changes in your plan if you find that

TABLE 4.2
INTERMEDIATE GOALS FOR A RESEARCH PAPER

Intermediate Goal	Date Completed
Phase 1: Prewriting	
Identify topic	
Find sources for topic	
Use correct bibliographic notation for sources	
Phase 2: Drafting	
Organize paper around two subtopics	
Write draft of subtopic 1	
Write draft of subtopic 2	
Write introduction to paper	
Write conclusion	
Phase 3: Revising and Editing	
Review drafts for grammar and writing style	
Check transitions among subtopics	
Edit complete paper	
Prepare title page, bibliography, and table of contents	

you miscalculated the time needed to complete a task. In some cases, you might find that you omitted an important task that needs to be added to your plan, such as researching a specific topic for a term paper. As you develop greater expertise in developing your plans, you will find they will require fewer modifications.

Step 5: Evaluating Your Progress

In Step 5, you will evaluate your plans and progress. Ask yourself the following questions after you have attained your goal or when you begin to realize that your plan is not working effectively (McCombs & Encinias, 1987, p. 41):

- "How well did the plan work?"
- "How many tasks did I complete?"
- "With which task(s) did I have the most trouble? Why?"
- "What strategies worked well?"
- "What problems came up?"
- "What did I learn about myself?"
- "What didn't I plan for?"

If you do not attain your goal, you can evaluate what went wrong. Evaluation can help you rethink your strategy and determine another way to reach your goal.

Table 4.3. presents the five steps you should use when setting your goals. As you read this book, you will acquire more information about

TABLE 4.3

Procedures for Goal Setting	
Procedures	Strategies
1. Identifying and defining the goal	Use SMART Goals
2. Generating and evaluating alternatives	Answer the following questions: "How would other people achieve this goal?" "Who can help me achieve this goal?" "How have I achieved similar goals in the past?"
3. Making an implementation plan	Use checklist to identify intermediate goals and related tasks
4. Implementing the plan	Identify the tasks that need to be completed
5. Evaluating your progress	Answer the following questions: "How well did the plan work?" "How many tasks did I complete?" "With which task(s) did I have the most trouble? Why?" "What strategies worked well" "What problems came up?" "What did I learn about myself?" "What didn't I plan for?"

developing and implementing goals. As you practice the process, you will develop greater expertise and enhance the likelihood that you will attain your chosen goals.

Key Points

1. One's values, long-range and intermediate goals, and daily tasks should be aligned.
2. Goals influence motivation and learning.
3. Setting and attaining intermediate goals can motivate students to attain long-range goals.
4. Three properties of goals influence motivation: specificity, proximity, and difficulty.
5. Each goal you set should be SMART: specific, measurable, action-oriented, realistic, and timely.
6. The following steps should be used each time you set a goal:

   1. Identifying and defining the goal
   2. Generating and evaluating plans
   3. Making implementation plans
   4. Implementing the plan
   5. Evaluating your progress

Follow-up Activities

1. Establish a Goal and Action Plan

Identify a short-term goal you would like to attain in the next few weeks. Develop a plan for attaining it and write a brief two- to three-page report on the extent of your goal attainment. Use the five-step sequence identified in the chapter as headings in your paper.

2. Analyze Student Behavior

Suppose you were working in your college counseling center as a peer counselor. Two students, Alan and Felicia, come to see you to discuss their problems. Read the brief description of each student and identify what you have learned to date that could be applied to each situation. Consider how you would start your discussion with Alan and Felicia? What issues would you raise? What advice would you give? Why?

Alan is a freshman music major who is an accomplished bass player. He has toured internationally with some of the best groups and is recognized as someone with a great deal of talent. His goal is to play professionally. He practices many hours a day and believes this activity is more worthwhile than taking general education courses. Alan believes he does not need a college education to attain his goal. Yet, his parents believe that the attainment of a college degree will benefit him throughout his life. He agrees to go to college to please his parents but is not very interested in some of his courses. As a result, his attendance is poor and his grades are low in freshman composition and psychology.

Felicia has always wanted to be a pediatrician. She is a freshman majoring in pre-med and is having difficulty in her first chemistry course. Although she did well in her high school chemistry course, she finds her college course more difficult because it is taught differently. The exams require more problem solving and higher level thinking than she experienced in high school. She begins to worry about her ability to excel in the sciences and to obtain admission to medical school.

Comments:

_____

_____

_____

_____

_____

_____

3. Evaluate the Productivity Pyramid

Figure 4.2 illustrates the fact that one's values should serve as the foundation for determining personal goals and creating a daily task list that is related to the attainment of long-range and intermediate goals. Smith (1994) stated: "If your daily activities are guided in this manner by your fundamental values, you will feel the satisfaction that comes from succeeding at those things that mean the most to you" (p. 67). Identify one of your values and determine the degree to which your long-range and intermediate goals and daily tasks are aligned with this value. If your goals and daily tasks are not well aligned with what you value, develop a plan to better align them.

Comments:

_____

_____

_____

_____

_____

_____

5

▌▌ ▌▌ ▌▌ ▌▌

Management of Emotion and Effort

In chapter 1, you learned the importance of managing your own motivation, and in chapter 3 you learned about the factors that influence motivation to learn. Thus far, you learned that values and goals are important determinants of motivation and that goal setting can be an important motivational strategy. In addition, you learned that the nature of your attributions can have an important impact on your motivation to learn because they influence your emotions and effort. More specifically, I suggested that you analyze how you interpret the causes of your successes and failures, especially ability versus effort attributions. You also learned that self-efficacy is an important belief that is related to academic performance. Thus, as you gain more expertise in "learning how to learn" and attain greater academic success, your efficacy beliefs, or judgments about your capabilities to learn, will be enhanced. In turn, these beliefs will lead to greater effort, persistence, and self-monitoring of your behavior. Finally, you learned that arranging or imagining rewards or punishments for success or failure at an academic task can be a useful motivation strategy.

In this chapter, I focus on procedures to help you manage your emotions and effort, with a special emphasis on reducing anxiety. I differentiate moods from emotions in terms of their intensity and duration. Moods are longer lasting, whereas emotions consist of short intense episodes (Rosenberg, 1998).

Academic emotions influence your learning and achievement. Positive emotions foster your control over your learning, whereas negative emotions lead to more passive behavior. Positive emotions predict high achievement, and negative emotions predict low achievement. In summary, your academic emotions are closely linked to your learning, self-control, and scholastic achievement (Pekrun, Goetz, Titz, & Perry, 2002).

There is increasing evidence that stress and depression among college students is on the rise (Reisberg, 2000). Peterson (2002) described a study finding that 30% of college freshman reported feeling overwhelmed a great deal of time.

There are many stressors in college life, such as greater academic demands, financial responsibilities, changes in your social life, preparing for life after graduation, and so forth. The National Institute for Mental Health has an excellent Web site that provides information about college students and depression (see www.nimh.nih.gov/publicat/students.cfm). If you have continuous feelings of sadness, decreased energy, fatigue, loss of interest or pleasure in your daily activities, feelings of hopelessness or guilt, or cry a great deal, you should seek help beyond the information provided in this chapter. Speak to your academic advisor or dorm advisor, make an appointment at your counseling center, or find out about the mental health resources in your community. There are many successful treatments for stress and depression.

After studying this chapter you will be able to:

- Change the way you think about events in your life so you have more positive feelings about yourself.
- Develop positive beliefs about your ability to attain goals.
- Use self-talk to reduce anxiety and other negative emotions.
- Use relaxation techniques to reduce anxiety.

EXERCISE 5.1: SELF-OBSERVATION: ASSESSING EMOTIONS

Directions: Assess your emotions by checking the appropriate response to each of the following questions. Write a summary statement in the space provided to describe the nature of your emotions.

	Always	Sometimes	Never
1. Do you get discouraged when you get a low grade on an exam or paper?			
2. Do you generally have a positive outlook on your ability to succeed in college?			
3. Do you find that panicky thoughts or worries frustrate your efforts to concentrate?			
4. Do you blame yourself when events do not go well for you?			
5. Do you easily get angry when people mess up?			
6. Do you have a high tolerance for frustration?			
7. Do you get depressed?			
8. Do you feel pride regarding your accomplishments?			
9. How often do you feel bored?			

Summary Statement:

_____

_____

_____

_____

_____

_____

WHAT IS THE ROLE OF EMOTIONS IN ACADEMIC PERFORMANCE?

What are emotions? How can negative emotions be modified? How do emotions impact academic achievement? These are the key questions that we will focus on in this chapter. My students write weekly journals in my learning and study strategies course. When I read the journals, I detect a wide range of both positive (e.g., enjoyment, hope, joy, satisfaction, pride, relief) and negative emotions (e.g., boredom, hopelessness, anxiety, disappointment, and shame). I particularly enjoy reading about the excitement that most students report during the first week in college. For example, there are numerous explanations about the pride they feel getting into college and working toward their long-range goals, or the excitement of meeting their roommates for the first time, and liking them. Other positive emotions pertain to receiving a good grade on their first quizzes or papers, or the satisfaction in meeting a new friend or having a great date.

Many students describe that their emotions resemble a roller coaster as they report the many ups and downs they experience throughout the semester. I recently saw a television advertisement for a hospital in my area with the slogan: "Bad things happen!" Unfortunately, the commercial not only applies to one's physical health, but one's psychological health as well. There are breakups in relationships, occasional poor test or paper results, misunderstandings with instructors or parents, and so forth. There are times when not all goes well. I find it interesting how students have different coping strategies to deal with adversity. Here is an example of negative emotions I recently read in one student's journal:

> I thought I was good in science before I started taking science courses at the university. The instructors cover more material in one lecture than I received in 2 weeks in high school. There doesn't seem to be any relationship between how much I study and my grades on exams. I'm beginning to feel dumb! I don't know what to tell my parents. They are going to be so disappointed in me!

This student is experiencing shame. Not only is he not receiving good grades, but he feels that he has little control over the events causing him to score low on examinations.

Some students are able to increase their motivation, make adjustments in their study strategies, and overcome feelings of shame. However, other students seem to crumple in the face of adversity.

What do we know about the difference between students who deal effectively with the feelings of shame and those students who do not (Turner, Husman, & Schallert, 2002)? Students who appear to be resistant to shame tend to focus on their valued future goals and are unwilling to give up. They maintain a belief in their academic ability and use motivation and learning strategies to make changes in their study behavior. Finally, they use positive thoughts to keep them on track. When something goes wrong, they remind themselves that they can do it. Most important, when they don't do well on an exam, they commit themselves to changing their learning and study behavior for the next exam. In fact, they even increase the number of study strategies they use. Here is what one student reported after a poor exam:

> I did more things. I studied harder . . . [like] trying to keep up with the reading and trying to just be a better student— going through the notes afterward, trying to do the right things, making flash cards, testing my knowledge, writing things down. (Turner, Husman, & Schallert, 2002, p. 85)

In contrast to the shame-resilient students, the students who are affected by shame (i.e., shame-nonresilient students) often are not able to sustain increased energy following their shame experiences. They are characterized by ambivalence, confusion, and conflict as seen by the statement by the student taking science courses. They are not sure of their future goals and can't seem to use learning or study strategies other than what they used for the first exam. This state of mind is best represented by the following remark (Turner et al., 2002): "I took really good notes. . . . [I] did all my readings, went over my readings very thoroughly. I just don't know what else I can do" (p. 86).

In summary, in dealing with negative emotional states like shame, disappointment, or both, it is important to have immediate and long-term goals to help maintain a focus for why it is worth overcoming obstacles. Without such goals, it is easier to quit or reduce effort, because there doesn't appear to be a purpose for trying harder. However, having goals is not sufficient to maintain one's learning activities. In addition to having the motivation to study, students also must acquire the necessary learning strategies and self-directed behaviors that will allow them to cope with academic difficulties (Turner et al., 2002). Remember the statement in chapter 1: "You must have both the will and the skill to achieve."

Boredom

Many students complain that they are bored in school or in various courses they must take. Boredom is a problem because it can diminish attention and interfere with academic performance. It can be related to both individual (i.e., personality) and situational factors (e.g., classes and instructors). Some individuals are more prone to boredom than others. In fact, one study found that students who report a high frequency of boredom in school also experience high rates of boredom outside of school (Larson & Richard, 1991). Explanations for boredom also include dislike of a course, instructor, or specific course content.

In a recent conversation about some reading material, one of my students reported that he found the material boring. When I tried to discover what aspect of the material he thought was boring, I quickly learned it was not "boredom" that was the problem, but his lack of understanding of the material. Therefore, when students report that they are bored with the material, they may use this state of mind to escape from learning tasks that are perceived to be beyond their capabilities.

Can something be done about boredom? The answer to this question may depend on how students attribute the causes of their boredom. For example, if students believe boredom is caused by external and uncontrollable factors (i.e., an uninspiring instructor or course), they will be less likely to think they can do something about their feelings as compared with students who attribute their boredom to internal and controllable factors (i.e., lack of understanding of the material or lack of effort). Successful students find ways to manage their boredom because they attribute it to controllable factors.

Try setting some personal goals to increase your motivation in a course. For example: Ask for help, locate reference books on topics that cause some difficulty, write papers on topics that interest you, talk to the instructor about the course, and study in a group. Think about the ways that you deal with boredom in your daily life.

HOW ARE EMOTIONS INFLUENCED BY EVENTS AND EXPERIENCES?

Okay, suppose I convinced you that it is good to have positive emotions. I think must students would agree with this belief. However, what do you do when you feel anxious or sad or depressed? Can one change his or her emotions? There is considerable evidence that individuals can be taught to change their emotions (e.g., Kanfer & Goldstein, 1991). Let's review one technique that you can use.

We often think that some environmental event causes some consequence. The following is such an example:

(A) "My friend didn't listen to my feelings when I said that I was upset."
(C) "I am really angry."

Ellis (1962) developed a system to deal with irrational ideas and beliefs and replace them with realistic statements about the world. He called his approach **rational emotive therapy**. His basic premise is that

Environmental ⟶ Beliefs, ⟶ Interpretation ⟶ Emotional–
     events   perceptions   self-talk   physical
                                       (irrational ideas)   reactions

FIG. 5.1. How beliefs influence your emotions (adapted from Davis, Eshelman, & McKay, 2000).

emotions have nothing to do with actual events. In between the activating event (A) and the emotion (C) are realistic or unrealistic beliefs and self-talk (B). It is the self-talk that produces the emotions. Your own thoughts, directed and controlled by you, are what create emotions like shame, anxiety, anger, and depression.

Figure 5.1 illustrates the relationship between environmental events and emotional and physical responses. It is your beliefs and perceptions that stimulate your feelings and your actions. A person or event can't make you feel bad. You make yourself feel bad. In other words, you feel the way you think.

The process can be depicted in the following manner:

(A) "My friend didn't listen to my feelings when I said that
      I was depressed."
(B) "I can't stand it when someone doesn't listen to me. I
      must not be very important to him or her."
(C) "I am really angry."

As you see in the example, your belief system (beliefs or perceptions) stimulates your feelings and your actions. You direct your actions by your belief that your friend doesn't think you are very important to him or her.

Whether you realize it or not, you spend most of the day engaging in self-talk, your internal thought language. (Yes, you do talk to yourself!) These are the words you use to describe and interpret the world. If your self-talk is accurate and in touch with reality, you function well and feel good about situations. If, however, your self-talk is irrational and untrue, then you will tend to feel stressful and uncomfortable. The following sentence is an example of irrational self-talk: "I must be liked by everyone!" Who says that everyone must like you? Can you get along knowing that one of your colleagues or peers may not like you?

Here's some other irrational self-talk: "I should never cry in front of other people" or "I can't allow anyone to hurt my feelings" or "I can't allow myself to fail at anything" or "There is only one person in the world who will truly love me."

Irrational ideas differ greatly. Some ideas are based on misperceptions (e.g., When the car's wheels shake, I know they are going to fall off"). Other irrational ideas are based on perfectionist shoulds, oughts, and musts (e.g., "I must be more successful than my brother"). The problem is that most irrational ideas lead to negative self-talk and negative emotional or physical consequences. Much of an individual's irrational thoughts can be changed to more rational statements. Therefore, instead of saying, "I need a best friend," you can change the statement to "I would like a best friend, but I have a number of people who like me. So, I don't absolutely need a best friend and can be happy with the friendships I have developed." Here is another irrational thought: "I'll never do well in this class, everyone is smarter than me!" You can change this thought by saying something like: "There are many bright students in this class, but if I use the learning strategies I have been taught, I can compete with them."

The following are eight irrational thinking patterns that influence individuals' emotions (McKay, Davis, & Fanning, 1997). As you read them, think of situations where you used any of the irrational thinking patterns:

1. **Filtering:** You focus on the negative details while ignoring all the positive aspects of a situation.
   Example: Your boss in a summer job tells you that your work is good, but he thinks you socialize too much with the other personnel in the workplace. You go home thinking that your boss doesn't like you.
2. **Polarized thinking:** Things are black or white, good or bad. You have to be perfect or you're a failure. There's no middle ground, no room for mistakes.
   Example: You have an argument with one friend and explain the problem to the second friend. You tell the second friend: "Either you support me or you are not my friend."
3. **Overgeneralization:** You reach a general conclusion based on a single incident or piece of evidence. You exaggerate the frequency of problems and use negative global labels. Popular phrases for overgeneralization are all, every, none, never, always, everybody, and nobody.
   Example: You break up with your boyfriend or girlfriend and say: "No one will ever love me!"
4. **Mind reading:** Without their saying so, you know what people are feeling and why they act the way they do. In particular, you have certain knowledge of how people think and feel about you.
   Example: "She is acting that way toward me because she is jealous of me."
5. **Catastrophizing:** You expect, even visualize, disaster. You notice or hear about a problem and start asking, "What if?" "What if tragedy strikes? What if it happens to me?"

Example: While talking the SAT exam, you have trouble concentrating because you keep saying to yourself, "What if I don't get into college?"

6. **Magnifying:** You exaggerate the degree or intensity of a problem. You turn up the volume on anything bad, making it loud, large, and overwhelming.
   Example: "This term paper is ridiculous. I'll never finish it."

7. **Personalization:** You assume that everything people do or say is some kind of reaction to you. You also compare yourself to others, trying to determine who is smarter, more competent, better looking, and so on.
   Example: "Everyone in this class appears smarter than me."

8. **Shoulds:** You have a list of ironclad rules about how you and other people should act. People who break the rules anger you, and you feel guilty when you violate the rules. Cue words used for this type of thinking are *should, ought,* or *must.*
   Example: "I never should appear hurt; I always need to appear happy and content."

EXERCISE 5.2: IDENTIFYING IRRATIONAL THINKING PATTERNS

Directions: Write the letter of the thinking pattern identified in the second column by the statement in the first column. The correct answers are listed at the end of this chapter.

Statement	*Pattern*
___1. I know that my friend is mad at me because I don't want to go to the concert with him.	a. Filtering
___2. If my parents don't like my boyfriend, they don't care about me.	b. Polarized Thinking
___3. My aunt spent a great deal of money to see the concert. Therefore, I should like it.	c. Overgeneralization
___4. I don't think I can do well in this class, everyone seems so smart.	d. Mind Reading
___5. I know my speech professor liked my presentation, but my closing argument wasn't that great. I'll probably get a C.	e. Catastrophizing

continued

Statement	Pattern
__6. I received a C on my first chemistry test. I will never become a doctor.	f. Magnifying
__7. My parents were not pleased with my final grade in English. I can't do anything to satisfy them.	g. Personalization
__8. My uncle has ulcers. It must run in my family, and I know that I am going to get ulcers.	h. Shoulds

HOW CAN THE RATIONAL EMOTIVE APPROACH BE USED TO CHANGE EMOTIONS?

The rational emotive approach proposes that irrational thinking follows an A-B-C-D-E model of development. "A" stands for an activating event. "B" stands for a belief (irrational) that follows the activating event. "C" stands for the consequence of the irrational negative thinking. "D" stands for disputing the irrational or helpless belief that followed the activating event and should be aimed at replacing the maladaptive beliefs with an adaptive and realistic belief. "E" is the new effect, that is, the improved way that one feels and acts after actively disputing the maladaptive belief that followed the adversity. Let's look at the process:

A (activating event)—Phil receives a D on his history examination

B (the irrational or helpless belief that follows the event)— "I'll never be a successful student."

C (consequence)—Phil feels helpless and anxious and believes that he will not succeed in the class.

D (disputing irrational beliefs)—"Ok . . . so I did poorly on this exam. I know that if I prepare early and use better study techniques, I can learn this stuff."

E (new effect)—"I still feel disappointed that I didn't do well, but I now have a plan to do better in the future. I can be a good student!"

As you review the process from A to E, you will note some skills that you must acquire (Merrell, 2001). First, you need to develop greater awareness of your own emotional states and how they vary over time. One good exercise to help you accomplish this goal is to draw a pie chart to describe how your feelings were divided up during a particular day or week. Label different slices of your "emotional pie," such as N = normal mood/ok, T = tense, H = happy, A = angry or mad, S = sad, W = worried. Add any additional emotions that are relevant to your life.

Second, you need to learn how to detect the automatic thoughts and identifying beliefs that underlie your thought processes and influence your emotions. Thinking about the list of the eight irrational thought patterns that were provided earlier is a good start. You also might want to keep a log whereby you identify negative automatic thought processes that may be typical reactions to situations you encounter during the day or week. When you identify each thought process, think about the beliefs that underlie them. For example, do you see yourself using musts or shoulds, or do you tend to see the worst consequence for most of your experiences?

Third, evaluate and dispute your automatic thoughts and beliefs. Ellis (1998) provided some questions for you to consider:

- Where is holding this belief getting me? Is it helpful or self-defeating?
- Where is the evidence to support the existence of my irrational belief? Is it consistent with reality?
- Is my belief logical? Does it follow from my preferences?
- Is it really awful (as bad as it could be)?
- Can I really not stand it?

Fourth, change the negative automatic thoughts and maladaptive beliefs. Note that this process involves both eliminating the maladaptive beliefs but replacing them with more positive beliefs and statements. Try to reframe and relabel negative thoughts, like the example provided earlier: Change "I'll never do well in this class, everyone is smarter than me!" to "There are many bright students in this class but if I use the learning strategies I have been taught, I can compete with them." Basically, you are changing negative self-talk to positive self-talk.

HOW DOES SELF-TALK INFLUENCE MY EMOTIONS AND BEHAVIOR?

I would like to discuss the role of self-talk in more depth in the process of changing emotions and behavior. You have learned that what we say to ourselves is an important factor in determining our attitudes, feelings, emotions, and behavior. This speech, or self-talk, as it is often called, is the running dialogue inside our heads. Some of our inner speech serves as a motivator to try new tasks and persist in learning (e.g., "I can do as well as anyone in this class" or "If

I keep studying this material, I know that I'll learn it"), whereas other forms of inner speech lead to unproductive behavior (e.g., "I'll never solve these problems" or "Why did I ever take this class?").

Self-talk is an important strategy for self-management. Individuals who exhibit inappropriate self-talk often act inappropriately. If more appropriate self-talk is introduced, behavior can be changed. The emphasis, therefore, is on changing negative self-talk to positive self-talk. The theory behind self-talk training is that inner speech influences cognition (thinking) and emotions, and ultimately guides our behavior.

Meichenbaum (1977) showed how self-talk can be used to modify the behavior of students who were anxious or impulsive. He successfully trained students to replace negative self-statements like "I can't do this" or "I'm not good at it" with positive self-statements like "If I concentrate I can solve the problems" or "I just need to relax and carefully read each problem." The training led to improved performance on tasks. Self-talk also has been used to control anxiety, mood, and other emotional responses.

A good example of the impact of self-talk is discussed by Gallwey (1974) in his book *The Inner Game of Tennis*. Gallwey said that tennis, like other sports, is composed of two parts, an outer game and an inner game. The outer game consists of mastering the techniques of how to play the game (e.g., how to serve and use one's backhand). The inner game takes place in the mind of the player and is basically the self-talk one uses while he or she is playing. Compare the dialogue of two different tennis players:

> I'm hitting my forehand rotten again today . . . Dammit, why do I keep missing those easy set ups . . . I'm not doing anything the coach told me to do in my last lesson. You were great rallying, now you're playing worse than your grandmother . . . (p. 82).

> The last three of my backhands landed long, by about two feet. My racket seems to be hesitating, instead of following through all the way. Maybe I should observe the level of my backswing . . . yes, I thought so, it's well above my waist. . . . There, that shot got hit with more pace, yet it stayed in (p. 83).

How do you think such talk influenced each player's game?

A sports commentator once said that there was little difference in the ability (i.e., outer game) of the top 20 ranked tennis players in the world. What sets them apart is their mental approach to the game (i.e., their inner game). There is evidence that the "inner game" plays an important role in individual success in all endeavors—at work, home, and school. For example, a student's motivation to learn is strongly influenced by his or her perceptions and beliefs about academic situations. These perceptions and beliefs often are identified by analyzing self-talk.

What types of self-talk have you experienced in athletic competition or in other performance situations? What about test situations?

HOW DOES SELF-TALK OPERATE?

Many individuals blame others for their negative emotional reactions: "He made me mad" or "My friend's response to my question made me depressed." People or events do not directly influence our emotional reactions. Instead, our self-talk related to events is the primary cause of our attitudes and emotions.

The following is how one psychologist believes the process operates (Ellis, 1962): An event or experience occurs (A). We then process the information and think about it (B). Finally, we react with our emotions and tend to take some action regarding the initial event or experience (C).

A. An event occurs	A. A low score on a test.
B. Thoughts about the event (self-talk)	B1. Self-talk: "I can't learn this stuff!" "What's the use of studying?" B2. Self-talk: "I have the ability to get these questions correct if I put forth extra effort." "I'm going to study differently next time."
C. Emotion caused primarily by the thoughts and self-talk	C1. Emotion: sadness and anger C2. Emotion: confidence

Note the different reactions—B1 and B2 to the event (A) and the resulting emotional responses. The first response (B1) is an example of harmful self-talk leading to negative emotional responses and often inappropriate behavior in future test preparation situations. The second response (B2) is an example of positive self-talk leading to a positive emotional response and possible changes in future test preparation situations.

Most of us use more positive than negative self-talk in dealing with the events and situations in our lives. By using positive self-talk, individuals are able to experience success in many different areas. When difficult or challenging events occur, individuals remind themselves that they have the ability, skill, or motivation to overcome any adversity. However, occasionally negative self-talk does play a role in emotion, attitudes, and behavior. The following are some examples of how self-talk affects students' emotional responses and behavior.

Student Reflections

When the notion of self-talk was first introduced in class, it sounded funny. After all, what normal person walks around talking to himself or herself? A week ago I started to analyze my own self-talk. I never realized how much I talk to myself! I talk to myself about my weight, my appearance, my academic progress, and life goals. When I am studying I wonder how I am doing in the subject or how well I will perform on the exam.

I find many examples of both positive and negative self-talk in my daily life. Recently, I was doing a scene in an acting class and I caught myself talking to myself, saying how bad I was doing. I was complaining to myself because I was not in the mood to do the scene. I stopped myself and just told myself to talk later and not now. My self-talk was not helping me get the job done.

Anxiety plays a different role in my life than I think it does for most other students. I do not experience much test anxiety, but I do experience task anxiety. When I am given an assignment for a class I spend more time worrying about how and when I am going to get the assignment done than I do actually working on the task.

I understand that instructors expect more out of students when they are given take-home assignments. These assignments make me nervous, because I do not know whether I can live up to the instructor's expectations.

I am trying to deal with my anxiety by finding out the instructor's criteria for grading the assignment. In this way, I feel more in control of my destiny.

Examples of Negative Self-Talk

Individuals express different types of negative self-talk. The following are four common types of self-talk that tend to be found in people who are prone to anxiety: the *Worrier*, the *Critic*, the *Victim*, and the *Perfectionist*. The Worrier creates anxiety by causing you to anticipate the worst-case scenario; the Critic is the part of you that constantly judges and evaluates your behavior; the Victim makes you feel helpless and hopeless; and the Perfectionist resembles the Critic, but its concern is not to put you down, but to push you to do better. Unfortunately, the Perfectionist generates anxiety by telling you that your

TABLE 5.1
NEGATIVE SELF-TALK

Type	Characteristics	Favorite Expression	Examples of Self-Talk
The Worrier	Imagines the worst situation	"What if . . ."	. . . "I get called on and I can't answer the question."
The Critic	Judges or evaluates your behavior; points out your flaws and limitations	"That was stupid!"	"My term paper needed more library research and another draft."
The Victim	Feels helpless or hopeless	"I can't." "I'll never be able to."	"I'm just too tired to do anything today."
The Perfectionist	Tells you that your efforts aren't good enough	"I should." "I have to." "I must." "I could have."	"If I take some time off from studying. I keep thinking: 'You should be studying.'"

Adapted from Bourne (1995) and Ottens (1991)

efforts are not good enough (Bourne, 1995). Individuals may display more than one type of self-talk in any situation. Table 5.1 summarizes information on each of the four types of self-talk. Do these characteristics play a role in your thinking, feelings, and behavior? If so, how?

EXERCISE 5.3: CLASSIFYING NEGATIVE SELF-TALK

The following are examples of negative self-talk. After studying Table 5.1, identify the type of self-talk—the Worrier, the Critic, the Victim, or the Perfectionist—depicted in each statement.

Type	Statement
	1. "I should have made an appointment to see my instructor."
	2. "I will never be able to make the dean's list, so what's the point in even trying."
	3. "I always find some way to screw up!"
	4. "What if I start stuttering in the middle of my speech?"
	5. "I could have done better."

HOW CAN I CHANGE MY SELF-TALK?

It is important to understand and to change your unproductive self-talk. After identifying and understanding the nature of your negative self-talk, you can counter it with positive, supportive statements. This requires writing down and actually rehearsing positive statements that directly refute your negative self-talk (Bourne, 1995).

Bourne provided some examples of positive counterstatements that can be used with each of the four types of negative self-talk. She recommended avoiding negative statements (e.g., "I'm not going to panic when I start the test") and focusing on positive statements: (e.g., "I'm prepared for this test"). She also suggested keeping counterstatements in the present tense and in the first person (e.g., "I can . . . " "I will now . . . " "I am learning to . . . ").

The Worrier
Instead of "What if . . . " say, "So what, I can handle this," "I can be anxious and still do this," "I'll get used to this with practice."

The Critic
Instead of self-criticism, say, "I'm okay the way I am," "I accept and believe in myself."

The Victim
Instead of feeling hopeless, say, "I can continue to make progress one step at a time." "I acknowledge the progress I've made and will continue to improve."

The Perfectionist
Instead of demanding perfection, say, "It's okay to make mistakes. Setbacks are part of the process and an important learning experience."

The procedure shown in Table 5.2 was developed by Butler (1981) to help individuals understand and change any self-talk that is preventing them from reaching their goals. Note how you can apply the self-management cycle in mastering this strategy: self-observation and evaluation (Steps 1–3), goal setting and strategic planning, and strategy implementation and monitoring (Steps 4–5). The fourth step in the cycle, strategic outcome and monitoring, becomes a function of your assessment of behavior change.

An Example of Analyzing Self-Talk

Sharon is graduating from high school and would like to major in biology in college because she plans to attend medical school. She decides instead to major in business, because her friends have told her about the many years of difficult study necessary to achieve her

TABLE 5.2

Procedures for Improving Self-Talk	
Procedures	Questions
1. Listen to your own self-talk *You can't alter inner speech unless you understand what you are telling yourself.*	"What am I telling myself?"
2. Decide if your inner dialogue is helpful or harmful. *Examine how your inner speech affects your emotions, motivation, and behavior. If your self-talk is helping, maintain it. If your self-talk is harmful, change it.*	"Is it helping?"
3. Identify the type of self-talk in which you are engaged. *Is it from the Worrier, the Critic, the Victim, or the Perfectionist?*	"What type of self-talk is maintaining my negative self-talk?"
4. Replace your harmful self-talk with positive self-talk. *Give yourself permission to try another strategy to deal with the event or situation. Identify your positive characteristics (e.g., desire, concentration, ability) that will help deal with the event. Try writing a counterargument to your negative self-talk.*	"What permission and self-affirmation will I give myself?"
5. Develop a guide: Decide what action to take consonant with your new supportive position. *If you decide that your self-talk is harmful, you want to change your behavior as well as your attitude or emotional response. Specify this new behavior.*	"What action will I take based on my new positive position?"

original goal. In addition, she doubts her ability and motivation to perform well in science. During the first semester at college, she becomes upset because she is not studying what she really wants and decides to explore her own self-talk.

Questions	Reply
What am I telling myself?	I'm saying to myself, "I really would like to go to medical school." Then I think, "Oh, come on, Sharon, you're being silly. Medical school is hard and you'll never be able to do the work."
Is it helping?	No. It's keeping me from doing what I really want to do.
What type of self-talk is maintaining my negative self-talk?	The Critic

continued

Questions	Reply
What permission and self-affirmation will I give myself?	I will tell myself that I need to stop listening to others and begin thinking for myself. After all, I did very well in high school and I am very motivated to succeed in college.
What action will I take based on my new position?	I'm going to see my advisor and find out what courses I need to major in biology. Next semester I will enroll in two science courses and see how I do. Then I'll have a better idea of both my ability and interest.

EXERCISE 5.4: SELF-OBSERVATION: USING SELF-TALK

Identify a situation or event in your life when you used negative self-talk. Use the following five-step process to change your talk. Briefly describe the situation or event and fill in the blanks indicating a possible reply to your self-talk.

Event:

Questions	Reply
What am I telling myself?	
Is it helping?	
What type of self-talk is maintaining my negative self-talk?	
What permission and self-affirmation will I give myself?	
What action will I take based on my new position?	

CAN RELAXATION REDUCE ANXIETY?

One of the most common strategies for reducing stress is to alleviate its symptoms. Sports competition occurs in a stressful environment that requires athletes to handle the effects of pressure. I have always been impressed with the athletic and mental ability of a field goal kicker on the 25-yard-line waiting to kick with 5 seconds left in the game and his team behind by 2 points, or the basketball player on the foul line waiting to shoot 2 shots that could tie or win the game. One of the factors that separate elite from nonelite athletes is the ability to control anxiety (Jones & Hardy, 1990).

For some individuals, preparing for or taking an exam, presenting an oral report, or writing a paper can present sufficient stress to negatively impact academic performance. In chapter 2, I stated that there were two effects of anxiety—worry and emotionality. Self-talk is a good strategy for dealing with worry, whereas relaxation techniques are successful in dealing with emotionality (i.e., psychosomatic illnesses such as headaches and stomach distress).

Relaxation techniques can be grouped into physical and mental techniques. For example, controlling one's breathing is an effective way to relax. Many experts in anxiety reduction teach individuals breathing exercises that involve long, slow exhalation. The diaphragm expands and tenses when taking in air and relaxes when the air is released. Thus, one way to relax is to increase the time you spend exhaling. This process is called *diaphragmatic breathing*. The following is a simple exercise to teach you to relax (Youngs, 1985). Experience the following technique by asking a friend to read each step so you can attempt it:

1. Get comfortable. Move your arms and legs around to make your muscles loose.
2. Close your eyes.
3. Take a deep breath in and count slowly: 1 . . . 2 . . . 3 . . . 4 . . . 5 . . . 6.
4. Let the air out very slowly, counting: 1 . . . 2 . . . 3 . . . 4 . . . 5 . . . 6.
5. Repeat Steps 3 and 4, but this time place your hands on your stomach and feel it filling up with air (pushing out) when you breathe.
6. Breathe in deeply while counting: 1 . . . 2 . . . 3 . . . 4.
7. Let the air out slowly while counting: 1 . . . 2 . . . 3 . . . 4 . . . 5 . . . 6 . . . (feel your stomach pull back in).
8. Repeat this a few more times.
9. Open your eyes.

Don't get too relaxed! You have more reading to do!

An example of mental relaxation is **transcendental meditation**. It involves assuming a comfortable position, closing your eyes, relaxing your muscles, focusing on breathing, and repeating a mantra, or key word. This technique has been associated with reduced oxygen consumption, decreased respiration, slower heart rate, and lower blood pressure. Most important, research has indicated that meditation can alter one's mood and emotions (Bourne, 1995).

Benson (1976), in his well-known book *The Relaxation Response*, developed his own version of meditation, which involved mentally repeating the word *one* with each exhalation of breath. The following is an adaptation of his procedure (Peurifoy, 1995):

1. Pick a time and place where you will not be disturbed and lie or sit in a comfortable position.
2. Close your eyes and choose a center of focus. This is a word or phrase that helps shift your mind from a logical, externally oriented thought to an internal, passive center of focus and stops your mind from wandering. The most common focal point is a word such as *one, calm,* or *relax.* However, a short phrase can also be used, such as *relax and be at peace.*
3. Repeat your word or phrase each time you exhale. As you do this, adopt a passive attitude. This is the most important element of this method. Avoid concern about how well you are performing the technique and adopt a "let it happen" attitude. Your mind will occasionally slip away from its concentration on the word or phrase you have chosen. When this happens, don't panic or abandon your practice. Simply redirect your mind to your breathing and continue repeating your chosen word or phrase after each exhalation.
4. Practice for 10 to 20 minutes, then open your eyes and resume your normal activities. (p. 317)

In summary, if you experience negative physiological symptoms to stressful events, you will want to explore strategies for dealing with your symptoms. Many students find jogging or walking, or listening to music helpful. You can find numerous books in the library or local bookstore on various relaxation techniques.

Key Points

1. What individuals say to themselves is an important factor in determining their attitudes, feelings, emotions, and behavior.
2. Individuals who exhibit inappropriate self-talk often act in an inappropriate manner.
3. People or events do not directly influence individuals' emotional reactions. Individuals' self-talk regarding events is the primary cause of their attitudes and emotions.

4. Responding with positive counterstatements is an effective way to change negative self-talk.
5. Relaxation techniques can be physical or mental.
6. Meditation can alter one's mood and emotions.

Follow-Up Activities

1. Use Rational Emotive Therapy to Change Emotions

Select some environmental event that disturbs you and demonstrate how you can change your irrational beliefs to more realistic beliefs leading to a more positive outlook regarding the event. Like most of the learning and motivational strategies you are learning in this course, you need to practice this procedure many times before it becomes effective (adapted from Merrell, 2001).

Activating Event (the situation I am disturbed about or the problem)

_____

_____

_____

_____

Belief (irrational or helpless belief that followed event)

_____

_____

_____

_____

Consequence (how I felt)

_____

_____

_____

_____

Disputing Irrational Beliefs (how I argue against the negative belief with a more realistic or rational belief)

_____

_____

_____

_____

New Effect (the way I feel and will behave after I disputed the irrational beliefs)

_____

_____

_____

_____

2. Identify Irrational Thinking

Individuals who experience negative emotions like depression, anxiety, hopelessness, and shame tend to adopt irrational modes of thinking. Therefore, it is important to identify patterns of such irrational thinking. Review the examples of irrational thinking identified in this chapter and identify a situation where you used any of these thinking processes:

- Filtering
- Polarized thinking
- Overgeneralization
- Mind reading
- Catastrophizing
- Magnifying
- Personalization
- Shoulds

3. Use the Self-Management Process to Reduce Anxiety

Complete the following self-study during a period of 2 to 3 weeks. Your report should include each of the following processes and should be approximately five to eight typed pages in length. See Appendix A for detailed information on how to conduct a self-management study.

Self-observation and evaluation. How does anxiety influence my academic and personal life? Do I need to change the way I deal with anxiety? If yes, what problem do I encounter? What are the symptoms of my problem (i.e., when, where, and how often does my problem occur)? What factors (e.g., beliefs, perceptions, feelings, physiological responses, or behaviors) contribute to this problem? What do I need to change to reduce or eliminate my problem?

Goal setting and strategic planning. What are my goals? What strategies will I implement to reduce my anxiety? When will I use these strategies? How will I record my progress?

Strategy implementation and monitoring. What strategies did I use to reduce my anxiety? When did I use these strategies? What method(s) did I use to record my progress (e.g., documents, charts, logs, tally sheets, checklists, or recordings)? When did I use these methods? How and when did I monitor my progress to determine if my anxiety-reducing strategies were working? What changes, if any, did I make along the way?

Strategic-outcome monitoring. Did I attain the goal(s) I set for myself? Has the reduction in my anxiety improved my academic performance or personal life? What strategies were the most and least effective? What changes, if any, do I need to make in the future?

4. Assess Self-Talk

During the next week, monitor your self-talk and evaluate how it affects your motivation and self-confidence. Consider all the situations and tasks in which you engage—academic, athletic and recreational, social, occupational, and personal. Include in your report the following information: date, situation (e.g., academic), setting (describe where you were and what you were trying to accomplish), and report the self-talk as specifically as possible. Finally, discuss what strategies you used to deal with any negative self-talk.

Date: _____

Setting: _____

Self-talk:_____

Strategy:_____

Date: _____

Setting: _____

Self-talk: _____

Strategy: _____

Date: _____

Setting: _____

Self-talk: _____

Strategy: _____

Date: _____

Setting: _____

Self-talk: _____

Strategy: _____

Comments: _____

_____

_____

_____

_____

_____

5. Explore Anxiety-Producing Situations in School

The following are common thoughts and worries expressed by individuals who have test anxiety (Smith, 1982, p. 179). Check those with which you can identify the most and then *add additional thoughts* in the empty spaces provided. Compare your thoughts and worries with those of other students in your class. Finally, discuss strategies you can use to deal with your negative thoughts.

a. Worry about performance
   _____ I should have reviewed more. I'll never get through.
   _____ My mind is blank, I'll never get the answer. I must really be stupid.
   _____ I knew this stuff yesterday. What is wrong with me?
   _____ I can't remember a thing. This always happens to me.
   _____
   _____

b. Worry about bodily reactions

_____ I'm sick. I'll never get through.

_____ I'm sweating all over—it's really hot in here.

_____ My stomach is going crazy, churning and jumping all over.

_____ Here it comes—I'm getting really tense again. Normal people just don't get like this.

_____

_____

c. Worry about how others are doing

_____ I know everyone's doing better than I am.

_____ I must be the dumbest one in the group.

_____ I am going to be the last one done again. I must really be stupid.

_____ No one else seems to be having trouble. Am I the only one?

_____

_____

d. Worry about the possible negative consequences

_____ If I fail this test, I'll never get into the program.

_____ I'll never graduate.

_____ I'll think less of myself.

_____ I'll be embarrassed.

_____

_____

Effective Strategies:

_____

_____

_____

_____

_____

_____

Answers to Exercise 5.2

1. D   2. B   3. H   4. G   5. A   6. C   7. F   8. E

Answers to Exercise 5.3

1. P   2. V   3. C   4. W   5. P

UNIT III

BEHAVIORAL STRATEGIES

Chapter 6: Time Management
Chapter 7: Management of Physical and
Social Environment

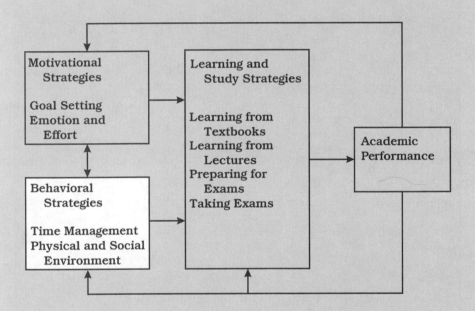

In this unit, I present strategies that will help you control your time and your physical and social environments. For the most part, these strategies involve behavioral changes that you can initiate to affect your learning. You cannot control your life without controlling your use of time. In chapter 6, I ask you to analyze your use of time and teach you a management system to use your time more effectively. In chapter 7, I describe procedures to help you manage your environment. Many students have academic problems because they do not manage their physical and social environments; instead, their environments manage them. The key aspect of management of the physical environment is one' study environment. Management of one's social environment focuses on knowing when and how to seek and obtain help.

6

Time Management

The goal in this chapter is to help you manage your time more effectively. Problems in time management can be related to one or more of the following: uncertainty of what is to be accomplished (i.e., lack of goals), failure to break down the goals into a series of tasks, or lack of awareness about how to manage time or how much time is needed to complete a given task (Britton & Glynn, 1989).

One of the most important factors influencing the attainment of goals is the efficient use of time. In high school, most of your time was structured for you because you were in school most of the day. For the most part, your time management involved structuring your study time after school. College life is more demanding because there are more tasks to accomplish. Your class schedule can vary greatly; for example, you may only have classes three or four times a week and might complete your classes by noon. In general, you have to manage more hours of time and often do not have your parents around to offer "suggestions" for how you should do it.

After studying this chapter, you will be able to:

- Analyze your use of time.
- Develop a time management system.
- Use strategies to reduce procrastination.

WHAT IS TIME MANAGEMENT?

Smith (1994) defined *time* as "a continuum in which events succeed one another from past through present to future" (p. 20). The basic aspect of time is an event. Everything in our lives is an event. Getting out of bed in the morning, driving or walking to class, reading this book are all events. Time is the occurrence of all the events in our lives in sequence, one after the other. When we talk about time management, we are really talking about event or task management. After all, the purpose of time management is to ensure that we complete all of our important tasks each day. It is not simply to manage time. Smith (1994) stated: "Controlling your life means controlling your time, and controlling your time means controlling the events in your life" (p. 20).

Student Reflections

I feel very hyperactive. I think that this state is really affecting the way I approach my work. I do one thing, and my mind races to another subject that I have to do. All of a sudden, I remember what I'm putting on hold, and I go back to finish my original task. At the same time, I don't finish what I set out to do in the second task. It's really annoying to be feeling this way, because I'm not getting a lot of things done. I keep jumping back and forth from one task to the next. I don't have any focus, and it's really hard to concentrate. I have no priority over any task, everything seems equal. At the same time, I feel like I'm postponing what I really have to do, because I'm too lazy or too distracted to do it at that time. I really feel like I'm avoiding what has to be done. I don't know exactly what that task is, but right now it feels like I'm avoiding everything that I have to get done.

What are your impressions of this student? I found three major concerns when I first read his journal. First, it is clear that he does not feel in control of his life. It appears that events are controlling his life. He mentions two other problems: He has no priority concerning the many tasks he must complete, and he is a procrastinator. As you read the material in this chapter, think about the suggestions you could give this student to help him deal with his problems.

HOW DO YOU USE YOUR TIME?

Everyone wastes some time. A problem occurs, however, when the amount of time that one wastes interferes with the attainment of personal goals. The purpose of the following exercise is to identify your major time wasters. Next, you will be asked to account for your time in a typical week to gain further insights into your use of time.

EXERCISE 6.1: SELF-OBSERVATION: ASSESSING TIME WASTERS

Directions: The following list identifies on a scale of 1 (highest) to 10 (lowest), the greatest time wasters reported by college students (Chaney, 1991). As you review the items, identify the time wasters you think give you the greatest difficulty. Rank them from 1 to 5 with the number 1 as your greatest time waster. Identify additional time wasters that you think should be added to the list since this study was conducted in 1991. Have you tried to eliminate your time wasters? If so, how successful have you been? Share some of your successful strategies with students in your class.

Time Wasters	My Rank
1. Procrastination	
2. Watching television	
3. Visiting with friends/socializing	
4. Daydreaming	
5. Figuring out how to do an assignment	
6. Physical problems, such as lack of energy	
7. Sleeping too much	
8. Lack of planning	
9. Waiting for others	
10. Talking on the telephone	

EXERCISE 6.2: SELF-OBSERVATION: ASSESSING USE OF TIME

Directions: Students who have difficulty with time management often lack awareness about how they spend their time. This exercise gives you an opportunity to evaluate your actual use of time. Fill in your activities last week in the following calendar. Next, using the Time

My Use of Time	Monday	Tuesday	Wednesday	Thursday	Friday	Saturday	Sunday
6–7 a.m.							
7–8							
8–9							
9–10							
10–11							
11–12							
12–1 p.m.							
1–2							
2–3							
3–4							
4–5							
5–6							

My Use of Time

	Monday	Tuesday	Wednesday	Thursday	Friday	Saturday	Sunday
6–7							
7–8							
8–9							
9–10							
10–11							
11–12							
12–1 a.m.							
1–2							
2–3							
3–4							
4–5							
5–6							

Time Analysis

Activities	M	T	W	TH	F	SA	SU	TOTAL
Eating								
Sleeping								
Class								
Studying								
Working								
Personal chores and responsibilities								
Social activities								
Sports and recreation								
Games								
Relaxing								
Miscellaneous								

Analysis table, determine how much time you spend in each activity listed for each day of the week, as well as the total for the entire week. When you total your time, *round to the nearest half hour* (e.g., 9 hours and 20 minutes sleeping = 9.5 hours).

List the three activities on which you are spending the most time (other than sleeping):

1.

2.

3.

Summarize what you have learned about your personal time-use habits. Be specific (e.g., When do you study? Do you spend more than 2 hours a day watching television or talking on the telephone? Do you tend to accomplish your goals?) Does your response differ from your original perception of time wasters reported in Exercise 6.1? What do you need to do to become more effective in achieving your goals?

WHAT ARE SOME GOOD TIME MANAGEMENT STRATEGIES?

Set Regular Study Periods

Setting a regular time to study each day helps "protect" you from constant conflicts with other tasks that you must complete. There always will be unexpected events that rob time from your studying. If circumstances arise that prohibit you from studying, adjust your schedule. If you do not establish a set time, the probability increases that you will become involved with other tasks.

Study in an Environment That Is Relatively Free of Distractions and Interruptions

Analyze your present study environment and determine whether it is the best place for you. Most college students study in one of five locations: home, dorm, apartment, fraternity or sorority house, or library. Wherever you decide to study, consider the level of distractions present. If you find you are constantly distracted by discussions, telephone calls, music, or other factors, consider another location (see Exercise 7.1).

Schedule Tasks So They Can Be Accomplished in 30- to 60-Minute Blocks of Time

There are two major reasons for block planning. First, it is wise to develop intermediate goals and specific tasks for each major goal identified. Organizing time around intermediate goals and daily tasks helps lead to a greater sense of efficacy as each intermediate goal and task is completed. For example, in developing a plan for writing a paper, you may decide to spend 30 minutes outlining the paper and another 30 minutes to determine what topics will be covered. Second, many students miss great opportunities for studying by neglecting time between classes. A few short intervals quickly add up to an hour or more of study during the day. Consider short intervals of study, as well as longer intervals when you plan your study schedule.

How to Get the Most Out of Even a Few Minutes

The 5-Minute Fanatic can . . .

- Set up a place to study for the day.
- Do a relaxation exercise to calm the mind before studying for an exam.
- Organize class notes in preparation for studying.
- Put in a load of laundry.
- Make phone calls to schedule appointments.

The 15-Minute Organizer can . . .

- Review class notes.
- Review the next day's activity schedule.
- Balance a checkbook.
- Outline a term paper assignment.
- Write a letter.

(Adapted from Scharf, 1985, pp. 78–79)

Take Short Breaks

How long you study is determined by your motivation and concentration. In general, most students need a short 5- or 10-minute break each hour. However, you may be able to concentrate for longer periods of time. You need to adjust the study intervals according to your own personal needs. If you find you are easily distracted, you may need a 2- or 3-minute break after 30 minutes or so.

Be Specific in Identifying How You Plan to Use Your Time

It is not how long you study, but how you study that determines academic success. If you break your goal into tasks, as suggested earlier, you will find it easier to determine how you will spend your time. Do not just write the course name or study topic (e.g., psychology) in your schedule. Specify what you plan to do during the time.

Alternate Subjects When You Have a Long Time Block Available for Study

There is no reason to complete studying a given subject before moving to the next subject. If you have a number of tasks to complete in a subject, you may find you can better control motivation and concentration by completing certain aspects of the assignment in one subject area and coming back to another part of the assignment at a later time. In addition, you should determine the sequence of studying different subjects so that you do not end up doing the same things for long periods of time (e.g., solving math problems and balancing chemical equations).

Estimate the Time Needed for Each Assignment

Successfully estimating the amount of time needed for each subject comes with experience. The better you estimate time, the more realistic your study plan will become. However, no one can be on target every time. It often is not until you begin studying or writing that you find that you underestimated the time needed to complete the task. If this occurs, there is nothing wrong with adjusting your schedule the next day.

Prioritize Tasks

One of the most important factors in developing an effective time-management system is prioritizing tasks. Not everything you have to do is of equal importance. You need to decide what task should be completed first. Smith (1994) discussed the difference between urgent and vital tasks:

> You need to understand that there's a big difference between important tasks and urgencies. Some tasks are never going to be urgent, even though they may be extremely vital. Other tasks may never be important, but they will be urgent. The secret is to identify your vital activities and infuse them with a sense of urgency built into them. . . . The only way to do these is to set up a system that takes your deepest values and translates them into daily activities. (p. 45)

An urgent task requires immediate attention. The most common urgent task is the telephone. When a phone rings, you say to yourself: "I need to pick up the phone." Yet, how many calls do you receive each day that can be classified as important? If you need a shirt to wear for an evening engagement and all your shirts are at the dry cleaners, going to the laundry becomes an urgent task. Spending time talking to a close friend may be a task you highly value: It is vital but not urgent, because your friend is always there. You can speak to him or her whenever you want. The problem is that we tend to put off highly valued tasks because we spend so much time dealing with urgent ones. Can you distinguish between vital and urgent tasks by providing some examples in your own life?

Do the Assignments for the Course You Dislike First

Do you have a tendency to put off difficult tasks? Do you recall stating the following: "I'll do it later in the day," or "I'll do it tomorrow"? If so, join the crowd. You are normal! Individuals tend to do first what they like the most. Later in this chapter, I will talk about procrastination to help you deal with the problem of delaying tasks.

Consider studying the course you dislike or have the most difficulty with first. There are many advantages in using this strategy: First, you become tired at the end of the day and should study difficult material when you are most alert. Second, one way to deal with the problem of procrastination is to deal with the disliked task immediately and get it out of the way instead of allowing it to "hang over your head." Finally, you often feel that you have something to look forward to when you leave the best for last.

Work Ahead of Your Assignments When Possible

Before the week begins, assess the workload for the upcoming week or even month, especially major events that may require changes in your schedule. For example, suppose you know that you are going home for the weekend or have an important social event coming up. In addition, you see that you have a major midterm on Monday morning following the big weekend. You will need to consider changes in your study schedule to prepare for the exam. Also, some assignments, like a major paper, may require more than 1 week of involvement. By knowing what future tasks are required, you can plan a strategy for completing them in a timely fashion.

Carry Your Calendar With You and Write Down Any Appointments as Soon as You Make Them

Have any of the following events happened to you? You take an appointment card from your doctor or dentist for your next visit and place it safely in your wallet or purse. Unfortunately, you fail to look at it and miss your appointment. You speak to your professor after class and make an appointment with him or her. You even write it down and put the date and time on a piece of paper. You lose the paper and forget the appointment.

I have experienced numerous situations in which I missed appointments because of poor time management. I cannot tell you how many times I have asked my wife if she found a piece of paper in one of my shirts as she was removing them from the wash.

Fortunately, I never (okay, rarely!) miss an appointment now because I no longer carry notes, cards, and slips of paper. Everything goes into my appointment calendar. A major advantage of carrying your calendar with you is that you can schedule meetings or make appointments around your planned schedule. If you have to make changes in your schedule, you can do it in the least disruptive manner.

Student Reflections

Things that worked for me in high school, I discovered, don't work for me in college. I really was unprepared for the amount of material that is presented here and the speed at which it is presented. It was a bit of a shock. Things I picked up quickly in high school I couldn't pick up as easily anymore.

Here at college I wasn't checked every day. I did not get off to a great start because I had never really learned to study this enormous amount of material in a systematic way. I tended to do one subject for a big time span and then neglect it for a week. Then I moved on to another subject and forgot about that for a week. So, there was no continuity within each course. That had a lot to do with it. Finally I figured it out. This year, I'm pushing myself to spend a little bit of time every day on each subject. (from Light, 2001, p. 24)

HOW DO I DEVELOP A SYSTEM OF TIME PLANNING AND MANAGEMENT?

I now use the information presented in this chapter to develop a system for time planning and management. The following are three forms useful in planning your time: a semester calendar, weekly priority tasks list, and a weekly schedule.

Semester Calendar

The semester calendar should be used to identify due dates each month for assignments and papers, dates of tests, and important nonacademic activities and events. This calendar should be on the wall in your room or on your desk. Semester calendars can be purchased in college bookstores and local stationery stores.

SEMESTER CALENDAR

Month _____

Sunday	Monday	Tuesday	Wednesday	Thursday	Friday	Saturday
				1	2	3
4	5	6	7	8	9	10
11	12	13	14	15	16	17
18	19	20	21	22	23	24
25	26	27	28	29	30	

Weekly Priority Tasks List

Week of _____ through _____

Tasks	Priority Ratings	Day(s) Scheduled

Goals

_____

_____

_____

_____

_____

_____

_____

_____

_____

Weekly Priority Tasks List

This form allows you to make a "to do" list for all the tasks that could or should be done during the week, based on your goals. Each week you will decide on the priority of each task and determine its order of importance. The following is an example of one student's weekly priority tasks list where A identifies the most important tasks to be completed, B identifies tasks needed to be completed only after the A tasks are completed, and C identifies tasks to be completed only after A and B tasks are completed. The number next to each letter further prioritizes the importance of each of the A, B, and C tasks.

Tasks	Priority Rating	Day(s) Scheduled
Rotate tires on car	C-3	F
Write poem for English	C-1	M–Th.
Send letter to cousin	C-2	F
Buy flowers for mother	C-4	Th.
Composition paper—outline and write	A-3	W, Th.
Calculus assignments		
Ch. 2—complete assigned problems	A-1	M
Ch. 3—complete assigned problems	A-2	W
Psychology		
Read ch. 2—outline main ideas	B-1	M
Answer end-of-chapter questions	B-2	T

Weekly Schedule

The final form is the weekly schedule, which identifies the time and order in which you will complete the tasks and activities for the week. This schedule is developed each week and reviewed each day to determine whether any changes are needed for the following day because

Name _____

WEEKLY SCHEDULE

	Sunday	Monday	Tuesday	Wednesday	Thursday	Friday	Saturday
6–7 a.m.							
7–8							
8–9							
9–10							
10–11							
11–12							
12–1 p.m.							
1–2							
2–3							
3–4							
4–5							
5–6							
6–7							
7–8							
8–9							
9–10							
10–11							
11–12							

of unforeseen circumstances (e.g., changes in appointments or the need for additional time to complete tasks).

Table 6.1 displays a summary of the procedures for developing and implementing a time-management plan.

TABLE 6.1

Procedures for Developing and Implementing a Time Management Plan	
Procedures	Examples
1. Establish a time for planning at the beginning of each week when you will not be interrupted. This time also should be used to review your prior week's use of time and performance.	Most students use Sunday night. Ask yourself the following questions: "Did I attain my goals last week?" Did I plan for sufficient study time?" "Do I need to make changes in my goals or priorities?" "Do I need to make changes in my time management?" "What are my goals for this week?"
2. Enter all fixed activities in your weekly schedule.	Fixed activities are those activities over which you have little or no control (e.g., job, meals, classes, athletic practice, sleep, appointments, etc.).
3. Review your written goals to determine what tasks need to be started or completed to bring you closer to attaining your goals.	"I want to practice my guitar four times a week for 40 minutes." "I want to achieve an 'A' in English this semester."
4. Check your semester calendar to determine whether there are any exams, papers, or other major assignments due in the next few weeks.	"I have a midterm in Spanish coming up in 2 weeks. I had better start developing a study plan to review all the material next week."
5. Identify all the personal and academic tasks you have to complete for the week on the weekly prioritized task list.	"I need to buy computer paper, complete my math problems, do my Spanish translation each day, write a short paper, and finish the assigned readings in sociology."
6. Prioritize daily tasks list by giving a value (A, B, or C) to each item on the list. Place an "A" next to items that must be done. Place a "B" next to any task that is important and should be done. That is, after all the "A" tasks are completed, and you have time, you would work on the "B" items. Finally, write a "C" next to any task that is less important and could be done. That is, after the "A" and "B" tasks have been completed, you'll do the "C" tasks.	"I am having some difficulty in Spanish so I can't afford to get behind (A). Therefore, I must spend extra time this week on my translations. My short English paper is due on Friday so I better write the first draft on Wednesday to give me time for a rewrite on Thursday (B)."

Continued

7. Give a numerical value to each item on the list. In other words, determine which "A" task is most important and label it "A-1." Then decide which "A" items is next most important and label it "A-2," and so on. Do the same for "B" and "C" tasks.

"I understood the sociology lecture so I'll do the reading after I finish my math assignments (C-1), and the first draft on my English paper. I'll practice my guitar before dinner (C-2)."

8. Complete your weekly schedule by transferring the items on your priority tasks sheet to your weekly schedule forms. Put the "A" items first, followed by the "B" items, and finally as many of the "C" items you think you can accomplish.

9. Each evening check your weekly schedule for the next day and make modifications as needed. (e.g., changes in appointments, unexpected assignments, or unusual demands on time).

"I thought I could write the first draft of my English paper Wednesday but found I have to do more library research. I need to spend at least 1 hour in the library tomorrow."

WHAT IS PROCRASTINATION?

It is time to deal with the most frequent time waster identified earlier in the chapter—procrastination: the behavior of postponing tasks (Burka & Yuen, 1983). Procrastination appears to be a universal problem negatively impacting the behavior of many individuals. Ellis and Knaus (1977) reported that between 70% to 90% of college students engage in academically related procrastination, including delaying the start or finish of papers, essays, studying for exams, registering for classes, making appointments with instructors, and turning in an assignment on time (Ferrari, 2001). It is particularly relevant from a self-management perspective because it is often discussed as a problem in self-control. By definition, you cannot be a self-directed learner if you fail to control your behavior.

Do You Procrastinate?

Everyone procrastinates from time to time. The issue is the extent of one's procrastination. You may have a problem with procrastination if you answer yes to any of the following questions: Do you delay starting assignments? Are you late handing in assignments? Do you tend to wait for the last minute to complete assignments? Are you often late for appointments? Do you often underestimate the amount of time needed to complete a task?

What Are the Causes of Procrastination?

Procrastination on academic tasks can lead to low academic performance, including poor grades and course withdrawal (Semb, Glick, & Spencer, 1979). Although there are different reasons for procrastination, Ferrari, Johnson, and McCown (1995) identified two patterns that should be of concern to college students. The first pattern is classified as a lack of conscientiousness and is associated with such behaviors as poor time management, work discipline, self-control, and responsibility. The second pattern is classified as avoidance and is associated with fear of failure and anxiety.

Fear of failure was discussed in chapter 2 under Covington's (1992) self-worth theory. He believes that academic procrastination serves the goal of preserving feelings of self-worth by avoiding situations in which students might fail. Closely related to fear of failure is perfectionism. Several authors have suggested that procrastination and perfectionism are related (e.g., Burka & Yuen, 1983). This relation is explained as follows: An individual procrastinates to gain additional time to produce the best product. Unfortunately, if the procrastinator has unrealistic or too high standards, he or she is rarely satisfied with the product and fails to turn it in on time. Psychologists have traced perfectionism back to experiences growing up in families where parents tend to be very demanding and critical of their children's behavior (Flett, Hewitt, & Martin, 1995). Another characteristic in the second pattern of procrastination is anxiety. If students are anxious, procrastination is seen as a way of avoiding the anxiety associated with studying or completing the assigned task.

It is beyond the scope of this book to determine specific diagnoses of procrastination problems. If you believe procrastination is a serious problem affecting your behavior and none of the following strategies identified in this chapter help you deal with your particular problem, you may want to consider discussing it with a counselor at your counseling center.

WHAT CAN I DO ABOUT MY TENDENCY TO PROCRASTINATE?

To begin, developing an effective time management plan is a good first step. Second, the self-talk strategy discussed in chapter 5 also can be effective in dealing with procrastination. In chapter 7, I also identify attention and concentration strategies that can be helpful in dealing with procrastination.

In this chapter, I discuss two additional strategies that you will find helpful. The first category of strategies involves taking some action to reduce or eliminate the tendency to procrastinate. The second strategy is an extension of self-talk procedures whereby you attempt to challenge and change some of the misperceptions that lead to procrastination.

Procrastination Elimination Strategies

The following are some procrastination elimination strategies to help you keep on task (Ellis & Knaus, 1977; Ferrari, 2001):

- *Time-Telling:* Procrastinators have difficulty estimating the time needed to complete tasks. For the most part, they underestimate the time necessary to perform a task. Practice estimating time needed to complete tasks and compare the accuracy of your estimation over a series of tasks.

- *Prompts/Reminder Notes:* Use physical reminder notes (e.g., Post-it notes) placed in specific locations to remind you to finish a particular task. For example, place a note on a bathroom mirror, in your appointment book, or palm pilot.

- *Reinforcement:* Make an agreement with yourself that after a period of working on a task, you will reinforce yourself. For example, "If I study for 50 minutes, I will call my girlfriend or boyfriend or eat some ice cream."

- *The Bits-and-Pieces Approach:* Set a goal to work on a task for a short period of time. For example, rather than ignore a paper assignment, commit to completing one or two pages per day.

- *The 5-Minute Plan:* Agree to work on a task for 5 minutes. At the end of 5 minutes, decide whether you will work on it for another 5 minutes. Often momentum builds as you near the end of the first 5 minutes, so you want to maintain your focus on the task.

- *The 80% Success Rule:* Don't expect to go from "total non-completion" to "total completion" of all tasks. Instead, take a realistic approach by setting a goal to complete at least 80% of the task. Give yourself some reinforcement when you reach this goal and plan the completion of the final 20% of the task.

- *Social Support for Task Completion:* Work with students who tend to complete tasks. These individuals can serve as positive models instead of fellow procrastinators who help maintain procrastination.

- *Establish a Set Time for a Routine:* Setting a precise time during the day for completing a task can help you get it done. For example, deciding to exercise soon after you wake up can help you establish regular exercise behavior.

- *Modify the Environment:* Your working environment can directly influence procrastination. For example, if you need to complete some reading or write a short paper, a room with a stereo, TV, or bed may not be the best place to begin and sustain motivation to complete the task. Changing the setting by going to another room in your home or going to the library where you may find fewer distractions can help you focus on the task.

Challenging and Changing Beliefs and Misperceptions

Another way of dealing with procrastination involves challenging and changing beliefs and misperceptions. The following misconceptions are frequent among most procrastinators (Ferrari et al., 1995):

- Overestimation of the time left to perform a task.
- Underestimation of time necessary to complete a task.
- Overestimation of future motivational states. This is typified by statements such as "I'll feel more like doing it later."
- Misreliance on the necessity of emotional congruence to succeed in a task. Typical is a statement such as "People should only study when they feel good about it."
- Belief that working when not in the mood is unproductive or suboptimal. Such beliefs are typically expressed by phrases such as "It doesn't do any good to work when you are not motivated."

Some misperceptions increase anxiety about a task, leading to a feeling of futility or hopelessness regarding the ability to complete it (e.g., "It's too late to complete this task"). Other misperceptions are characteristic of individuals who are not very conscientious about completing tasks (e.g., "I do my best work when I do it at the last minute").

EXERCISE 6.3: CHALLENGE IRRATIONAL BELIEFS

The following is a list of rationalizations and corresponding suggestions for challenging the first three misperceptions (adapted from Ferrari, et al., 1995, p. 198). Provide your own challenges for the remainder of the beliefs. As you attempt to deal with reasons for procrastination, ask yourself the following: Is my belief or explanation reasonable? Is my belief accurate? Am I being objective? What argument or statement can I use to discredit my irrational belief?

Irrational Beliefs	Self-Talk Challenges
It's too late to complete this task.	"It's never too late! If I get started now, I can make good progress and get the task done."
I'm very good at getting things done at the last minute, so I don't have to worry.	"I fool myself in thinking that I do a good job when I wait until the last minute. The truth is I rush to find all the material I need, I don't have time

continued

Irrational Beliefs	Self-Talk Challenges
	to review a draft of the assignment and make necessary changes. My main concern is finishing the task rather than determining how I can do the best job."
I won't get this task done unless I relax first or get in the right mood.	"I need to stop kidding myself. I may never be in the mood to complete the assignment or get in the mood after the assignment is due. If I get started on the assignment, I may get in a better mood to do it."
I'm too nervous or stressed to get this task done.	
I've missed so many opportunities so far, so why should I bother?	
I'll do it tonight so I don't have to worry.	
I'm not smart enough to do this task.	
If I don't think about doing this task, I won't have to worry as much.	
I'm too tired to do this task well, so why bother.	
I can't work without (a specific person, study, room, etc.) being available.	

Key Points

1. Individuals control their lives by controlling, whenever possible, the timing of events in their lives.
2. Students with better time-management skills tend to have higher grade-point averages.

3. The problem for most individuals is not lack of time but poor time management.

4. Assessing present use and waste of time is essential before changing or modifying a daily or weekly schedule.

5. Individuals must always consider personal goals before scheduling tasks in a time-management plan.

6. Three forms are needed for time planning and management: a semester calendar, a weekly priority tasks list, and a weekly schedule.

7. One of the major problems in time management is failure to prioritize tasks.

8. Two major patterns of procrastination are lack of conscientiousness and avoidance associated with anxiety and fear of failure.

9. Strategies for dealing with procrastination include improving time management, maintaining attention and concentration, using specific behavioral changes, such as the 5-minute plan, reducing anxiety, and challenging irrational beliefs.

Follow-up Activities

1. Use the Self-Management Process to Improve Your Time Management

Complete the following self-study during a period of 2 to 3 weeks. Your report should include each of the following processes and should be approximately five to eight typed pages in length. See Appendix A for detailed information on how to conduct a self-management study.

Self-observation and evaluation. How do I manage my time? Do I need to change the way I plan and manage my study schedule? If yes, what problem(s) do I encounter? What are the symptoms of my problem (i.e., when, where, and how often does my problem occur)? How much of an impact does this problem have on my academic performance? What factors (e.g., beliefs, perceptions, feelings, physiological responses, or behaviors) contribute to this problem? What do I need to change to reduce or eliminate my problem(s)?

Goal setting and strategic planning. What are my goals? What strategies will I implement to improve my time management? When will I use these strategies? How will I record my progress?

Strategy implementation and monitoring. What strategies did I use to improve my time management? When did I use these strategies? What method(s) did I use to record my progress (e.g., documents, charts, logs, tally sheets, checklists, or recordings)? When did I use these methods? How and when did I monitor my progress to determine if my new time-management plan was working? What changes, if any, did I make along the way?

Strategic-outcome monitoring. Did I attain the goal(s) I set for myself? Have the modifications in my time management improved my academic performance or personal life? What strategies were the most and least effective? What changes, if any, do I need to make in the future?

3. Identify Your Escapist Techniques

On a separate sheet of paper, create a chart using the following headings and jot down all of the methods you use in a 1-week period to avoid doing your work. What can you do to keep from repeating these avoidance patterns (taken from Van Blerkom, 1994, p. 52)?

Date	Assignment or Study Task	What did I do to escape?	Why did I want to escape?	What strategies can I use to keep from trying to escape my work?

4. Identify Your Favorite Procrastination Beliefs

The following is a list of common beliefs and misperceptions of procrastinators (Bliss, 1983). Identify your top *five* cop-outs and write a challenge for each of them.

1. It's unpleasant.
2. It's not due yet.
3. I work better under pressure.
4. Maybe it will take care of itself if I just don't do anything.
5. It's too early in the day.
6. It's too late in the day.
7. I don't have any papers with me.
8. It's difficult.
9. I don't feel like doing it now.
10. I have a headache.
11. Delay won't make much difference.
12. It may be important, but it isn't urgent.
13. It might hurt.
14. I really mean to do it, but I keep forgetting.
15. Somebody else may do it if I wait.
16. It might be embarrassing.
17. I don't know where to begin.
18. I need a good stiff drink first.
19. I'm too tired.
20. I'm too busy right now.
21. It's a boring job.
22. It might not work.
23. I've got to tidy up first.
24. I need to sleep on it.
25. We can get by a little longer as is.
26. I don't really know how to do it.
27. There's a good TV program on.
28. As soon as I start, somebody will probably interrupt.
29. It needs further study.
30. My horoscope indicates this is the wrong time.
31. Nobody is nagging me about it yet.
32. If I do it now, they'll just give me something else to do.
33. The weather's lousy.
34. It's too nice of a day to spend doing that.
35. Before I start, I think I'll take a break.
36. I'll do it as soon as I finish some preliminary tasks.
37. My biorhythms are out of sync.
38. The sooner I fall behind, the more time I'll have to get caught up.

39. I'll wait until the first of the year and make a New Year's res-
     olution.
40. It's too late now, anyway.

Cop-out #1: _____

Challenge Statement: _____

Cop-out #2: _____

Challenge Statement: _____

Cop-out #3: _____

Challenge Statement: _____

Cop-out #4: _____

Challenge Statement: _____

Cop-out #5: _____

Challenge Statement: _____

7

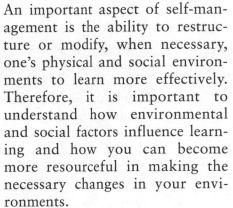

Management of Physical and Social Environment

An important aspect of self-management is the ability to restructure or modify, when necessary, one's physical and social environments to learn more effectively. Therefore, it is important to understand how environmental and social factors influence learning and how you can become more resourceful in making the necessary changes in your environments.

You can take actions to adapt to your environment, as well as change your environment to fit your needs. For example, although you cannot control the room assignment for a course, you often can determine where you sit, as well as your level of concentration during the period. If you sit near students who are carrying on a conversation during a lecture, you can move your seat. If you are in a discussion and there is considerable noise outside, you can ask to shut the window or close the door. In other words, even when you cannot select the optimal learning environment, you can take steps to adapt or modify the physical environment. Even when you do select the environment for learning, modifications to the environment can be made by disconnecting the phone, allowing the answering machine to pickup messages, or placing a "Do Not Disturb" sign on the door.

Some of the students in my classes are athletes and fraternity or sorority members who are required to attend a "study table" for a number of hours per week to study under supervision in a specific location. Because of their many time pressures, the requirement of a specific place for study is not a bad one. However, many students report that their mandated study environment often is not conducive for effective study. Some complaints include too many individuals in the room, high noise levels, and friends more interested in talking or listening to music (i.e., headphones) than studying. This is a situation where management over one's physical environment is not an easy task but can be achieved with some ingenuity. The following strategies have been used by students in this environment: setting specific study goals for each evening, selecting a location in the room that is most conducive for study, reducing visual contact with certain individuals, and limiting socializing to breaks outside the room.

Self-management of social environment relates to the ability to determine when you need to work alone or with others, or when it is time to seek help from instructors, tutors, peers, and nonsocial sources such as a reference book, additional textbooks, or the Internet (Zimmerman & Risemberg, 1997).

A recent experience provides a good example of the need for self-management in this area. A student mentioned in class that she did not do well on her biology exam, because she did not prepare for the type of questions it contained. I suggested she meet with her instructor to discuss her present performance and learn more about future exams. She agreed. When she returned to class the following week, I asked her about the meeting. She stated that she went to the instructor's office, but because other students were waiting to see him, she left and did not return. In chapter 1, I mentioned that when certain learners confront obstacles, they find ways to succeed; they don't give up! If a meeting with an instructor can lead to higher academic performance, you must develop strategies to obtain the information. This may mean making an appointment, waiting outside the office, finding out when the instructor arrives in the morning, or walking with the instructor to his or her next class. In other words, your job is to obtain the information. It is easy to convince yourself that you sufficiently tried to complete a task or that the task was too difficult. Unfortunately, these attributions do not help you attain the information you need.

Motivational beliefs and perceptions often play an important role in explaining individual differences in the willingness and ability to manage physical and social environments. For example, as reported in chapter 3, students who perceive themselves as academically competent, feel in control of their academic success, and have a mastery orientation view help seeking as an effective learning strategy and are more likely to seek help (Newman & Schwager, 1992). In a study of the characteristics of students who attend voluntary review sessions, Ames and Lau (1982) found that students' participation was related to their attributional patterns and past performances. Students who did poorly on earlier exams, but attributed their poor performance to low effort and a lack of knowledge rather than to low intelligence, were much more likely to seek help than students who attributed their poor performance to lack of interest, the difficulty of the exam, or the instructor. After studying this chapter, you will be able to:

- Improve your attention and concentration.
- Select or modify study environments.
- Work more effectively in groups.
- Prepare for and benefit from meetings with tutors and instructors.

IS THERE A DIFFERENCE BETWEEN ATTENTION AND CONCENTRATION?

In chapter 3, I pointed out that a student may be motivated to engage in a task but may have difficulty persisting, because he or she easily becomes distracted. The problem is that even though the student may be capable and motivated, he or she may lack the self-discipline or self-management to overcome environmental distractions, anxiety, or competing emotional or physical needs.

It is necessary to learn how to deal with attention and concentration. Although these terms often are used interchangeably, there is a slight difference in meaning. **Attention** is a selective process that controls awareness of events in the environment. During the discussion of the information processing system (chapter 2), I pointed out that the nature of attention determines the stimuli that are processed or neglected. Because of our limitations in attention span and ability to focus on a stimulus, it is necessary to constantly refocus on the stimulus or message. **Concentration** is the term used to identify the continual refocusing on a perceived stimulus or message. Note that *focus* is the key word identifying attention and *refocus* is the key word identifying concentration (Wolff & Marsnik, 1992).

Chapter 2 discussed the key to learning as attention. Information cannot be acquired unless one is attentive. Unfortunately, many students are not aware when they are not paying attention. Have you ever caught yourself daydreaming as you turned pages in a textbook and realized that you did not recall anything you read? Have you tried to study but had so many things on your mind that it was impossible to accomplish anything? If you answered yes to any of these questions, you will benefit from the information in this chapter.

EXERCISE 7.1: SELF-OBSERVATION: EVALUATING STUDY ENVIRONMENTS

Directions: The purpose of this exercise is to help you identify your best study environment. You may study in many different locations: dorm room, apartment, home, fraternity, sorority, or athletic study hall, and library. Identify two or three different study locations that you have used to study this term and rate your behavior in each location on a 5-point scale. Identify the location by writing it next to the letters A, B, or C. Complete your ratings by writing in the number 1, 2, 3, 4, or 5 for each location.

A:

B:

C:

1	2	3	4	5
Very descriptive of my behavior		Moderately descriptive of my behavior		Not at all descriptive of my behavior

	Locations		
Behavior	**A**	**B**	**C**
1. I begin studying immediately.			
2. I study with little interruption from others.			
3. I spend time on the phone.			
4. I spend time daydreaming or sleeping.			
5. I find the temperature conditions satisfactory.			

Behavior	Locations A	B	C
6. I find the chair, table, and lighting satisfactory.			
7. I concentrate on what needs to be accomplished.			
8. I take the appropriate number and length of breaks to maintain concentration.			
9. I return to studying immediately after my breaks.			
10. I attain my study goals.			

Average Rating   —   —   —

Average your ratings for each of the locations you rated. The lower the score, the better you rated the location. Which location did you rate the best? Is the information consistent with your perceptions? How can you make use of the information in this exercise? Do you need to alter or change your study environment? If, so, what changes might you make?

_____

_____

_____

_____

_____

_____

WHAT FACTORS INFLUENCE ATTENTION AND CONCENTRATION?

Students have difficulty concentrating on tasks, because of external and internal distracters. External distracters are environmental sources of interference (e.g., noise, such as the TV), interruptions (e.g., telephone calls), uncomfortable study areas (e.g., clothes and books piled all over the room), and disruptive roommates. Internal distracters refer to sources of interference from within, such as irrelevant thoughts (e.g., "I forgot to return my library books today"), worry (e.g., "I don't know if I can learn this material"), physiological and emotional distress (e.g., headache), and daydreaming (e.g., thinking about next weekend's party).

EXERCISE 7.2: SELF-OBSERVATION: BECOMING AWARE OF MISDIRECTED ATTENTION

It is important to identify the types of distracters that tend to interfere with attention (Ottens, 1991). Think about academic situations in the present or past where your attention was misdirected. In the following space, identify the situation and type of distraction. Consider the following questions: Do your distractions tend to be more internal or external? Do your distractions tend to occur in certain situations (e.g., tests or lectures) or locations (e.g., studying at home or school or in the library)?

Where Attention Got Misdirected	Type of Distraction (Internal or External)

HOW CAN I IMPROVE MY ATTENTION AND CONCENTRATION?

You will be better able to enhance your concentration if you deal with known distracters before you begin studying, reading, or listening to a lecture; adopt strategies that encourage concentration; monitor your concentration as you study; and deal with distractions when they occur. Table 7.1 contains a list of suggestions to help you manage both external and internal distractions.

TABLE 7.1
MANAGEMENT OF EXTERNAL AND INTERNAL DISTRACTIONS

Ways to Reduce External Distractions	Examples
Establish a study area with minimal distractions	Study in the library or designated study area in the dorm.
Have necessary materials available	Borrow notes before a study session.
Control noise levels	Ask your roommate to lower or shut off the stereo, close the window, or change your seat location in lecture hall.
Move to the front of the lecture room	
Reduce interruptions	Place a sign on the door: "Midterm Exam: Do Not Disturb," place a message on the answering machine: "Call after 10 p.m."
Protest	"Please, I'm trying to concentrate on this reading." Avoid visual contact with distracter.

Ways to Discourage Internal Distractions	Examples
Pay attention to, and whenever possible deal with, your physical state	Take a short nap before your study, get something to eat or drink, or take an aspirin for your headache.
Carefully determine when you will study in your time-management plan	If you get tired late in the evening, don't schedule study times when you are likely to be tired or don't attempt to study during your dinner hour.
Daydreaming	Make a checkmark on a notepad whenever you catch yourself daydreaming. Monitoring concentration can help keep you ontask.
Deal with boredom	Alternate different subjects when you study, take study breaks every 50 minutes or so.
Instead of worrying, take action	Talk to the instructor or teaching assistant about course issues or problems, find a tutor, call your girlfriend or boyfriend to resolve a recent disagreement before you begin studying.

Use Strategies that Encourage Concentration	Examples
Monitor concentration	Constantly ask yourself questions like: "Did I understand what I just read?" "Am I beginning to daydream?" "Am I trying to understand the lecture?"

continued

TABLE 7.1
MANAGEMENT OF EXTERNAL AND INTERNAL
DISTRACTIONS   (CONTINUED)

Use self-reminders or self-directives	"You're starting to worry again about your test performance, just relax and get back to the question" or "I better start asking myself questions because I didn't understand what I just read."
Set goals	"I want to complete chapter 4 this evening and answer all questions in the study manual."
Manage your time	"I need to find 3 hours in my study plan this week to research library material for my paper."
Take breaks	Take a 10-minute break for every 50 minutes of study or work longer if you can maintain your concentration.
Use active learning strategies	Write and answer questions, outline, or summarize material.

EXERCISE 7.3: DEALING WITH DISTRACTERS

For each of the following situations, identify the type of distracter by placing an *I* (for internal) or an *E* (for external) in the space provided. Next, refer to the suggestions in the previous section on ways to improve concentration and recommend how each student could improve his or her concentration.

___ 1. Alicia is about to study for her history exam when her roommate comes rushing in to tell her about her date for Saturday night.
Recommendation:

_____

_____

___ 2. While Tony is working on his calculus assignment, he remembers that he forgot to put money in his checking account and his tuition check will bounce.
Recommendation:

_____

_____

___ 3. While Ralph is taking notes in his biology class, workers start drilling outside the window of the lecture hall.
Recommendation:

_____

_____

___ 4. Each time Carole starts studying for her French exam, she is reminded of her low quiz scores and wonders if she is going to pass the course.
Recommendation:

_____

_____

___ 5. As Mary is reading her economics text, she realizes that she turned five pages and does not remember one thing she read.
Recommendation:

_____

_____

___ 6. Alex has trouble concentrating when his professor starts talking too fast. He gets frustrated with the professor and stops taking notes.
Recommendation:

_____

_____

___ 7. Felicia starts studying at about 10 p.m. and soon finds she is too tired to complete her history assignment for the next day.
Recommendation:

_____

_____

Student Reflection

I was never the one to receive help in high school. If I could not understand any subject matter, I just told myself that it was too complex for me. I thought that students who sought extra help in subjects they did not understand were people who were "teachers' pets." I often believed that they were too concerned with their academic learning. I reasoned that these types of students developed into nerds, because they did nothing but study. My fear was that if I gained extra help I would become one of them.

Table 7.2 summarizes the procedures for monitoring and dealing with attention and concentration problems.

TABLE 7.2

Procedures for Monitoring and Dealing With Attention and Concentration Problems	
Procedures	Examples
1. Review your time-management plan and determine which tasks you will attend to during each study session.	"I need to read and study two chapters in my psychology textbook today."
2. Before you begin studying, determine whether there are any distracters that may influence your concentration.	"I have one internal and one external distracter that will interfere with my reading. My two roommates are playing cards in my room and I must call my mother and wish her a happy birthday."
3. If a distracter is present, determine whether it is internal or external and refer to the list of strategies to deal with it. If no distracter is present, begin using strategies that encourage concentration.	"I'll go to the library tonight to study and call my mother before I leave."
4. Monitor concentration as you study.	"I have turned two pages but don't remember what I read."
5. If attention gets misdirected, refer to the list of strategies to maintain concentration. If concentration is broken, maintain your use of learning strategies and take short breaks during the study session.	"I better start asking myself questions so I can maintain my focus on the material."
6. At the end of the study session, make a check next to each task that you completed in your time-management plan.	"Ok, I'm finished with my math problems and research for my anthropology paper. What's next on my list?"

HOW DO I SEEK ACADEMIC HELP?

Earlier in the chapter, I presented research to indicate that students who perceive themselves as academically competent and who feel in control of their academic success are more likely to seek help. The paradox is that students who need the most help are often less likely to obtain it. Students who are comfortable and capable of eliciting help from others are often able to solve their problems and, in addition, acquire greater knowledge of how to obtain help in the future. Newman (1991) identified a sequence of decisions and actions that play an important role in both help seeking and the self-management of learning:

- *Awareness of a need for help.* The student is aware that knowledge is lacking or comprehension is incomplete. Awareness is a key factor in both seeking and benefitting from help. Individuals are not likely to seek help if they do not know what they do not understand. You should not wait to be jolted by a low exam score or poor grade on a paper to decide that you need help. Instead, you should evaluate your understanding of the content in each of your courses on a regular basis throughout the semester.

- *Decision to seek help rather than taking alternative actions.* When some students realize they are in trouble, they head for the registrar's office to drop a course rather than consider alternative strategies such as obtaining a tutor, joining a study group, or meeting with the instructor or teaching assistant.

  At times, many self-directed learners have academic difficulties. However, they learn how to use the services and resources available to them. Are you aware of the services provided by your college or university? Do you have a learning center for academic assistance? Are tutoring services available?

- *Decision regarding the type of help to seek.* Some problems can be solved by seeking nonsocial assistance. For example, students in math or science courses can benefit from purchasing review books that provide numerous opportunities to solve different types of problems. They can also borrow other textbooks from the library that explain information in different ways.

- *Decision regarding the target person from whom to seek help.* The target person could be a friend, study group, professor, or tutor. Keep in mind that you're not limited to one source of help. Ask yourself: How soon do I need the help? Who is most likely to provide help in the shortest time frame? Who is most competent in providing the help?

- *Employment of a help-seeking strategy.* Prepare before you meet with the person who can help you. First, determine what it is that you do not understand about the material. Second, make an appointment (if possible) with your tutor, teaching assistant, or instructor. Third, carefully review the content and make a list of the specific questions you want answered at the meeting. Categorize the different problems you have trouble solving (e.g., underline foreign language passages that you have trouble translating or list terms that you don't understand). You will benefit more from these sessions if you are prepared for the meeting. It is not acceptable to walk into a session and say something like: "I don't get it," or "I don't know what is going on in this course." Many times, you will spend more time *preparing* for a productive session than you spend with the person in the session.

- *Processing of the help*. Good notes should be taken concerning the advice obtained so they can be referred to after the session. You may wish to bring a tape recorder so you can listen and think during the session instead of writing.

    Consider the advice you received when you sought help in terms of how it could change your learning and study behavior for the remainder of the course. What did you learn that could be applied to new chapters or units in the course? What are some immediate changes you should make to improve your performance in the course? How can you best keep pace with the new material in the course?

HOW CAN I WORK MORE EFFECTIVELY IN GROUPS?

Each semester, when I introduce a group project, one or two students will ask to work individually because of negative experiences with group projects. Many students do not realize that it is difficult to escape team involvement in the workplace. That is to say, it is unlikely that one would approach his or her supervisor and ask: "Can I work on a project by myself?"

Recently, I had an opportunity to teach an educational psychology course to training specialists working for some of the most successful computer companies in the country. During a discussion in class, the students mentioned that their companies had no difficulty hiring bright mathematicians, scientists, or computer specialists. Their problem was that some of their personnel did not function well in group settings. Because teams complete most projects, there are often delays in completing projects because of problems in interpersonal relations.

One of the most productive sources of social support is working in learning or study groups. Reports from studies indicate that cooperative

TABLE 7.3

Procedures for Forming and Studying in Groups

1. Notice who is in your class.
2. Identify two, three, or four interested students.
3. Contact the students to arrange a meeting time and place.
4. At the first session:
   - Exchange names and phone numbers.
   - Conduct an overview of the subject matter.
   - Discuss each member's particular interest in a topic.
   - Assign each member an equal number of text pages or notes to lead the discussion of each topic in the course.
   - Discuss possible test questions.
5. Before you end the first meeting:
   - Make sure every member has a clear set of goals for the next session.
   - Be certain that each member understands his or her particular assignment.
   - Discuss any problems that occurred during the first session.
6. At the second meeting, discuss the content and begin testing each other. (Smaller groups may begin testing each other during the first meeting if they complete their planning over the phone or in person before the meeting.)
7. Identify topics or sections of the content that the group had difficulty understanding.
8. Decide how the group members can obtain additional help, if needed (e.g., one group member may contact the instructor or teaching assistant to answer questions, another member may decide to research a question or topic in greater depth).

learning can promote higher academic achievement, higher level thinking skills, and increased friendships (Johnson & Johnson, 1987). Table 7.3 presents some recommended procedures for forming and studying in groups (Frender, 1990). The following are examples of how one student found different ways to use cooperative learning in different classes:

Student Reflections

During the course of the semester, I have found group studying to be an essential part of my success in my different classes. The following are examples of how I have used group study this semester:

- Before a test in biology, I met with two friends to review the material for the exam. We heard that the professor's exams came straight from his lectures. Therefore, we basically went straight through the notes and discussed what was presented each day. As we proceeded, we learned some information from each other that we did not have in our notes. Also, discussing the material helped us learn it more thoroughly.

- There are practicals in my biology laboratory in which students are required to identify different things seen in the lab and perform different tasks learned in lab throughout the semester. I studied in a group for my practical so we could quiz each other. We used pictures and drew diagrams, and asked each other to label them. We wrote down different procedures learned in lab as we discussed how we did them. Most important, we discussed the reasons behind each activity that occurred during the lab.

- In chemistry, there are many problems that must be done after reading a chapter to prepare for a test. My friends and I usually read the chapter by ourselves, then get together to do the problems. This way, if we don't understand something, we can ask each other and get help solving the problems. This procedure speeds up the learning process because we don't need to go back and refer to the chapter as much.

- In math, I meet with my friends to discuss problems that we couldn't solve individually. The individual who solved a problem correctly explains to the rest of the group how he or she did it.

- In my English course, I get together with one of my friends to read each other's papers. Usually after I write a paper, it is hard for me to identify my own errors. When someone else reads it, he can tell me what parts he doesn't understand and what needs improvement so I can make the necessary adjustments.

HOW CAN I HELP MAKE MY STUDY GROUP MORE PRODUCTIVE?

Not all group experiences are as positive as the examples identified in the student reflection section. Numerous interpersonal skills affect the success of group learning and study. A key factor in determining how one deals with group problems is influenced by how the group was formed. For example, one may have more freedom in developing policy and procedures in your group when the members self-select, such as a study group, as compared with a situation where an instructor places students in specific groups to complete an assignment or project. The following are four categories of important skills used in collaborative settings (adapted from Johnson, Johnson, & Holubec, 1994).

Forming skills are needed for organizing the group and for establishing minimum norms of appropriate behavior. One of the major problems facing most groups is dealing with individuals who do not meet their responsibility to the group. Group members need to discuss their expectations and how they will deal with problems that occur when they first meet. It is important to be fair in dealing with group members. For example, a group member may have had a serious personal or family problem that prevented completion of a task. This is no reason to exclude the person from the group. However, if during a project a member does not complete his or her work, the rules established at the beginning of the work should be used to deal with the problem. The basic rule should be: fair, but firm!

Another area of concern is how group members treat each other. Some of the principles groups might adopt include:

- There are no dumb ideas. People should feel free to be imaginative.
- When you disagree with an *idea*, be sure you don't attack the *person*.
- Mutual respect will allow the project to flow much more smoothly.
- Be slow to draw conclusions about your fellow group members. We are all more complex than we first appear to be. Avoid prejudging.

Group members should discuss additional behaviors they believe are vital for effective interpersonal relations at the first meeting. One of the most important behaviors to stress is that personal criticisms are not a part of effective group functioning.

Functioning skills are the second category of cooperative skills. They involve the management and implementation of the group's efforts to achieve tasks and to maintain effective working relationships among members. Such skills include expressing support and acceptance for the contribution of group members, asking for help or clarification about what is being said or done, offering to explain or clarify another student's position, and motivating the group with new ideas or suggestions when enthusiasm wanes.

Formulating skills are directed at helping group members understand and remember the material being studied in the group. Such skills include encouraging group members to summarize what was covered, adding important information when something is left out of the summary, reviewing important information, and using learning strategies to remember important ideas. Formulating skills can be implemented as group members fill different roles. Depending on the task to be completed, the following roles should be assigned:

- A facilitator, whose job is to help organize the workload and keep the group focused, and who reminds members of the policy and procedures of the group.
- A recorder, whose job is to take notes and keep attendance.

If possible, specific responsibilities should be assigned to all group members.

Fermenting skills are used to stimulate academic controversy so that group members will rethink and challenge each other's positions, ideas, and reasoning. Examples of such skills include challenging ideas but not people, formulating a coherent and defensible position on an issue, and probing and eliciting information for achieving answers and solutions to problems. The major concern at this level is to ensure that the group members do not stop investigating when the first solution is presented. Sometimes the first answer or the quickest solution is not the best one. Each group member needs to help stimulate the thinking and intellectual curiosity of others.

HOW CAN I IMPROVE MY COMMUNICATION SKILLS?

Sending Messages Effectively

One of the most important functioning skills in group dynamics is learning how to send messages effectively. Johnson (2003) identified some key skills for this purpose:

1. *Clearly "own" your message* by (a) using personal pronouns such as I, me, and my and (b) letting others know what your thoughts and feelings are. You "disown" your messages when you use expressions such as: "most people," "some people," and "our group," making it difficult to tell whether you really think and feel what you are saying or are simply repeating the thoughts and feelings of others.

2. *Describe the other person's behavior* without including any judgment, evaluation, or inferences about the person's motivates, personality, or attitudes. When reacting to the behavior of other people, be sure to describe their behavior ("You keep interrupting me") rather than evaluating it ("You're a rotten, self-centered egotist who won't listen to anyone else's ideas").

3. *Describe the ways the relationship can be changed* to improve the quality and quantity of interaction among the individuals involved. To maintain and improve a relationship, the quality of the relationship needs to be discussed and reflected on periodically.

4. *Make the message appropriate to the receiver's frame of reference.* This same information will be explained differently to an expert in the field than to a novice, to a child than to an adult, or to your boss than to a coworker.

5. *Ask for feedback* concerning the ways your messages are being received. To communicate effectively, you must be aware of how

the receiver is interpreting and processing your messages. The only way to be sure is to seek feedback continually as to what meanings the receiver is attaching to your messages.

6. *Describe your feelings by name, action, or figure of speech.* When communicating your feelings, it is especially important to be descriptive. You may describe your feelings by name ("I feel sad"), by actions ("I feel like crying"), or by figures of speech ("I feel down in the dumps").

7. *Use nonverbal messages to communicate your feelings.* Nonverbal messages are very powerful but inherently ambiguous. When people cry, for example, it may be because they are sad, happy, angry, or even afraid. When utilized with verbal messages, however, nonverbal messages clarify, strengthen, enrich, emphasize, and frame the message.

8. *Make your verbal and nonverbal message congruent with each other.* Every face-to face communication involves both verbal and nonverbal messages. Usually these messages are congruent, so by smiling and expressing warmth nonverbally, a person can be saying that she has appreciated your help. Communication problems arise when a person's verbal and nonverbal messages are contradictory; if a person says, "Here is some information that may be of help to you," with a sneer and in a mocking tone of voice, the meaning you receive is confused by the two different messages being sent simultaneously.

9. *Be redundant.* Repeating your message more than once and using more than one channel of communication (such as pictures and written messages, as well as verbal and nonverbal cues) will help the receiver understand your messages (pp. 132–133).

Receiving Messages Effectively

One of the most important skills in receiving messages involves giving feedback about the message in ways that clarify and encourage the continuation of discussion. Gordon (2001) provided some helpful information when he encourages listeners to become **active listeners.** This means letting others know that we recognize the feelings behind what they are saying. Read the following possible dialogue between you and a friend. Which comment do you think will gain the most response from your friend? Why?

Friend: "That was the worst test I ever took."
You: "Don't worry about it. Let's get a pizza!"

Friend: "That was the worst test I ever took."
You: "You are really upset about the test."

Gordon believes that the second dialogue would most likely encourage greater dialogue, because you attempt to communicate that you understand your friend's feelings. Active listening involves recognizing the feeling and meaning of others, and then restating this meaning so others feel understood and accepted. This type of listening provides a sort of mirror for the person to see himself or herself more clearly.

Many individuals do not use active listening. Instead, they want to give advice as to what others should do about their situation without recognizing feelings. In fact, in some families, students grow up without being able to openly express their feelings. Here's an example:

> Student: "I can't complete all the work demanded in my courses."
>
> Parent: "I have many pressures in my job, too. I wish I was in college and all I had to think about was my courses!"

Is this the type of response that will encourage you to discuss your feelings, or is it more likely to encourage you to walk away or change the topic? Think about your closest friends. Are they more likely to recognize your feelings than other individuals in your life? If you were the student's parent, what type of active listening response would you give? Remember, don't start by trying to give advice.

The following is a partial list of feeling words. Think of other words that could be added to each list.

Happy Feelings	Upset Feelings
accepted	angry
appreciated	anxious
better	disappointed
cheerful	embarrassed
joyful	hurt
excited	irritated
good	sad
proud	stupid
satisfied	worried

The following are other examples of active listening:

> Message: "I can't complete all the work demanded in my courses."
>
> Response: "You seem upset about your course work."

> Message: "I can't believe it that my boyfriend [or girlfriend] said that I was an inconsiderate person!
>
> Response: "Your boyfriend [or girlfriend] really hurt you."

> Message: "I finally made the dean's list."
> Response: "You seem proud of yourself."

As you can see from these examples, the responses reflect back the meaning of the message in a clear manner. The listener focuses on the feeling expressed and avoids trying to solve problems for others. This strategy helps to confirm and validate an individual's feelings, as well as to set the stage for any necessary problem solving by getting individuals to discuss the reasons behind their feelings. Try using active listening with a member of your class, close friend, or parent and evaluate the nature of your communication with this individual.

Key Points

1. Successful learners restructure their physical and social environments to improve their learning.
2. Self-management of one's social environment relates to the ability to determine when one needs to work alone or with others, to seek help when needed from instructors, tutors, or peers, or to seek help from nonsocial sources (e.g., textbooks and reference materials).
3. Students may lack the self-discipline or self-management to overcome environmental distractions, anxiety, or competing emotional or physical needs.
4. Motivational beliefs and perceptions account for individual differences in the willingness and ability to control one's physical and social environment.
5. Students have difficulty concentrating on tasks, because of external and internal distracters.
6. Interpersonal skills for group learning and study can be categorized into four levels: forming, functioning, formulating, and fermenting.
7. Students can improve their communication skills by learning how to send and receive messages more effectively.
8. Learning how to become an active listener can impove communication with others.

Follow-up Activities

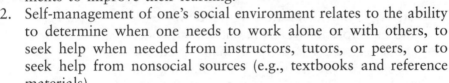

1. **Use the Self-management Process to Improve Attention and Concentration**

Complete the following self-study during a period of 2 to 3 weeks. Your report should include each of the following processes and should be approximately five to eight typed pages in length. See Appendix A for detailed information on how to conduct a self-management study.

Self-observation and evaluation. What problem(s) do I have regarding attention and concentration? What are the symptoms of my problem (i.e., when, where, and how often does my problem occur)? How much of an impact does this problem have on my academic performance? What factors (e.g., beliefs, perceptions, feelings, physiological responses, or behaviors) contribute to this problem? What do I need to change to reduce or eliminate my problem(s)?

Goal setting and strategic planning. What are my goals? What strategies can I use to reduce distracters and maintain concentration? When will I use these strategies? How will I record my progress?

Strategy implementation and monitoring. What strategies did I use to improve my attention and concentration? When did I use these strategies? What method(s) did I use to record my progress (e.g., documents, charts, logs, tally sheets, checklists, or recordings)? When did I use these methods? How and when did I monitor my progress to determine if my new plan was working? What changes, if any, did I make along the way?

Strategic-outcome monitoring. Did I attain the goal I set for myself? Have the modifications in my attention and concentration improved my academic performance or personal life? What strategies were the most and least effective? What changes, if any, do I need to make in the future?

2. Assess Group Dynamics

Use the procedures for forming and studying in groups discussed in this chapter and evaluate the effectiveness of one of your study groups according to each of the necessary group skills: forming, functioning, formulating, and fermenting. In other words, report on how well your study group effectively performed in each skill area and make recommendations on how your group could function more effectively.

3. Visit With an Instructor

Newman (1991) identified a sequence of decisions and actions that play an important role in both help seeking and self-management of learning. Use Newman's suggestions discussed in this chapter to meet with one of your instructors. Write a summary of how you used his recommendations and evaluate the effectiveness of the meeting.

4. Practice Active Listening

The following are a series of statements made by my college students. Provide responses to each statement that demonstrate active listening responses.

1. This course sucks!
   Response:

2. I don't know how I will ever finish this term paper.
   Response:

3. I can't believe my girlfriend left me!
   Response:

4. I'm so tired, I can't study any longer.
   Response:

5. My instructor must think I am an idiot by asking me such an easy question.
   Response:

6. It doesn't matter how much I try, I can't get higher than a C in my writing course.
   Response:

7. I know I will make first string on the volleyball team.
   Response:

Answers to Exercise 7.3

1. E   2. I   3. E   4. I   5. I   6. E   7. I

UNIT IV

LEARNING AND STUDY STRATEGIES

Chapter 8: Learning From Textbooks
Chapter 9: Learning From Lectures
Chapter 10: Preparing For Exams
Chapter 11: Taking Exams

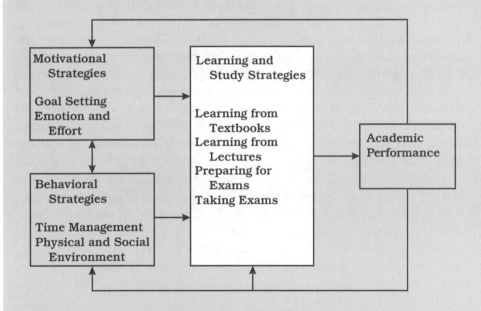

This unit includes four chapters focusing on important study strategies used to learn, remember, prepare, and take exams. One of the important ideas presented in this unit is that preparation for exams *begins* when students first take notes or read the first chapter on a topic. Exam preparation should not begin when an instructor announces an exam! The manner in which one takes notes and reads textbooks determines how much information is learned and remembered. Therefore, the more content one understands and remembers while moving from one topic to another in a course, the easier it is to prepare and perform successfully on an exam.

It is often difficult to make up for ineffective learning by studying. Reviewing incomplete information, confusing theories, or improper procedures for solving problems generally leads to less than satisfactory results on examinations. At times, intensive studying or cramming can help students get through certain exams that simply require regurgitation of basic material. However, as questions become more complex and require greater understanding of material, it is more difficult to succeed without using effective learning and study strategies.

An important issue to consider is motivation. What is the goal in taking a course and learning its content? Is it simply to get through the material, or learn it? If the goal is to master the material, cramming is not an efficient study strategy. Ask yourself: "How much of the material do I understand? Could I adequately explain the content to others and answer questions about it?"

Another important idea emphasized in this unit is that reading or taking notes and remembering are two separate activities. Just because one reads a textbook or takes notes does not mean that he or she will remember what was read or written down. Additional steps are needed to ensure remembering the material learned. These steps involve the use of elaboration and organization strategies to move information into long-term memory (Cortina et al., 1992).

A final point before beginning the unit: there are common learning strategies used in both learning from lectures and textbooks that should be undertaken *before, during,* and *after* each learning session. These strategies make the differences in how information is learned and remembered. They involve preparing for learning, paying attention to specific signals provided by a lecturer and author to identify main ideas, keeping track of main ideas, and identifying organizational patterns within the material (Pauk, 1993). Many of the same learning strategies used to learn and remember material in textbooks apply to learning by lectures, and vice versa. Remember that individuals learn best when they recognize or impose patterns of organization on content rather than studying isolated bits and pieces of information.

8

Learning From Textbooks

Individuals spend a good deal of time reading throughout their lives. They read for enjoyment, relaxation, or knowledge. As a result, they often read differently depending on the purpose for reading. For example, students do not read a college textbook the same way they read popular magazines or best-sellers. Have you ever watched people read a magazine? How often do you see them underlining or taking notes on what they read? For the most part, these individuals do not care about how much they remember, because they do not expect to be tested on the material. Yet, because of their interest in the material, they often remember a great deal of what they read. College students are expected to read and remember material in courses whether or not they are interested in the content or believe it has any relevance to their future occupational goals. Success in different courses depends on learning to use effective reading strategies for a variety of college textbooks.

Do you enjoy making checks on "to do" lists after completing reading assignments? The checks tell you that you completed the assignment, but do not tell you how much you learned or remembered.

You may have completed your readings but cannot recall much of the information you read a short time ago. In fact, you may have forgotten much of what you read by the time you finished reading the assignment.

What else do you do beyond simply reading a textbook? Do you ask yourself questions about what you have read? Do you attempt to summarize the author's main points? How do you know that you have identified the main ideas in a chapter? What strategies do you use to remember what you read?

Many students underline passages in their textbooks as they read. Unfortunately, underlining is a rehearsal strategy that does not require much thinking about the content and, as a result, does not help move material into long-term memory. Another problem is that irrelevant information is often underlined along with relevant information. When it comes time to review the understanding of the text, the underlining may be confusing. Thus, it is possible to spend considerable time underlining a textbook and still not remember most of the important ideas in a chapter. Underlining must be used in concert with other reading strategies.

I ask you to assess your present reading strategies in this chapter and determine how successful they are in helping you achieve your academic objectives. After studying this chapter, you will be able to use effective learning strategies to improve your reading comprehension and retention.

WHAT DOES RESEARCH TELL US ABOUT GOOD READERS?

Good readers attempt to comprehend and remember what they read by using specific learning strategies to manage their understanding. The following is a summary of these strategies (Dole, Duffy, Roehler, & Person, 1991):

- *Determining importance.* Good readers identify main ideas and separate them from examples and supporting details. Poor readers often underline or highlight text as they read and do not differentiate between important and less important ideas.
- *Summarizing information.* Good readers summarize information by reviewing all the ideas in a passage or chapter, differentiate important from unimportant ideas, and then synthesize the ideas to create a statement that represents the meaning of the passage or chapter. Poor readers do not stop to summarize what they have read.
- *Drawing inferences.* Good readers use inferencing extensively to fill in details omitted in a text and to elaborate on what they

read. In other words, they ask questions like: What is the author implying? What is the implication of the actions suggested in the passage? How do these ideas relate to other points of view on the issue? Poor readers rarely go beyond the written words in the text.

- *Generating questions.* Good readers maintain active involvement by generating questions and attempting to answer them while they read. Poor readers tend to be more passive and fail to generate such questions.
- *Monitoring comprehension.* Good readers are not only aware of the quality and degree of their understanding but know what to do and how to do it when they fail to comprehend material. Poor readers fail to monitor their understanding. As a result, they frequently rely on others to determine their degree of understanding.

The five reading activities just described have an important element in common. Reading for understanding and remembering requires an active involvement on the part of the reader. The following exercise provides an opportunity to evaluate your own reading strategies.

EXERCISE 8.1: SELF-OBSERVATION: ASSESSING READING STRATEGIES

Directions: For each question, place a check in the corresponding box that best describes the strategies you presently use to complete your reading assignments. When you have responded to all of the items, write a brief summary statement describing what this brief assessment tells you.

	Always	*Sometimes*	*Never*
1. I preview all my text-books to review the learning aids provided by the authors.			
2. I preview each chapter before I read.			
3. I think of questions as I read.			
4. I underline my textbook as I read.			

Continued

	Always	Sometimes	Never
5. I look for main ideas as I read.			
6. I use maps or charts to organize the content I read.			
7. I complete exercises or answer questions at the end of each chapter when I am finished reading.			
8. I make notes to identify material I don't understand.			
9. I constantly monitor my understanding as I read.			
10. I read my assignments before attending lectures.			

Summary Statement:

_____

_____

_____

_____

_____

_____

_____

Compare your reading strategies with the following student responses. How are strategies similar or different from the behavior reported?

Student Reflections

When I started college, I mostly underlined and highlighted everything I thought was important (which unfortunately happened to be just about every other sentence). This strategy proved to be detrimental in studying for exams. I even thought that highlighting sentences or key phrases in different colors would make a difference, instead, this strategy was worse. I ended up with endless pages that looked like rainbows of pink, blue, yellow, and green marks. I could never decipher the information any better than I could before I highlighted it.

# # # #

High school textbook reading was certainly an easier task than it is now in college. College-level reading requires more time and energy in absorbing ideas and information. In high school, I always read assigned reading once and highlighted and memorized vocabulary words and facts. Now that I am in college, I allocate more time to study and read all the necessary information. I begin looking over all the headings throughout the chapter, both headings and subheadings. I then review vocabulary and boldface terms in each chapter. Following readings, I review the key points at the end of the chapter. I answer the questions given at the end of the chapter, as well as the questions I developed from the reading.

# # # #

A majority of high school reading is related to worksheets and other assignments where you are required to find specific details to finish an assignment. This demand got me into the habit of reading just for the specific facts, which didn't focus on the big picture. In college, you are often asked higher level questions on exams that require much more thought about a topic. It is helpful to own your own books, because you can mark in them.

WHAT LEARNING STRATEGIES CAN I USE TO IMPROVE MY READING COMPREHENSION AND RETENTION?

Now that you have some understanding as to what it takes to become a good reader and have evaluated your own reading behavior, you are ready to learn some new reading strategies. The strategies discussed in this section are separated into activities to be completed during three stages of reading—before, during, and after (adapted from Cortina, Elder, & Gonnet, 1992).

Before Reading

1. Preview the Book for Learning Aids.   If you were to review each of your textbooks, you would find that they differ greatly in design and readability. Think about two different textbooks you are currently reading. What makes one appear more "reader friendly" and another less "reader friendly"? Are you influenced by color, large type, headings, pictures, summaries, or wide columns?

Have you considered the learning aids included by the author to help you comprehend the material? The following are some of the most common learning aids provided in textbooks:

- Chapter objectives or questions
- Glossaries
- Boldface or italics
- Answers to problems or exercises
- Summary or review sections
- Tables and figures
- Research or application boxes

Think about how each of these learning aids help you learn. *Objectives* and *questions* help you determine what you learned in each chapter. When you are finished reading, you need to determine whether you attained the objectives of the chapter. If questions are presented at the beginning or end of the chapter, you can check to determine whether you can answer the questions. If you cannot answer the questions, you did not learn the material. A *glossary* defines the key terms in a textbook and often is listed in the back of the book. Some books have what is called a running glossary, where key terms are defined on the page where they first appear. Some authors *boldface* all words in the glossary and use *italics* or bullets to identify an important term or phrase. These elements are used to signal important information. *Answers to problems and exercises* are very useful in mathematics, business, and science courses, where solving problems is an important objective of the course. Most authors only provide answers to the even or odd problems in the textbook. Summary and review sections help identify main points in the chapter and serve as a useful reminder of what should have been learned. *Tables and figures* can be useful in summarizing a large amount of information on a topic. Finally, *research or application boxes* either describe specific investigations that have been conducted by researchers or provide special insights regarding the relevancy of the information to daily life.

In summary, authors include various learning aids in textbooks to help you comprehend and retain information. Recognizing and using these aids can help you check your understanding and encourage you to become more actively involved in your reading assignments. Can you identify the learning aids provided in this textbook?

2. Survey the Assignment Before Each Reading Session. Before you go on a trip, you usually spend time planning where you are going, how long you will be there, where you are going to stay, and how you will get to each location. Effective planning increases the probability of a satisfying vacation.

Planning before reading also can help you achieve satisfying results, because it forces you to make decisions about how to deal with the assigned material. Before you begin reading a chapter, survey the table of contents and read the major headings. Then read the chapter summary and any questions posed by the author. This surveying will help you identify some of the main ideas, topics, or issues of the chapter before you begin reading.

When you first preview a textbook, look for learning aids. When you survey a chapter before reading, you are preparing to make some decisions. Surveying is analogous to viewing the coming attractions for a film. The film preview gives the viewer an idea of the type of movie he or she will view in terms of the plot and characters. It prepares an individual for the viewing of the movie. Surveying a reading assignment not only provides insights for what you will learn, but it also helps you evaluate the difficulty of the material. This evaluation helps you determine whether you should read the entire chapter at one time or divide the reading into several sessions.

3. Read Questions That Are Provided at the Beginning or End of Each Chapter, in Accompanying Study Guides, or Provided by Your Instructors. These questions provide important guidelines for what you are expected to learn in the chapter. By reading questions before you begin reading the chapter, you have a better idea of what to focus on.

During Reading

1. As You Begin Reading, Think of the Text as a Conversation Between the Author and Yourself. Ask the following questions: What is the author trying to tell me? Which sentences state the main idea? How do these ideas relate to other points of view on the issue?

2. Turn the Headings in Your Textbook into Questions and Answer Them. Write questions in the margin of a textbook if there are no headings, or between the headings if there are long sections of text.

There are two broad levels of questions: lower level and higher level. Lower-level questions tend to focus on factual information and ask you to retrieve information that was previously presented. They involve responses regarding facts, dates, terms, or lists. The following are examples of lower level questions:

- What is the definition of a molecule?
- What are the three major categories of marine life?
- Why do experimental psychologists formulate hypotheses before beginning research investigations?
- What are the reasons for the start of the World War II?
- What is the law of definite proportions?

Higher level questions require you to *apply* the information that you learned in a new situation, *solve* problems, *analyze* information, *develop* a novel plan or solution, or *make judgments* about the value of the information. The following are examples of higher level questions:

- Why does the temperature of the water influence the velocity of sound? (Analyze)
- How effective was the president's State of the Union address in urging Congress to increase the defense budget? (Make judgments)
- What is the density of iron if 156 g of iron occupies a volume of 20 cm^3? (Solve problems)
- What are the differences in the Keynesian and monetarist views on how money affects the economy? (Analyze)
- How do behavioral and cognitive psychologists differ in the explanation of human motivation? (Analyze)

As you attempt to determine the main ideas presented by the author, think about the level of questions that might be asked on exams. In this way, you will move beyond factual or low-level questions. Students who spend considerable time studying for an exam and still do not do well often find that they failed to ask appropriate higher level questions in their exam preparation. Underline the answers to your questions.

The headings in a textbook often indicate the subject matter of a series of paragraphs. Therefore, if you can answer the questions generated from the headings, you will focus on the main ideas and supporting details in the specific passage in the textbook. For example, if you are reading a book and come to the heading "Physical Properties of Matter" you should ask yourself: What are the different physical properties of matter? As you read the passage, you will learn that they are *solid*, *liquid*, and *gas*. If your question is on target, you can write it as part of the heading and underline the answer in the textbook. If you develop a question and find that the passage focuses on something else, you can change your question and underline the answer to the alternative question. For example, you read the heading

"Taxation" in an economics textbook but have no specific idea as to what about taxation the author will discuss. You read on and learn how the federal government uses tax policy to allocate different resources. You then go back to the heading and write: "How does the government effect the allocation or resources through tax policy?" You then go back to the text and underline the answer to the question. Sometimes you can ask more than one question. For example, if you find the heading "Gun Control" in a political science book, you might want to know: What are the different views on gun control? What organizations support and oppose gun control? What legislation currently exists regarding gun control?

The following are examples of headings in textbooks turned into questions:

Headings	Questions
Improving Listening Skills	What methods can students use to improve their listening skills?
Interest Groups	How do interest groups influence political elections?
Gender Identification	What is gender identity? What are the different theories of gender identification?

The following are two excerpts from textbooks where a student has turned the heading into a question and underlined relevant phrases in the passage to answer the question. Notice the selective use of underlining:

What are the different types of computer crimes?
~~High-Tech Crime: The Criminal and the Computer~~

Technological change advances criminal opportunities as well as non-criminal ones. Nowhere is this more in evidence than in the realm of electronics. We live in an era of high technology, one in which electronic brains and silicon chips rule much of the behavior of people and machines. The more computers we have and the more things we can get them to do, the more opportunities there are for computer crime. Estimates of the annual losses from computer-related crimes go as high as $5 billion, and in all likelihood the figure will go much higher.

The range of computer crimes is vast and growing....Embezzlement, industrial espionage, theft of services (for example, using a computer that belongs to someone else for one's private business), invasion of privacy, copyright violations, destruction of information or programs, falsification of data, and a host of fraudulent transactions are just a few of the computer-related abuses that have come to light.

The potential for computer crime is staggering, and that fact is now recognized in legislative and enforcement circles. But most of the preventive work so far initiated is privately organized and paid for. Hundreds of companies have sprung up in recent years peddling advice and technology to counteract the new breed of high-tech criminals.[1]

What are

Barriers to Listening?

There are several reasons why people are poor listeners. One reason is that the complex human mind can comprehend many more words per minute than speakers can produce. Listeners can process more than 400 spoken words per minute, yet the average speaker only produces between 125 and 175 words per minute. This time lag between slower speaking rates and faster rates of thinking is known as the **speech–thought differential**. Stated in a different way, the listener needs only 15 seconds of every minute to comprehend the spoken message. The resulting time lag creates special problems. In this excess time, listeners' thoughts may begin to stray. Can you recall a time when you began listening to a speaker but soon found yourself thinking about lunch, an upcoming test, or a date? This tendency for our thoughts to stray poses many problems for the speaker trying to convey an understandable message, especially if the subject matter is complex.[2]

3. Underline and Annotate Textbooks. In the introduction to this unit, I mentioned that underlining was an ineffective learning strategy. The purpose of underlining is to identify main ideas and supporting details (e.g., examples, facts, and illustrations). When underlining is done without determining the main points, or if too much material is underlined, both relevant and irrelevant information is highlighted. Therefore, it is often difficult to make sense of the underlining, because everything appears to be important. It is not necessary to underline each word in a sentence to capture the idea in a passage. One way to test for successful underlining is to read through underlined passages to determine whether the main ideas have been identified. You accomplish this task by determining whether you have answered the questions asked in the textbook or answered the questions generated from the headings in the text. Sometimes you find that it is necessary to underline more information.

[1]From Barlow, H. D. (1984). *Introduction to Criminology* (3rd ed.). Boston: Little, Brown, p. 252.
[2]From Gronbeck, B., et al. (1992). *Principles of Speech Communication*. New York: HarperCollins.

Underlining must be a selective process. The most important advice I can give about underlining is to underline *after* reading a paragraph or passage, not during the reading. The main idea in any paragraph can be in the first sentence or the middle or end of the paragraph. If underlining is begun as the reading is started, the critical phrases in the passage may be missed. The basic rules of underlining are to read first and then underline, and select only main ideas and supporting details.

In some situations, it may be important to do more than generate questions and underline main ideas. Another strategy to improve comprehension is to annotate or mark textbooks. Annotations are words or symbols usually written in the margin of the textbook that help one to organize and remember important information. There are many different ways to mark or annotate a textbook. Consider the following guidelines:

- Mark selectively.
- Mark pages only after they have been read.
- Develop symbols that make sense.

Figure 8.1 identifies various types of symbols for annotations in textbooks. Other types of annotations include summary words or phrases in the margin that identify key ideas in the text, such as "causes of the illness" or "3 characteristics of." Finally, you can write critical comments in the margin to help prepare for discussion of essays, short stories, or poems. *Do not annotate a book that you do not own, especially library books.*

4. Comprehension Monitoring. The following is a question you should ask yourself each time you read: "How well am I understanding what

Symbol	Explanation
?	Use a question mark to show material you don't understand.
*	Use a star to identify important ideas.
def	Use an abbreviation to identify definitions.
|	Use a vertical line to identify important ideas that are several lines in length.
◯	Use a circle to identify unknown words.

FIG. 8.1. Types of annotations.

I am reading?" If you are not understanding what you are reading, *stop*. Ask yourself why. The following are some common reading problems and possible strategies to solve them (adapted from Cortina et al., 1992, p. 34):

Problem	Strategy
There are words that I don't know.	• Try to use the rest of the sentence or paragraph to figure out the meaning of those words. • Check a glossary or a dictionary. • Ask someone.
I am having difficulty concentrating.	• Identify what is bothering you and take some action (read chapter 7).
The topic is difficult because I know nothing about it.	• Reread the passage. • Read ahead to see if it becomes clearer. • Read supplemental material or simpler material on the same topic (perhaps an encyclopedia, another textbook, or a book from the library). • Ask someone to explain the material.

After Reading

Many students make the mistake of assuming that they are done once they read the last paragraph in their assignment. This is the critical time to take the necessary steps to ensure that you *remember* what you have just read. Because forgetting occurs very rapidly, it is important to get the information you read into long-term memory immediately. Here is what you can do:

1. Answer Out Loud the Questions You Generated From the Headings, Printed in Your Textbook, or Given to You by Your Instructor. If you cannot answer a question, you do not understand part of the content. Go back and reread the section of the textbook where the answer should be found. Once you find the answer, check your underlining or annotations to ensure that the answer is identified.

2. Consider Summarizing the Material.   A summary is a brief statement that identifies the major ideas in a section of a textbook, play, newspaper article, or story. It is particularly useful in preparing for essay exams or when reading literature. For example, writing a summary of the plot in a novel incorporating information describing who did what, when, and where can be useful in determining that you understood the reading.

The following are some suggestions for writing summaries (McWhorter, 1995, p. 238):

- Start by identifying the author's main point; write a statement that expresses it.
- Next, identify the most important information the writer includes to support or explain his or her main point. Include these main supporting ideas in your summary.
- Include any definitions of key terms or important new principles, theories, or procedures that are introduced.
- Try to keep your summary objective and factual. Think of it as a brief report that should reflect the writer's ideas, not your evaluation of them.

3. Consider Outlining the Material.   At times, answering questions is sufficient to confirm that you remembered what you read. However, sometimes because of the complexity of the material, you may decide to outline or graphically represent (i.e., map) the information. Both strategies organize the material by identifying the relation between main ideas and supporting details.

The easiest way to show the relationship between ideas and details in an outline is to use the following format:

I. Major topic
   A. First main idea
      1. First important detail
      2. Second important detail
      3. Third important detail
   B. Second main idea
      1. First important detail
         a. Minor point or example
      2. Second important detail
II. Second major topic
   A. First main idea

Notice that the most important ideas are closer to the margins, with less important ideas or examples indented toward the middle of the page. The purpose of this format is to be able to look at the outline and quickly determine what is most important.

McWhorter (1995, p. 235) made the following suggestions for developing an effective outline:

- Don't get caught up in the numbering and lettering system. Instead, concentrate on showing the relative importance of ideas. How you number or letter an idea is not as important as showing what other ideas it supports or explains. Don't be concerned if some items do not fit exactly into outline format.
- Be brief; use words and phrases, never complete sentences. Abbreviate words and phrases where possible.
- Use you own words rather than lifting most of the material from the text. You can use the author's key words and specialized terminology.
- Be sure that all information underneath a heading supports or explains it.
- All headings that are aligned vertically should be of equal importance.

Here's a brief outline of the information-processing system discussed in chapter 2:

I. Information Processing System
  A. STSS
    1. Memory lasts few seconds
    2. Capacity is large
  B. WM
    1. Memory limited in capacity and duration
      a. 7 ± 2
      b. Memory lasts 5 to 20 seconds
  C. LTM
    1. Storage of info is permanent
    2. Organization is like filing cabinet
    3. Flow of info in two directions

4. _Consider Representing or Mapping the Material._ I'm sure you have heard the expression "A picture is worth a thousand words." In learning, students often find it helpful to represent knowledge in terms of maps or diagrams to show how a topic and its corresponding information are related. Sometimes academic content is more easily learned by using a visual display of its organization rather than reviewing an entire chapter or section of a textbook. Consider, for example, how much discussion it would take to describe the functioning of a human heart. A good graphic representation in the form of a diagram can quickly illustrate the key components of a heart and the flow of blood through it.

Information in texts and lectures is often presented linearly, one idea at a time. Many students view academic subjects in terms of a large number of isolated facts. No wonder little information is remembered. Learning involves constructing meaning by combining ideas so that relations and patterns are apparent. When students view information solely in a linear format, they miss important relations among ideas.

One of the advantages of recognizing different organizational patterns used by authors and lecturers is that it allows the reader or listener to anticipate the type of information likely to be presented. A second advantage is that understanding how ideas and information is organized makes it easier to remember the information. If the author's or lecturer's organization patterns are understood, more of the material will be understood and remembered (Cortina et al., 1992).

The discussion in this section is based on the work of Kiewra and DuBois (1998), who have developed a useful approach to the representation of knowledge. They identified four different representations—**hierarchies, sequences, matrices,** and **diagrams**—and provided suggestions for constructing them. This information is appropriate both for learning from reading and lectures. Kiewra and DuBois favor representations over outlines. They believe that representations provide better comparison of content and a more precise overview of the structure of the content than outlines. Each of the four representations is reviewed here.

Hierarchies.   Hierarchies organize ideas into levels and groups. Higher levels are more general than lower levels. Hierarchies are organized around class-inclusion rules. These rules are based on the notion that something is a part of or a type of something else. Examples of class inclusion rules are the classification of reptiles as part of animals, and neutrons as part of atoms.

Take another look at the hierarchy of minerals that was first introduced in chapter 2 (Fig. 2.2). Level 1 represents the class (minerals), Level 2 includes two types of minerals (metals and stones), Level 3 includes three types of metals and two types of stones, and Level 4 includes specific examples of each of the type of metals and stones. The number of levels in a hierarchy can vary from one or more. It is important to reflect all the important levels and groups in any hierarchy that is developed.

The following is an excerpt from a child psychology textbook (Vasts, Haith, & Miller, 1992, p. 31) that will be used later in the chapter to illustrate how sequences and matrices can be used to organize information. Read the excerpt before moving to the next section of this chapter:

> **Stages of Development.** Piaget was a stage theorist. In his view, all children move through the same stages of cognitive development in the same order. Each stage is a qualitatively distinct form of functioning, and the structures that

characterize each stage determine the child's performance in a wide range of situations. There are four such general stages, or periods, in Piaget's theory.

The **sensorimotor** period represents the first 2 years of life. The infant's initial schemes are simple reflexes. Gradually, these reflexes are combined into larger, more flexible units of action. Knowledge of the world is limited to physical interactions with people and objects. Most of the examples of schemes given earlier—grasping, sucking, and so on—occur during infancy.

During the **preoperational** period, from roughly 2 to 6 years, the child begins to use symbols to represent the world cognitively. Words and numbers can take the place of objects and events, and actions that formerly had to be carried out overtly can now be performed mentally through the use of internal symbols. The preoperational child is not yet skilled at symbolic problem solving, however, and various gaps and confusions are evident in the child's attempts to understand the world.

Many of these limitations are overcome when the child reaches the period of **concrete operations**, which lasts approximately from ages 6 to 11. Concrete operational children are able to perform mental operations on the bits of knowledge that they possess. They can add them, subtract them, put them in order, reverse them, and so on. These mental operations permit a kind of logical problem solving that was not possible during the preoperational period.

The final stage is the period of **formal operations**, which extends from about age 11 through adulthood. This period includes all of the higher level abstract operations that do not require concrete objects or materials. The clearest example of such operations is the ability to deal with events or relationships that are only possible, as opposed to those that actually exist. Mentally considering all of the ways certain objects could be combined, or attempting to solve a problem by cognitively examining all of the ways it could be approached, are two operations that typically cannot be performed until this final stage.

Sequences. Sequences order ideas chronologically by illustrating the ordering of steps, events, stages, or phases. Sequences usually appear in a left-to-right pattern, with arrows between steps. Figure 8.2 provides an example of the stages of cognitive development described in the preceding excerpt. Timelines in history also can be used to visualize the sequence of events by drawing a horizontal line and marking it off in intervals. The times when different events in history

Sensorimotor ⟶ Preoperational ⟶ Concrete ⟶ Formal

FIG. 8.2.   Stages of cognitive development.

occurred can be illustrated by adjusting the intervals at which the dates are placed on the line.

Matrices.   Matrices display comparative relations. They are developed from a hierarchy or sequence and have three parts: *topics, repeatable categories,* and *details* located inside the matrix cells. These parts are shown in Fig. 8.3. The topics appear across the matrix (e.g., amphetamines, depressants, and hallucinogenics). The repeatable categories appear down the left margin. They are the characteristics by which the topics are compared (e.g., function, street terms, and example). They are called repeatable categories, because each category is repeated for each topic. The author often identifies repeatable categories. However, sometimes categories will have to be identified from the information provided by the author. The details are the facts that pertain to the intersection of topics and repeatable categories. They appear inside the matrix in the cells at the intersection of topics and repeatable categories.

Any hierarchy or sequence can be extended downward to form a matrix. Fig. 8.4 illustrates a hierarchy extended into a matrix framework, and Fig. 8.5 illustrates a sequence extended into a matrix framework from the reading on cognitive development. In Fig. 8.5, the repeatable categories (i.e., age and characteristics) are provided for you. Fill in the details for each of the four stages of cognitive development and compare your representation with a classmate.

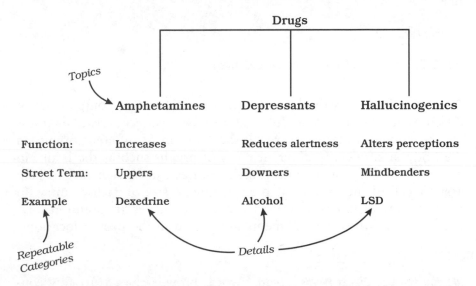

FIG. 8.3.   Components of a matrix.

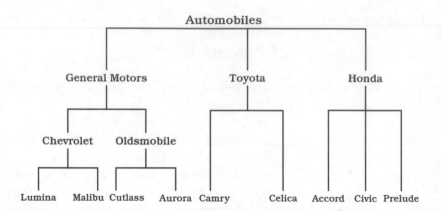

Performance:

Comfort and
Convenience:

Safety and
Reliability:

FIG. 8.4. Road tests for different automobiles.

Sensorimotor ———→ Preoperational ———→ Concrete ———→ Formal

Age:

Characteristics:

FIG. 8.5. Stages of cognitive development.

Diagrams. Diagrams display or illustrate the parts or components of different objects and are useful in almost every subject area. Diagrams can be drawn in biology to recall the location of different organs in the body or to identify different parts of organs such as the brain. In geography, a map of the European countries can be sketched to help assist recall of the location and approximate size of each country. In mathematics, diagrams of different geometric shapes are useful in solving problems when measurements are placed in the proper locations.

How Can I Construct Representations?

Identify and Use Signal Words. Signal words provide clues as to how content is related and what representation (hierarchy, sequence, matrix, or

TABLE 8.1
EXAMPLES OF SIGNAL WORDS

Hierarchy	Sequence	Matrix
kinds of	first	like
types of	before	similarly
classified as	in the center	equally
composed of	lower	in contrast
parts of	outside	on the other hand
groups of	after	alternatively
properties of	next	similar
characteristics of	last	in comparison
perspectives	steps	
	stages	
	phases	
	cycle	
	as a result	
	consequently	
	therefore	

Adapted from Kiewra and Dubois (1998).

diagram) to construct. A representation should not be selected solely on a signal word without the entire passage being read to confirm the representation. Table 8.1 includes examples of different signal words. Signal words for diagrams include parts, appearance, position, and movement.

EXERCISE 8.2: IDENTIFYING DIFFERENT REPRESENTATIONS IN ACADEMIC CONTENT

Directions: The following are brief statements that introduce discussion of various topics. For each of the statements, identify which representation would most likely depict the information to follow by writing H for hierarchy, S for sequence, M for matrix, and D for diagram in the space provided. The answers are provided on p. 216.

__1. There are a number of similarities and differences between mitosis and meiosis.
__2. Once food has been chewed, it is swallowed and passed down the esophagus to the stomach.
__3. Eating disorders are grouped into three categories: obesity, bulimia, and anorexia nervosa.
__4. There are several perspectives on gender identification.
__5. The development before birth, called gestation, takes place in three stages: germinal, embryonic, and fetal.

continued

——6. The cerebellum is the coordinating center of voluntary movements and is located behind the cerebrum.
——7. The framers of the Constitution devised alternative methods
of selection and terms of service for national officials.

Identify and Develop Repeatable Categories.   Signal words are useful in
determining what representation will be used (i.e., a hierarchy,
sequence, matrix, or diagram). However, because all hierarchical and
sequential representations can be extended to form matrix representations, it is important to learn how to identify the matrix's repeatable categories.

It is important to be aware of the structure of different academic
disciplines. For example, history courses tend to focus on who, what,
why, and when questions that can be developed into repeatable categories such as causes, major battles, resolution, and so forth. In literature, short stories have a plot, a setting, and characters that can
be used as common characteristics for comparing stories. In psychology, learning theories are used to explain how students learn. Therefore,
repeatable categories to consider might be the definition of learning,
role of the teacher, role of the student, and factors that influence
motivation.

Often authors and lecturers identify the repeatable categories. Suppose you read about gender identity and the author points out that
he will discuss four different theories of gender identification and the
key processes and basic beliefs of each theory. Once you have completed the opening paragraph of the section in your textbook, you
have already identified the repeatable categories: key processes and
basic beliefs.

In some cases, you will read considerable material and have to
identify the repeatable categories on your own. Suppose you read in
a history book about different Asian cities. The author provides information about living conditions in the cities but does not specifically
categorize the differences. For example, you may find reference to the
congestion in one city, the slow pace of the inhabitants in another
location, and so forth. If you were to develop a matrix of the information, you might consider lifestyle as a repeatable category to compare the cities you studied.

Like any other skill you develop, learning to construct representations takes practice. As you read textbooks this week and take notes,
think about how the information you are learning can be organized
more effectively. As you begin constructing representations, you will
find it easier to understand important relationships in the content of
your courses.

EXERCISE 8.3: CONSTRUCTING DIFFERENT REPRESENTATIONS IN ACADEMIC CONTENT

Directions: Read the following passages from different academic textbooks and, in the space provided, construct a complete representation for the material.

Cells are composed of chemicals. The chemicals of life (biochemicals) tend to be large and are therefore called **macromolecules.** The macromolecules that make up and fuel cells include **carbohydrates** (sugars and starches), **lipids** (fats and oils), **proteins,** and **nucleic acids.** Cells need vitamins and minerals in much smaller amounts, but they are also vital to health.

Carbohydrates provide energy. Lipids form the basis of several types of hormones, produce insulation, and serve as an energy reserve. Proteins have many diverse functions in the human body. They participate in blood clotting, nerve transmission, and muscle contraction. Proteins called **enzymes** are especially important, because they speed, or catalyze, biochemical reactions so that they occur swiftly enough to sustain life.

Most important to the study of heredity are the nucleic acids **deoxyribonucleic acid** (DNA) and **ribonucleic acid** (RNA). DNA and RNA form a living language that converts information from past generations into specific collections of proteins that give a cell its individual characteristics.[3]

Representation:

Stocks and Bonds

Our discussion of the earnings of an investor in corporate securities introduces a subject of interest to millions of Americans—*stocks* and *bonds*, the financial instruments that provide funds to the corporate sector of the economy.

[3]From Lewis, R. (1997). *Human Genetics: Concepts and Applications* (2nd ed.). Dubuque, IA: Brown, p. 18.

Common stock represents ownership of part of a corporation. For example, if a company issues 100,000 shares, then a person who owns 1,000 shares actually owns 1% of the company and is entitled to 1% of the company's dividends, which are the corporation's annual payments to stockholders. The shareholder's vote counts for 1% of the total votes in an election of corporate officers or in a referendum on corporate policy.

Bonds differ from stocks in several ways. First, whereas the purchaser of a corporation's stock *buys* a share of its ownership and receives some control over its affairs, the purchaser of a bond simply *lends* money to the firm. Second, whereas stockholders have no idea how much they will receive for their stocks when they sell them, or how much they will receive in dividends each year while they own them, bondholders know with a high degree of certainty how much money they will be paid if they hold their bonds to maturity. For instance, a bond with a face value of $1,000, with an $80 coupon that matures in 2004, will provide to its owner $80 per year every year until 2004 and, in addition, it will repay the $1,000 to the bondholder in 2004. Unless the company goes bankrupt, a *prior claim* on company earnings, which means that nothing can be paid by the company to its stockholders until interest payments to the company's bondholders have been met. For all these reasons, bonds are considered less risky to their buyers than stocks.[4]

Representation:

---

[4]From Baumol, W. J, & Blinder, A. S. (1994). *Economics: Principles and Policy* (7th ed.). Orlando, FL: Dryden, pp. 330–331.

TABLE 8.2

Procedures for Learning From Textbook

Before Reading

1. Preview the book for learning aids.
2. Survey the assignment before each reading session.
3. Read questions at the beginning or end of each chapter or study guide that may accompany your textbook, or that are provided by your instructors.

During Reading Each Passage or Section

1. As you begin reading, think of the text as a conversation between the author and yourself. Ask the following questions: "What is the author trying to tell me?" "Which sentences state the main idea?"
2. Turn the headings in a textbook into questions and answer them. If there are no heads, write questions in the margin of the textbook.
3. Underline the answers to your questions and annotate the textbook.

After Reading Each Passage or Section

1. Answer out loud the questions that you generated from the headings, printed in your textbook, and given by your instructor.
2. After you have underlined the material, reread questions to check whether underlining provides sufficient clues to answer questions. If necessary, make modifications in underlining.
3. Check your understanding of the material you read by attempting to answer the questions.
4. Consider summarizing, outlining, or representing the material.

Table 8.2 contains a review of the different reading procedures discussed in this chapter:

Key Points

1. Good readers use specific learning strategies to manage their understanding.
2. Simply underlining textbooks as one reads is not an effective learning strategy unless it is used with the generation and answering of questions.
3. Reading or taking notes and remembering are two separate activities. Just because you read or take notes does not mean you will remember what you read or wrote down.
4. Learning from textbooks and lectures involve activities undertaken *before, during,* and *after* each activity.
5. Good readers monitor their understanding as they read.

6. Summarizing, outlining, and representing textbook content are useful strategies for learning and remembering material.
7. Information in textbooks and lectures is often presented in a linear fashion, one idea at a time. This form of presentation obscures the relation among ideas.
8. To construct meaning, it is unusually necessary to organize information.
9. The four types of representations that can help learners understand relationships include hierarchies, sequences, matrices, and diagrams.

Follow-Up Activities

1. Use the Self-management Process to Become a More Successful Reader

Complete the following self-study during a period of 2 to 3 weeks. Your report should include each of the following processes and should be approximately five to eight typed pages in length. See Appendix A for detailed information on how to conduct a self-management study.

Self-observation and evaluation. How effective are my reading strategies? Do I need to change the way I read and study? If yes, what problem(s) do I encounter? What are the symptoms of my problem (i.e., when, where, and how often does my problem occur)? How much of an impact does this problem have on my academic performance? What factors (e.g., beliefs, perceptions, feelings, physiological responses, or behaviors) contribute to this problem? What do I need to change to reduce or eliminate my problem(s)?

Goal setting and strategic planning. What are my goals? What strategies will I implement to improve my treading comprehension? When will I use these strategies? How will I record my progress?

Strategy-implementation and monitoring. What strategies did I use to improve my reading comprehension? When did I use these strategies? What method(s) did I use to record my progress (e.g., documents, charts, logs, tally sheets, checklists, or recordings)? When did I use these methods? How and when did I monitor my progress to determine if my new reading comprehension plan was working? What changes, if any, did I make along the way?

Strategic-outcome monitoring. Did I attain the goal(s) I set for myself? Have the modifications in my reading comprehension strategies improved my academic performance? What strategies were the most and least effective? What changes, if any, do I need to make in the future?

2. Assess Reading Behavior

The self-management model at the beginning of the chapter indicates that the use of motivational strategies (i.e., goal setting and mood and effort) and behavioral strategies (i.e., time management and physical and social environmental control) influence learning and study strategies. Explain how motivation and behavioral strategies impact your reading behavior. In addition, explain what steps you could take to deal with your reading concerns.

3. Analyze Use of Reading Strategies

In the beginning of this chapter, you learned about the strategies that good readers use: *determining importance, summarizing information, drawing inferences, generating questions,* and *monitoring comprehension.* Select a chapter in a textbook in another course and explain how you used these strategies in comprehending the material. If you did not use one or more of the strategies, explain the reason for your decision.

4. Improve Reading Comprehension and Retention

Directions: The following passages are taken from college textbooks in different academic areas. Only the first two passages have headings. Read each passage and (a) generate a question; (b) underline relevant parts of the passage that answer the question; (c) identify the type of representation you could use to comprehend the material, including the topics and repeatable categories; and (d) circle the signal words in the passage. You will not be able to complete the representation, because the paragraphs do not include all the details you would need.

Passage 1: **Types of Organisms**

Although there is a great diversity of marine life, it is commonly separated into only three major categories: plankton, nekton, and benthos. These subdivisions are based solely on the general habit of the organisms and have nothing to do with their scientific classification, their size or complexity, or whether they are plant or animal.

The plankton are organisms that live within the pelagic zone and float, drift, or swim feebly; that is, they cannot control their position against currents. The plankton include plants, which are called phytoplankton, and animals, which are called zooplankton. Nekton are those organisms that swim. Only animals are included in this group. The benthos are those organisms that live on or within the bottom, the benthic environment.

The plankton are the most diverse and numerous, with the benthos not too far behind. Many groups of organisms spend a portion of their life cycle in more than one of these modes of life. It is common for a particular group to be planktonic in the larval or juvenile stage and then nektonic or benthonic as adults.[5]

Type of representation:

Passage 2: Federation Versus Confederation

In a federation, the national government is fully sovereign; the states may not withdraw without the consent of the national authorities; and the people create both the national government and the state governments, delegate powers to both, and may restrict both through a written constitution. The national government may act directly on the people; it can tax and draft them. In contrast, in a confederation, the states are sovereign; they may join the nation or withdraw from it at will. They delegate specified powers to national institutions and reserve all others to themselves. The national "government" is a creature of the states and can deal only with the states, not directly with their citizens.

Confederation is an ancient form of government; it has bound people together throughout history, from the time of the alliances of the Israelite tribes to the Renaissance and the

[5]From Davis, R. A. (1986). *Oceanography: An Introduction to the Marine Environment.* Dubuque, IA: Brown, p. 129.

confederacies that flourished in what is today Germany, Italy, the Netherlands, and Switzerland. Federalism is more modern; it was developed first in the United States and later was adopted by one third of the countries of the world, including the Soviet Union, Brazil, India, Nigeria, Mexico, Switzerland, Yugoslavia, West Germany, Canada, and Australia.[6]

Type of representation:

Passage 3

Three different accounts have been proposed to explain why stereotypes develop. The first, the shared distinctiveness account, is a purely cognitive account; it proposes that the tendency to form stereotypes of people is a natural consequence of the way we process information. In particular, David Hamilton has proposed that a phenomenon well-known in general psychology, the illusory correlation, can explain the development and maintenance of stereotypes without needing to posit that we have any motivational biases at all with regard to our thinking about groups of people. The second account also sees stereotypes as a consequence of the way we think about people, but it suggests that stereotyping depends on our having categorized people into ingroups and outgroups. The essence of this account, the outgroup homogeneity account, is that once we divide people into ingroups and outgroups, we are likely to form stereotypes of the outgroups. The third account, the cultural account, argues that we cannot understand the stereotypes we have of various groups in cognitive terms alone; it suggests that the stereotypes we have are a consequence of the specific way our culture has structured interactions between ingroups and outgroups. According to this view, the history of a culture determines the particular content that various stereotypes have. Let us consider these explanations one at a time.[7]

[6]From Pious, R. M. (1986). *American Politics and Government*. New York: McGraw-Hill. p. 64, 66.
[7]From Sabini, U. (1995). *Social Psychology* (2nd ed.). New York: Norton, p. 125.

Type of representation:

4. Construct a Representation

Construct a representation for a textbook you are currently reading. Copy the pages in the textbook where the information came from. Identify the type of representation you used and include the repeatable categories and details.

Answers to Exercise 8.2

1. M   2. S   3. H   4. M   5. S   6. D   7. M

9

Learning From Lectures

Suppose immediately after the completion of a lecture, you were asked to explain the major ideas presented by the instructor. How often could you adequately respond to the request? Could you provide the information for all classes or some of your classes? Would you have to refer to your notes? If so, would your notes provide all the information you need?

Much of the information learned about a subject in college is presented in lecture form. Remember the discussion of the information-processing system in chapter 2. Because human memory fades quickly, it is important that you learn how to record major ideas and supporting details. Also, unless your notes are organized, it will be difficult to understand what you recorded weeks after you first took the notes. The most frustrating experience is to look at your notes and ask yourself: What does this mean?

One of the major differences between learning from texts and lectures is that in reading you can control the flow of information. If you do not understand something, you can reread it, take notes, or put down the text and return to it at another time. However, in lectures, the pace is controlled by the instructor. As a result, you need to use strategies to capture the main ideas more rapidly.

In this chapter, you will learn that what you do with your notes is just as important as how you record them. Educational research indicates that students who take notes and review them shortly after class learn more than students who take notes but do not review them (Kiewra, 1989). Part of the benefit of reviewing notes is that it allows further elaboration and integration of the material. Therefore, you should not simply skim your notes, but think actively about the ideas in the notes and relate them to other information you already know.

I notice that the amount of notes students take in my class is related to my instructional methods. When I am standing in front of the podium presenting information, students take many notes. However, if I move away from the podium and lead a discussion, note taking is reduced. What many students fail to realize is that a great deal of information is presented during discussions. It is the students' responsibility to capture the main ideas presented or discussed in all classes.

After studying this chapter, you will be able to:

- Evaluate your present note-taking practices.
- Use an effective method for taking and reviewing notes.

EXERCISE 9.1: SELF-OBSERVATION: ANALYZING NOTE-TAKING STRATEGIES

Directions: Assess your current note-taking strategies by checking the appropriate responses to each of the following questions. Be prepared to discuss in class your perception of the effectiveness of your current strategy. Think about why each of the following questions below is relevant to taking effective notes.

	Always	*Sometimes*	*Never*
1. Do you complete the assigned readings before each lecture?			
2. Do you try to sit as close as possible to the lecturer?			
3. Do you doodle during a lecture?			

	Always	*Sometimes*	*Never*
4. Do you avoid listening when difficult information is presented?			
5. Do you condense the main ideas rather than write complete sentences?			
6. Do you use abbreviations?			
7. Do you daydream during lectures?			
8. Do you separate main ideas from examples and other secondary information?			
9. Do you make a notation in your notes for information you don't understand?			
10. Do you attempt to control distractions around you?			
11. Do you try to determine the organization of the lecture?			
12. Do you review your notes each day after class?			
13. Do you understand your notes when you begin preparing for an exam?			

Comments:

_____

_____

_____

_____

_____

_____

_____

_____

Read the following student reactions to their experience with note-taking strategies. Are your experiences different or similar to the following comments?

Student Reflections

Note taking is far more difficult in college than in high school. The note-taking strategy that I learned in high school would be inappropriate and ineffective if used in a college course. High school teachers often spoon-fed the notes and emphasized what was important for you in the lecture. You were guided very thoroughly on what the specific main points and supporting details were. Key points often were written on the board, were illustrated in worksheets, and repeated many times. In addition, teachers would interact regularly with students while lecturing, allowing them to ask questions freely while emphasizing important information.

#   #   #   #

In college, taking notes requires more critical thinking and concentration. Good listening skills are essential for effective note taking because you have to determine the main points for yourself. Professors often move through a lecture with lightening speed, forcing you to determine key points quickly.

My note-taking strategies were very poor in high school. I would write down everything that the teacher said and that the teacher wrote on the board. I thought that if I got everything written down on my paper, it would be easier for me to study, even if I did not know what the notes were about. At least I wrote all the information down! My notes were very disorganized, and I had no idea of the main purpose or idea of my notes. Everything appeared to be thrown together, and it was very difficult to return to my notes, because I didn't know where to find certain things, and sometimes I really didn't know the meaning of the information I wrote.

#   #   #   #

In high school, my notes were very confusing to me. I would just write down whatever I felt like at the time. My notes had very little structure to them. They would consist of very fragmented thoughts. When trying to review them for tests, I had a very hard time trying to figure out what went on in that particular lecture. I wouldn't even date my notes to know when a particular topic was discussed in class. At the time when I was in high school, I thought that my notes were just fine. I now look back on them, and they didn't do the job.

HOW CAN I TAKE BETTER NOTES?

There is more to taking notes than recording ideas in a notebook. Like reading textbooks, taking good notes and remembering what was written also involves activities in three important stages—before, during, and after the lecture.

Before the Lecture

1. Complete Assigned Readings Before Class. If you read textbook assignments related to the lecture, you will learn more from the lecture for the following reasons (Ormrod, 1995): First, you will be able to direct your attention appropriately. One of the most important tasks in a lecture is to determine the main ideas. If you have already read the textbook, you will have a better idea of what is important than will another student who knows nothing or very little about the topic. Second, you are more likely to engage in meaningful rather than rote learning. That is to say, you will be better able to make sense of the lecture. Third, you will be able to organize the information, because you will have a framework for understanding the material. Fourth, you will to able to use information from the textbook to elaborate on the information by filling in missing details or clarifying ambiguities.

2. Review Notes From the Previous Class.   This activity should not take more than 5 or 10 minutes, but the time is very worthwhile. Under-standing previous material often provides a foundation for learning new material. The more information you do not understand, the more difficult it is to make sense of new material. Look up definitions of terms you do not understand and review computations in math and science courses after each lecture.

3. Bring All Necessary Materials (e.g., Notebook, Pen, Handouts, Syllabus, and Textbook) to Class.   Prepare at least 20 sheets of note paper in the fol-lowing format: draw a line down a sheet of paper, allowing for a 3-inch margin on the lefthand side of the page. Write lecture notes in the wide righthand column and reserve the 3-inch margin for ques-tions derived from the lecture notes. Many college bookstores sell notebooks with 3-inch margins.

Keep your course syllabus in your binder or notebook, because instructors sometimes change assignments or dates of examinations. Placing changes directly in your syllabus will ensure that you do not miss some important information.

Instructors often mention material in the textbook, use the text for class discussions, or follow the text closely in their lectures. There-fore, if you bring your textbook, you can mark the text or identify specific pages in your notes.

4. Sit Toward the Front of the Room if You Have Difficulty Concentrating.   The closer you sit to the lecturer, the better able you are to see and hear the instructor and to maintain eye contact. The further you sit from the lecturer, the easier it is to be distracted by other students talking or passing notes.

5. Date and Number Each Day's Notes.   There are two major reasons for dating and numbering notes. The first is to be able to check the notes with the assigned textbook reading. The second is to obtain notes for days when you are absent. It is difficult to identify information in your notes when you do not know the exact day of the lecture. If you have a friend in class, it is easier to discuss your notes when you can easily locate any given lecture.

During the Lecture

1. Listen Carefully to the Instructor and Take Notes That Focus on Main Ideas and Supporting Details.   Be alert for signals that indicate the importance of information and suggest possible representations you can construct after class.

Different instructors have different ways they communicate the importance of lecture material. The following are signals that indicate you should copy information in your notes:

- If the instructor *repeats* or *emphasizes a point,* you can usually assume it is important. You might write *R* (repeat) or place an asterisk (*) in the margin to mark the importance of the information.
- Copy whatever the instructor *writes on the board* or *shows on the overhead projector.*
- Always *write definitions and listings,* such as: "The three steps in this process are . . . " "The two effects were . . . " "Five characteristics are. . . . "
- Listen for *important comments,* such as: "This is an important reason . . . " "Don't forget that . . . " "Pay special attention to. . . . "

In the previous chapter, I discussed four different representations—hierarchies, sequences, matrices, and diagrams. Listen for the signal words listed in Table 8.1. The same words used by authors to signal organizational patterns also are used by lecturers. When you hear a signal word in a lecture, make a notation in your notes to review the information for a possible representation after class. Leave room in your notes for the construction of the representation.

2. Condense the Main Ideas and Supporting Details Into Short Phrases or Sentences, Using Abbreviations Whenever Possible.

Lecturer: "There are three parts to the information processing system: the short-term sensory store, working memory, and long-term memory."

Condensation: Three parts to IPS—STSS, WM, LTM

Words	Abbreviations
pound	lb
and	&
positive	+
negative	−
without	w/out
compare	comp
example	eg.
feminine	fem
masculine	masc
point	pt.
introduction	intro.
that is	i.e.

versus	vs
equal to	=
number	#
achievement	ach
continued	cont'd

3. Use an Indenting Form for Writing Notes. Start main points at the margin and indent secondary ideas and supporting details. Further indent material that is subordinate to secondary points. The outline format helps you see how the lecture was organized and helps identify the relative importance of the content when studying for an examination (see Figs. 9.1 and 9.2). If the instructor's presentation is not well organized, do not spend too much time during the lecture trying to figure out the outline. Get the main ideas down in your notes and reorganize them after class (McWhorter, 1996).

4. When the Instructor Moves to Another Idea or Topic, Show This Shift by Skipping Two Lines. One of the most confusing aspects of analyzing notes after class is following the instructor's main ideas. By skipping lines in your notes, you are alerted to the fact that the instructor moved on to another idea or topic. This procedure helps make sense of your notes.

After the Lecture

The most important part of note taking is the activities that are completed after you take notes. The activities presented here were developed by Heiman and Slomianko (1993). They involve generating and answering two types of questions from notes. The first is called a *mirror question*, because it directly reflects the information in your notes (see Figs. 9.1 and 9.2). The second is called a *summary question*, because it reflects the major theme or main idea of the total lecture. If you know the answers to these questions, you understand your notes.

You need to set aside about 5 to 10 minutes per lecture shortly after class to review your notes and complete the following activities:

1. Add Any Important Information You Remember the Instructor Saying but You Did Not Write Down.

2. Locate Information You Did Not Understand in the Lecture From the Instructor, Another Student, or the Textbook.

3. Play a Form of Academic Jeopardy and Think About Notes as Answers to Questions. After class, carefully read over the notes. Write mirror questions (in complete sentences) that the notes answer in the lefthand column of your note paper (see Figs. 9.1 and 9.2).

Ask yourself: "If the information I wrote in my notes was an answer to a test question, what would the questions be?" In general, you should have three to four questions for each page of notes. If you cannot think of questions for certain parts of your notes, you probably do not understand the content or did not write enough information

---

Biology - Heart - 9/17

Heart —muscular pump that provides pressure to pump blood throughout body

What are the different chambers of the heart?

What are the functions of the different chambers?

Four chambers

> *rt. & left atria—collect blood from major veins and empty it into ventricles*

> *right & left ventricles—muscles whose contract. forces blood to flow-through arteries to all parts of body*

Atrioventricular valves—between atria and ventricles that allow blood to flow from the atria to the ventricles, prevent flow in opposite direction.

Semiliunar valves—valves in aorta and pulmonary artery

> *aorta—carries blood from the left ventricle to body*

> *pulmonary artery—carries blood from the right ventricle to the lungs.*

What happens if the valves in a heart are damaged?

If valves are damaged, the efficiency of the heart as a pump is diminished.

> *person may develop sympt. such as enlarged heart. Diagnosed by abnormal sounds as blood passes through them—heart murmurs.*

What happens if the ventricles in a heart are damaged?

If vent. are weakened by infection, lack of exercise, etc. the pumping efficiency of the heart is reduced

Symptoms—chest pain, shortness of breath

pain caused by heart not getting suff. blood.

Portion of heart muscle not receiving blood will die n time

Summary question (for complete lecture):

How does the heart function?

FIG. 9.1.   An example of the note-taking method in biology.

What are the different budget strategies that a president can use?	**Presidential budget strategies - 9/15** *Veto strategy—often used as a defensive weapon that prevents Congress from funding at a higher level than the president wants.* *president lack line item veto would allow them to veto particular items rather than whole measure.* *Impoundment strategy—have the Congress and the OMB withhold funds from agencies* *president Nixon made most use of this strategy* *Reconciliation strategy—a method of changing budget politics*
What strategies did Reagan use?	*Types of* *fast track—budget committee compiles a single, omnibus reconciliation bill allowing proposed budget shifts all at one time.* *national agenda—use public opinion to develop support for policy* *Outcome*
Why did early reconciliation work for Reagan?	<u>*Reagan was able to dominate budget politics by compressing process*</u> <u>*A single package made budget cuts highly*</u> <u>*visible—susceptible to national agenda*</u> <u>*made it difficult for party members to go against him*</u>

Summary question (for complete lecture):

How do budgetary strategies allow presidents to implement their political agendas?

FIG. 9.2. An example of a note-taking strategy in political science.

to make sense of the specific section of the notes. Write a question mark in the margin and ask a friend or the instructor about the information.

In science and math classes, it is important to identify the type of problem in the lefthand margin and the solution of the problem in the righthand column. For example, if your math instructor is demonstrating the procedure to find the reciprocal of different numbers, the righthand side of your notes identifies the procedure and the lefthand side lists the question: How do you find the reciprocal of different numbers?

4. Once a Question Has Been Identified, Return to the Lecture-Note Text and Underline a Key Term or Phrase That Triggers an Answer to the Question. Different students given the same notes may underline different words or phrases, because the information that triggers an answer for one person may do nothing for another. As in reading textbooks, do not underline too much. Focus on only enough information to help answer the mirror question you wrote. The following are additional procedures to help you learn the content in your notes:

5. Read the Key Terms or Phrases to Verify That They Help You Recall the Information in the Notes. If the key terms or phrases trigger only partial answers to the questions, underline more information.

6. Cover the Notes With a Blank Sheet of Paper and Attempt to Answer Questions.

7. If Appropriate, Construct Representations to Depict the Organization of the Material in the Lecture.

8. Write a Summary Question for the Total Lecture at the End of Your Lecture Notes for the Day. Place a circle or box around this question so it will be easily recognized when you review your notes. Here you want to ask: "What is the one major question that reflects the purpose of today's lecture?" or "What is the relationship between my mirror questions?" If you can answer both of these questions, you would understand the theme or main idea of the total lecture. Think about the usefulness of summary questions in studying for essay examinations. In some classes, you may be able to predict 75% or more of the essay questions on your examinations.

EXERCISE 9.2: PRACTICING THE NOTE-TAKING STRATEGY

Directions: The following is a lecture excerpt on the psychology of learning. Take notes on this passage in the space provided. Be sure to use the indenting format. After taking notes, write one or more mirror questions in the lefthand margin and, finally, underline parts of your lecture notes that answer your mirror question(s). If possible, have a friend play the role of the instructor and read the lecture to you as you take notes.

I would like to begin my presentation this morning by comparing three major perspectives on human learning. Each of these perspectives has generated a great deal of research on human learning.

Contemporary behaviorists view environmental factors in terms of stimuli and resultant behavior in terms of responses. They attempt to demonstrate that behavior is controlled by environmental contingencies of external reward or reinforcement, which are links between behavioral responses and their effects (or stimuli). Teachers who accept the behavioral perspective assume that the behavior of students is a response to their past and present environment and that all behavior is learned. For example, classroom troublemakers "learn" to be disruptive because of the attention (reinforcement) they get from peers; withdrawn students "learn" that their environment does not reinforce gregariousness, and they become reserved and silent. As a result, any behavior can be analyzed in terms of its reinforcement history. The logical extension of the behavioral principle of learning is a method to change or modify behavior. The teacher's responsibility, therefore, is to construct an environment in which the probability of reinforcing students for correct or proper behavior is maximized. This goal is best attained by carefully organizing and presenting information in a designed sequence.

In contrast to the behavioral perspective, cognitive psychologists focus more on the learner as an active participant in the teaching–learning process. Those who adhere to this perspective believe that teachers can be more effective if they know what knowledge the learner already has acquired and what the learner is thinking about during instruction. More specifically, the cognitive approach tries to understand how information is processed and structured in an individual's memory. Many cognitive psychologists believe that teachers should instruct students in ways to use techniques or strategies to learn more effectively. Weinstein and Mayer (1986) state that effective instruction "includes teaching students how to learn, how to remember, how to think, and how to motivate themselves" (p. 315).

Humanistic psychologists believe that how a person feels is as important as how the person behaves or thinks. They describe behavior from the standpoint of the believer rather than of the observer, and they are especially concerned with "self-actualization"—the growth of persons in whatever area they choose. The humanistic teacher is interested in creating an educational environment that fosters self-development, cooperation, and positive communication because of the belief that these conditions will foster greater learning.

(Adapted from Dembo, 1994).

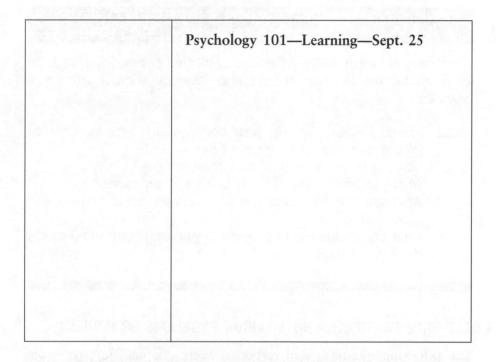

Psychology 101—Learning—Sept. 25

HOW CAN I ASK GOOD MIRROR QUESTIONS?

When students first begin writing mirror questions, most of the questions tend to be factual. As you write and answer mirror questions, it is important that the level of your questions reflect the same level of the instructor's focus. For example, if the main purpose of a lecture is to compare and contrast differences in major wars during the last century, the instructor is likely to focus on content that will be answered by such questions as: "What is the difference between . . . ?" "What were the causes of . . . " "What might have happened if . . . ?" However, if most of your questions focus on factual information like: "What is . . . ?" or "Who are . . . ?" you are going to miss the major focus of the lecture and may not be properly prepared for the examination.

There are two broad levels of questions: lower level and higher level. Lower level questions tend to focus on factual information and ask you to retrieve information that was previously presented. They involve responses regarding *facts*, *dates*, *terms*, or *lists*. Higher level questions require you to *apply* the information that you learned in a new situation, solve problems, *analyze* information, *develop* a novel plan or solution, or *make judgments* about the value of the information.

EXERCISE 9.3: IDENTIFYING DIFFERENT LEVELS OF QUESTIONS IN LECTURES

Directions: For each of the questions identified below, write an *L* for lower level question or an *H* for higher level question in the space provided.

___1. Should Timothy McVeigh have been given the death sentence for the bombing in Oklahoma City?

___2. How many individuals died in the bombing?

___3. What materials were used to make the explosives?

___4. What are the differences in trial procedures in federal and state courts?

___5. What arguments would you use if you had to defend Timothy McVeigh in court?

HOW DO I DEAL WITH PARTICULAR NOTE-TAKING PROBLEMS OR ISSUES?

The following questions and responses were adapted, in part, from Heiman and Slomianko (1993) and McWhorter (1995):

Should I copy over my notes?

No. Recopying notes is primarily a rehearsal strategy that requires little thinking. Your time is better spent writing and answering questions about the notes using the system described in this chapter.

Should I take notes in my textbook?

Generally, no. Most lectures do not follow information directly from textbooks. Therefore, you will miss information by trying to locate the material in the textbook. One exception to this advice is books in literature classes. If the instructor refers to specific lines or pages while discussing a play, poem, or novel, notations in the margin may be helpful.

Should I tape record the lecture?

Generally, no. Listening to the lecture again takes up considerable time from other more useful study methods like organizing the information. However, if English is not your primary language and you have serious difficulty following lectures, you might consider taping lectures for a short time until you improve your language skills.

Should I try to listen and not write when I don't understand something?

No. Keep taking notes; use blanks to indicate that you missed some material and question marks indicating that you didn't understand something. Ask another student or your instructor to explain material you didn't understand.

I can't write as fast as my professors talk. What should I do?

Do not try to take verbatim notes. Paraphrase and use abbreviations. Insert blank lines and ask a student in your class for the notes you missed.

How can I better concentrate on the lecture?

Sit in the front of the room. Be certain to preview assignments. Think about questions you may be expected to answer on exams.

How do I deal with an instructor who constantly wanders from one topic to another?

Be sure to read the textbook to discover organizing principles, and attempt to organize notes after class. Compare your notes with other students.

What can I do about all the technical terms in the lecture that I can't spell?

Write them phonetically, the way they sound; fill in correct spellings during editing.

Table 9.1 presents a summary of the note-taking procedures discussed in this chapter.

TABLE 9.1

Procedures for Note Taking

Before the Lecture

1. Complete assigned readings before class.
2. Review notes from the previous class.
3. Bring all necessary materials (notebook, pen, handouts). Prepare at least 20 sheets of note paper in the following format: Draw a line down a sheet of paper allowing for a 3-inch margin on the left-hand side of the page. Write lecture notes in the wide right-hand column and reserve the 3-inch margin for questions derived from the lecture notes.
4. Sit in the front of the room, if possible.
5. Date and number each day's notes.

During the Lecture

1. Listen carefully to the instructor and take notes that focus on main ideas and supporting details. Be alert for *signals* that indicate the importance of information.
2. Condense the main ideas and supporting details into short phrases or sentences using abbreviations whenever possible.
3. Use an indenting form for writing notes. Start main points at the margin and indent secondary ideas and supporting details. Further indent material that is subordinate to secondary points.
4. When the instructor moves to another idea or topic, show this shift by skipping two lines.

After the Lecture

1. Add any important information you remember the instructor saying but you didn't write down.
2. Locate information you didn't understand in the lecture from the instructor, another student, or the textbook.
3. Play a form of academic *Jeopardy* and think about notes as answers to questions. Shortly after class, read the notes over carefully. Write the questions that the notes answer in the left-hand column of your note paper.
4. Once a question has been identified, return to the lecture-note text and *underline a key term or phrase that triggers an answer to the question.*
5. Read the key terms or phrases to verify that they help you recall the information in the notes. If the key terms or phrases trigger only partial answers to the questions, underline more information.
6. Cover the notes with a blank sheet of paper and attempt to answer questions.
7. If appropriate, construct representations to depict the organization of the material in the lecture.
8. Write a summary question for the total lecture at the end of your lecture notes for the day.

Key Points

1. Taking good notes and remembering what was written also involves activities in three important stages—before, during, and after the lecture.
2. Use an indenting form for writing notes. Start main points at the margin and indent secondary ideas and supporting details.
3. Be alert for signals that indicate the importance of information.
4. Think about notes as answers to questions.
5. Write mirror questions (in complete sentences) that the notes answer in the lefthand column of the note paper.
6. Use lower and higher level questions.
7. Once a question has been identified, return to the lecture-note text and underline a key term or phrase that triggers an answer to the question.
8. Write a summary question(s) that reflects the theme or main ideas of the total lecture.
9. Use mirror and summary questions to prepare for exams.

Follow-up Activities

1. Use the Self-management Process to Become a Better Note Taker

Complete the following self-study during a period of 2 to 3 weeks. Your report should include each of the following processes and should be approximately five to eight typed pages in length. See Appendix A for detailed information on how to conduct a self-management study.

Self-observation and evaluation. How effective is my note-taking strategy? Do I need to change the way I take notes? If yes, what problem(s) do I encounter? What are the symptoms of my problem (i.e., when, where and how often does my problem occur)? How much of an impact does this problem have on my academic performance? What factors (e.g., beliefs, perceptions, feelings, physiological responses, or behaviors) contribute to this problem(s)? What do I need to change to reduce or eliminate my problem(s)?

Goal setting and strategic planning. What are my goals? What strategies will I implement to improve my note taking? When will I use these strategies? How will I record my progress?

Strategy implementation and monitoring. What strategies did I use to improve my note taking? When did I use these strategies? What method(s) did I use to record my progress (e.g., documents, charts, logs, tally sheets, checklists, or recordings)? When did I use these methods? How and when did I monitor my progress to determine if my new note-taking strategy was working? What changes, if any, did I make along the way?

Strategic-outcome monitoring. Did I attain the goal(s) I set for myself? Have the modifications in my note taking improved my academic performance? What strategies were the most and least effective? What changes, if any, do I need to make in the future?

2. Analyze Note-Taking Experiences

Identify your easiest and most difficult class in which you take notes. Explain why you selected these classes and what steps you have taken (or will take) to deal with the problems in the "most difficult" class.

Comments:

_____

_____

_____

_____

_____

_____

3. Edit and Review Your Notes

Select lecture notes from a class you took recently. Rewrite the notes to fit the format discussed in this chapter. Submit both sets of notes and write an analysis of the difference in the two sets of notes.

4. Analyze Your Instructors' Clues for Signaling Important Information

Instructors differ in the way they signal important information. Identify each of your instructors and list the verbal or nonverbal clues that he or she uses to signal main ideas or other important information presented in lectures.

Instructor   **Clues**

_____

_____

_____

_____

_____

_____

5. Compare Notes With Another Student

Select a lecture at which another student in your class was in attendance and took notes. Compare the number of main ideas identified by each of you and the mirror questions written after the lecture. Discuss how the two sets of notes differ.

Model answer to Exercise 9.2

	Psychology 101—Learning—Sept. 25

What are the differences between the beh., cog, and humanistic theories of learning?	Behaviorist
	    S and R
	    beh. controlled by environ.
	    <u>all beh. is learned reinforcement</u>
	
	Cognitive
	    learner as active partic.
	    <u>information processing</u>
	    teach sts. how to learn
	Humanistic
	    self-actualization
	    develop educ. Environ.
	    <u>feeling is important</u>

Answers to Exercise 9.3

1. H   2. L   3. L   4. H   6. H.

10

Preparing for Exams

Although I titled this chapter "Preparing for Exams," an alternative title could be "Studying." All of the self-management processes discussed thus far are factors that can be used to plan and implement more effective study sessions (Zimmerman, 1998a). For example, to self-manage academic studying, students must determine whether they will study and deal with the potential distractions and anxiety interfering with studying (motivation), plan how much time to spend studying (time management), determine how to study (methods of learning), select or create effective environments for study (physical environment), and ask instructors and other students to assist in learning (social environment).

Early in a term, most instructors remind students of a scheduled exam. It is not uncommon for many students to think: "Already . . . the class just started!" If you were to listen in on a conversation about exam preparation, you might hear the following: One student mentions she will set aside next Sunday to study, the day before the exam; a second student mentions that he began studying last week; a third student asks about organizing a study group. When the students begin talking about what material

237

to study, one student remarks that he only plans to study his notes, because he heard that the instructor stresses lecture notes over textbook readings; a second student states that she hopes much of the test comes from the textbook, because she did not take many notes and has difficulty understanding the notes she took; a third student mentions that she plans to review the summary section of each chapter of the book and read through her notes a few times.

Students use a variety of study strategies for exam preparation. These strategies lead to different levels of success. In general, it is difficult to become a successful student by selectively studying course material. Yes, at times, some students will correctly predict the questions on an exam, but at other times, they will have wished they took a different approach. My advice is to approach exam preparation with the notion that all relevant content will be reviewed. In this way, you will be prepared no matter what the instructor asks on an exam.

Sometimes a student can acquire some valuable tips from friends about exam preparation. However, students' comments also can negatively impact self-confidence if a student assumes that other students better understand the content or know more about exam preparation. Although it is helpful to discuss the content or even study with classmates, be sure to develop your own plan for success on an exam.

Each year I hear the following comment (although in different forms): "I can't believe this grade, I studied so hard!" or "I thought I really knew this stuff, I can't believe I didn't do well on the exam!" Remember the term—the *illusion of knowing*—introduced in chapter 2? The term describes the fact that some students *think* they know something when they really do not. Such an illusion occurs when students do not accurately test their knowledge to determine whether or not they understand and can recall the necessary content. Unfortunately, they wait for feedback from the instructor, who grades the exam, to find out whether or not they learned the material. An important aspect of exam preparation is to learn how to self-assess one's understanding of the course content. The primary method of self-assessment is predicting and answering questions. Simply stated: *If a student does not generate and answer questions during study sessions, he or she is not adequately preparing for an exam!*

Remember the discussion of the information-processing system, in chapter 2? The goal of learning is to move material into long-term memory, where it can be stored for retrieval. This goal can best be reached by using elaboration and organizational strategies rather than rehearsal strategies. Therefore, students who only use reciting, recopying, or rereading (i.e., rehearsal strategies) may have difficulty recalling information or answering higher level questions during an exam. An important goal of this chapter is to encourage students to use a variety of study strategies appropriate for the different types of questions asked on exams.

Finally, the material in chapters 10 and 11 is interrelated. You will learn that after you take an exam, you should evaluate the effectiveness of your preparation. As you learn more about taking exams, you should apply this knowledge to improving your preparation.

After studying this chapter, you will be able to develop and implement effective study plans for examinations.

EXERCISE 10.1: SELF-OBSERVATION: ASSESSING EXAM PREPARATION

Directions: Assess your current exam preparation strategies by checking the appropriate responses to each of the following questions. Think about why each of the questions is relevant to effective preparation and summarize your exam preparation strategies in the following space.

	Always	Sometimes	Never
1. Do you determine what content material is to be covered before you begin studying?			
2. Do you set goals for what you hope to accomplish each time you study?			
3. Do you set aside sufficient time to prepare for exams?			
4. Do you develop a study plan over a number of days?			
5. Do you identify the specific study strategies you will use in each of your study sessions?			
6. Do you select a quiet environment in which to study?			
7. Do you study in groups?			
8. Do you use study strategies other than rehearsal (e.g., reading over notes and textbooks, underlining content in textbooks, reciting definitions)?			

continued

	Always	*Sometimes*	*Never*
9. Do you review your mistakes on past exams?			
10. Do you write questions to answer while studying?			
11. Do you combine information from your lecture notes and texts together according to themes or topics when you study?			

Summary Statement:

_____

_____

_____

_____

_____

_____

HOW DO I DEVELOP A STUDY PLAN?

Successful athletes, musicians, artists, and writers often develop plans for how they will practice, prepare for performances, or make progress toward attaining their goals. For example, novelists often write many outlines and develop scenes and characters before they begin writing. Musicians set daily practice session goals and work carefully on separate passages of a composition. Students also plan for their performances, which are judged by examinations of the knowledge acquired in their courses. Therefore, sufficient time must be given to developing a "game plan" to prepare for each examination.

An effective study plan includes *what, how*, and *when* content will be reviewed. It organizes and separates material into small sections for study over a period of days. In addition, it includes a variety of learning and study strategies that will help the student respond correctly to both lower and higher level questions. As you might expect, time management plays an important role in the development of a study plan.

I will now review a six-step procedure for how you can develop a study plan for each of your scheduled exams:

Step 1: Determine the Content Coverage and Question Format of the Exam

Exam questions come from many different sources. Omitting any of the following sources can result in incomplete information for exam preparation:

Course Syllabus. The course syllabus is a good place to start to determine the specific course content covered during the term. It is normally distributed at the first or second class session and includes all (or most of) the assignments (e.g., textbook chapters, exercises, and papers), as well as exam dates. Some instructors provide more information than others in a syllabus. This is why syllabi can range from about 2 pages to 10 pages. A review of the course syllabus will help you determine the exact content covered on the exam. If there are questions about the information in the syllabus, they can be raised in class. This review will prevent you from realizing midway through an exam that you failed to study some of the content covered on the exam.

Textbook Chapters. After checking the textbook chapters covered on an exam, make sure the instructor did not announce any changes during the term. If the instructor failed to emphasize certain chapters or paperback books, do not assume they will not be covered on the exam. If you have questions, ask the instructor whether he or she will emphasize certain material in the course. Finally, assess how well you understand the material in each chapter and determine which chapters need more extensive study.

Lecture Notes. Review your notes to determine whether you have all the lecture notes. When notes are dated, it is easy to determine whether any notes are missing. If notes are missing or incomplete, borrow them from another student. Finally, ask your instructor or classmates questions about confusing aspects of your notes.

Previous Exams and Quizzes. Some instructors hand out copies of past exams, place them on reserve in the library, or allow students to review them in his or her office. If no mention is made of such exams, ask your instructor if it is possible to review an exam. The purpose of reviewing past exams is to identify possible topics or issues that are likely to appear on future exams. Although reviewing past exams can be helpful, do not assume that the exam coverage will be the same. Instructors often change textbooks or course content, and their exams reflect these changes.

The following are some questions you might want to consider when reviewing past exams: Does the instructor tend to ask questions from all the major areas in the course, or does he or she tend to focus on specific areas? Do the questions reflect both the lecture and text, or is one source of information favored over the other? What type of questions are asked? Do they tend to be factual, or do they ask you to engage in higher level thinking such as solving problems, giving opinions, or analyzing information?

Instructor's Handouts. Do not limit your review to lecture notes and textbook reading. Many instructors pass out summaries, outlines, lists of terms, sample problems, maps, or charts that provide information for exams. Any information that your instructor gives you is likely to be important. Date and label handouts as you receive them. The labeling should identify the lecture topic to which the material corresponds. It is important to place these handouts in your notes so you do not lose them.

Information From Other Students. Did you miss any lectures during the term? Is there information you do not understand? Do not hesitate to ask students in your class questions about the course content. In addition, consider whether you could benefit from participating in group study sessions.

Information From the Last Class Before the Exam. Review the content covered for the exam before class so you will be better prepared to ask questions in class and understand the instructor's reply to other students' questions. Although students can learn important information about a course from each lecture, the last lecture before an examination is especially important for several reasons. First, instructors may give a brief overview of the exam by discussing both content and format (i.e., number of essay and objective test questions). Second, instructors may provide last-minute suggestions, such as "Pay particular attention to . . . " or "Be sure to look over . . . " Third, instructors may provide important information by the manner in which they reply to students' questions.

Information about the format of the exam can be helpful in determining the study strategies selected. Is the exam a combination of essay and objective questions (e.g., multiple-choice or true–false), or will the exam include only one type of question? The instructor can cover a broad field of knowledge by using objective questions, because they can be answered quickly. However, essay questions usually cover a limited field of knowledge, because they take longer to answer. The selection of study strategies for an exam depends both on the format and nature of the course content. For example, focusing on the summary questions after each lecture may be more important in preparing for an essay exam; whereas focusing on factual information may be more important when studying for certain objective exams.

Step 2: Organize and Separate the Content Into Parts

Many students open their textbooks and notes and proceed sequentially through the content. They focus on dates, facts, formulae, or definitions found in textbooks or lecture notes. Often, studying textbooks and studying lecture notes are viewed as separate activities. The problem in this approach is that it is easy to lose sight of the important ideas and issues in the course. An alternative approach is to use *thematic study*, which involves organizing all relevant content, no matter where it is found, around specific topics or themes. For example, a unit covering different wars in history might be organized as follows: causes, major battles, military leaders, and political and economic consequences (repeatable categories in a matrix). All the factual information could be studied within each of the repeatable categories.

The advantage of thematic study is that it forces students to determine which topics are most important and to integrate the information from lectures and chapters in the textbook. Here are some suggestions for using this approach (McWhorter, 1996): First, review the course syllabus, introductory chapter, and lecture notes to determine whether the instructor or textbook author identified themes or topics for the course. A review of the table of contents in a textbook can be helpful in identifying themes. Second, identify how the lectures relate to the material in the textbook. Finally, try to integrate related material from the textbook and lectures.

As illustrated in the earlier example of the study of wars in history, one useful way to determine major topics and themes is to use representations for as much of the material as possible. Such representations can be helpful in organizing the material and provide help in generating possible exam questions.

Step 3: Identify Specific Study Strategies

Table 10.1 identifies a list of learning strategies that can be used in a study plan. You may use one or more of these strategies in the preparation for exams depending on the difficulty of the material and your own experience as to which strategies work best for you.

Predicting Exam Questions.   You will notice that the major study strategies identified in Table 10.1 focus on the prediction of exam questions. If you follow the procedures for reading texts and taking lectures notes described in chapters 8 and 9, respectively, you already have been generating and answering questions related to the content in your courses. Therefore, you do not have to start from scratch. Your mirror and summary questions for each lecture will be useful for study. The questions in your textbook or the self-generated questions from the headings are another useful source. Finally, the representations developed after reading or note taking can help you generate questions. If you

TABLE 10.1
STUDY STRATEGIES FOR USE IN A STUDY PLAN

Preparation Strategies	Review Strategies
Create representations and identify possible exam questions	Replicate representations or answer self-generated questions
Outline	Recite main points from outline
Summarize	Recite out loud
Predict essay questions	Answer essay questions
List steps in a process	Recite steps from memory
Read textbook questions	Answer textbook questions
Identify self-generated questions from textbooks	Answer self-generated questions
Prepare material for study group	Explain material to group members
Make question cards	Recite answers
Make formula cards	Practice writing formulas
Make problem cards	Work problems
Identify mirror and summary questions from notes	Answer mirror and summary questions from notes
Make self-tests	Take self-tests

Adapted from Van Blerkom (1994).

have not developed such representations, you should consider doing so during your final preparation for an exam.

In earlier chapters, you were taught to write questions from your notes and turn headings in textbooks into questions. The purpose of this elaboration strategy was to help you become actively involved in the content so you would focus on the most relevant material when preparing for exams. The extra work that you did to complete these tasks will now pay off as you use these questions for self-testing.

The questions you formulated from your lecture notes and textbook material need to accurately cover the possible questions that could be asked on an exam. Remember that lower level questions involve responses regarding *facts*, *dates*, *terms*, or *lists*. Questions beginning with Who . . . ? What . . . ? When . . . ? and Where . . . ? are appropriate for lower level questions.

Higher level questions require you to: *apply* the information that you learned to a new situation, *solve* problems, *analyze* information, compare and contrast information, develop a novel *plan* or *solution*, or *make judgments* about the value of the information. The following examples are stems for higher level questions: Why . . . ? How . . . ? What if . . . ? How does A affect B? What are the advantages or disadvantages of . . . ? What are the strengths or weaknesses of . . . ? What are the differences between . . . ? What is your opinion of . . . ? Make a list of other higher level questions that could be asked on exams in the different courses you are taking.

Front of Card	Back of Card
What were the causes of ...	The causes were 1) 2) 3)
What are the differences between_____and_____?	The differences are 1) 2) 3)
Convert .742 kg to grams	.742 kg × 1000g/1kg = 742g
Learning strategies	Techniques or methods students use to acquire information. Rehearsal (e.g. underlining) Elaboration (e.g., analogy) Organizational (e.g., outline and map) Certain learning strategies are more effective in moving information to LTM.

FIG. 10.1.   Examples of different types of study cards.

Figure 10.1 presents different types of study cards students can develop for different courses. Note that the study cards can include both lower and higher level questions. A study card can focus on one major point or can combine a great deal of information about a topic. In this way, you can reduce the number of cards you need to produce.

When you approach the last evening before an exam, you should not be rereading the textbook or class notes, but instead use the representations you developed along with questions, note cards, and summaries as your primary review material.

Step 4. Identify the Amount of Time Needed for Each Strategy

Different study strategies involve different amounts of time. For example, making study cards to review definitions of terms often requires less time than developing a representation of content in a chapter or summarizing a short story. Therefore, after you determine how you will study for an exam, it is important to estimate the amount of time needed. No one can accurately predict the exact time needed for projected study sessions. Base your projections on previous experience and modify them as you acquire greater skill in using a strategy.

Step 5: Allocate Time for Each Study Strategy in a Weekly Schedule

Remember the discussion of massed versus distributed practice in chapter 2. Although mass practice may be effective in learning a large amount of information in a short time, it is a poor method of learning if retention of information is the goal. Think about the examinations on which you used massed practice. How much of the content did you remember a few days after the examination?

For each exam you take, consider how much time each of the study strategies you plan to use will take and then identify time in your weekly schedule for each of the strategies. For example, in some cases you may need 1 or 2 days to prepare for short quizzes or exams, whereas for more detailed exams, you may need a week or more to prepare.

Step 6: Modify the Plan as Necessary

The fact that you developed a study plan does not mean you always will follow it as planned. Students constantly make changes in their initial plans, because of an underestimation or overestimation of time needed to study different content. Many different factors influence the need for change, such as: the unavailability of certain study material, the inability to study because of interruptions and distractions, or the realization that you need to review certain material that you do not understand or cannot recall.

The following student reaction illustrates that learning any new strategy takes time. How would you respond to the question asked in the last sentence?

Student Reflections

I have read the chapter on test preparation and I am trying to implement the strategy of generating and answering questions for my next exam in anthropology. I am outlining the required chapters, studying the vocabulary words, and generating some questions that I think will be on the exam. I think I am doing everything possible to prepare for the exam. Why don't I feel confident? There are so many possible questions that could be on the exam. I don't know if I am generating enough questions. My instructor makes it sound like test preparation is easy when it is not. I am never sure what an instructor will ask on an exam. Everything seems important to me! How do I deal with this situation?

AN EXAMPLE OF A STUDY PLAN

Figure 10.2 presents a study plan developed by a student in a child development course. As you review the procedures, think about how you could develop your own plans for exams in different courses.

Day	Study Strategy	Time	Completed
Monday	Reread Chapter 10 and generate questions from headings (A)	2 hrs	X
	Develop study cards for key terms (B)		X
	Make a list of major research findings (C)		X
Tuesday	Answer questions generated from Chs. 10 and 11 and related lecture notes (D)	2 hrs	X
	Review study cards (E)		X
Wednesday	Develop three representations from content and generate and answer possible exam questions (F)	$1\frac{1}{2}$	X
	Review lecture material not emphasized in textbook (G)		X
Thursday	Review summary section at the end of each chapter (H)	3 hrs	X
	Make a short list of possible essay questions from summary questions, lectures, representations, and textbook (focus on theories and developmental characteristics) (I)		X
	Outline or develop representations to assist in responding to the questions (J)		X
	Review study cards (K)		X
	Review list of major research findings (L)		X
Friday	Take exam		

FIG. 10.2. Janis' study plan.

Content Coverage and Question Format

Janis prepared for an examination in Human Development, which included 30 multiple-choice and 4 short-essay questions. Her instructor announced that the exam would include two chapters on adolescence development and related lecture notes. Janis read one of the chapters thoroughly and skimmed the second chapter. She realized from her dated notes that she needed to obtain a copy of one day's notes from her friend.

Organize the Content for Study

The two chapters and lecture notes were on the physical, intellectual, personality, and social development in adolescence. Janis reviewed the textbook and lecture notes and decided that the best organizing topics or themes for her review should be based on the four topics. The textbook was already organized around these topics, and the lecture notes needed to be reorganized to fit this organization. Because she used a three-ring binder for all her class notes, it was easy for her to place the notes in a different order from which they were originally presented.

Based on meeting with her instructor and her review of the course syllabus, Janis decided that she needed to learn the (a) key terms found in the readings and lecture notes, (b) important research findings, (c) theories of development, and (d) typical behavior of adolescence in each of the four areas.

Identify Specific Study Strategies

Janis decided to make study cards for all the major terms in the two chapters, as well as the terms introduced by her instructor. The definitions were written in her own words rather than verbatim from the text so she was sure that she understood each term. She also added examples, when appropriate, to enhance her recall of specific course content. For example, one key term was *personal fable,* which is defined as a belief in adolescence that one is special, unique, and not subject to the rules that govern the rest of the world. Janis wrote on the back of the study card: belief that one is special such that bad things affect others, not oneself (e.g., other people have sex and get pregnant, but not you).

One of the topics discussed in the readings and lecture notes was eating disorders. She decides it would be important to compare the three types of eating disorders—obesity, anorexia, and bulimia—in a matrix form. Figure 10.3 includes the matrix she developed.

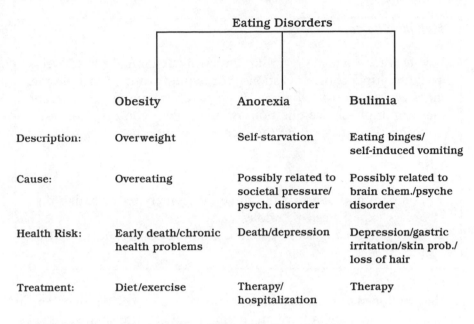

FIG. 10.3.   A matrix depicting different eating disorders.

From the matrix, she identified both multiple-choice and essay questions that could be asked about the material. The following are examples of some of the questions she generated and answered in her study notes from the representation:

Multiple-Choice

Which one of the following eating disorders is difficult to treat without hospitalization?

a. Obesity
b. Anorexia
c. Bulimia
d. All of the above

Self-starvation is a major problem in adolescents with

a. Gonorrhea
b. Anorexia
c. Bulimia
d. Herpes

---

continued

Multiple-Choice

If you are studying in a group and your assignment is to write a few multiple-choice questions, you would want to include the incorrect responses. However, if you are attempting to generate many multiple-choice questions on your own, you may not want to spend the time writing the incorrect responses.

Essay

1. Compare and contrast the three different types of eating disorders experienced by adolescents.
2. Discuss the causes for different eating disorders identified in adolescence.

She developed a second matrix comparing physical development in males and females and a third on common sexually transmitted diseases. Finally, she constructed a sequence representation on different stages of moral development. She found the sequence helpful in understanding and recalling this important theory of development. In each case, she attempted to predict test questions that might appear on the exam.

Because she carefully read, generated questions from headings, and underlined the answers for the first chapter, she only had to review the answers to the questions. However, for the second chapter, she needed to reread the material, generate questions, and underline the answers in her textbook.

Finally, she reviewed the questions generated from her notes and attempted to identify material that was not covered in her questions from her textbook. Because her instructor was interested in cultural differences in adolescent development, there was considerable material in the lecture notes that was not included in the textbook.

Identify the Amount of Time Needed for Each Strategy

In determining the amount of time needed for each strategy, Janis considered (a) her experience and knowledge using a strategy and (b) the time she thought she needed to spend on each strategy. For example, she believed that writing definitions for the key terms on study cards could be done in 30 minutes, but developing three representations could take $1^1/_2$ hours. Because she turned headings into questions for one chapter, she believed that the chapter could be reviewed in 20 minutes. However, she did not generate questions when she read the second chapter. She needed to reread the chapter and write questions, which she estimated would take at least an hour.

Allocate Time for Each Study Strategy in a Weekly Schedule

Janis was taking four other courses and could not stop reading and studying in her other courses to prepare for her child development course. For example, she also had a math quiz and had to write a short essay for English. Her task, therefore, was to integrate her exam preparation with her other learning and study activities.

Janis labeled all the activities in her study plan from A to I. This labeling allowed her to identify each activity in her weekly schedule by a letter. Using this procedure, she did not have to recopy the description of the study activity in her weekly schedule. She simply referred to her study plan when it was time for the activity. Notice in Fig. 10.2 that she prioritized her study sessions by starting with the chapter she did not carefully read. Janis also included time during the day to study for her child development exam so that she would have some time each evening for her other courses.

Janis' study plan was presented to provide a concrete example for how to develop such a plan. Such plans can greatly differ from course to course and student to student, depending on the nature of the content and ability of the student. For example, a study plan for a math course would involve the identification of the different type of problems studied in the unit with problem solving as the major study activity. In a science course, the study strategies would focus both on learning the content knowledge and solving problems.

Janis did not choose to study in a group for this exam but has formed study groups for other exams in the same and other courses she is taking. In general, she has found group study very helpful in reviewing answers to questions and reviewing solutions to problems.

Finally, once you start developing your own plans, modify the format to fit your own needs. The most important factor is not the format of the plan, but the selection and use of learning and study strategies to improve your retention and retrieval of information on the exam. Table 10.2 provides a summary of the procedures for developing a study plan.

TABLE 10.2

Procedures for Developing a Study Plan	
Procedures	*Examples*
1. Determine the content coverage and question format of the exam	"I never miss the class before an exam because the instructor usually reviews the content coverage. I also take the time to check that I have all the needed resources (i.e., books, notes, and handouts) before I begin studying."

continued

TABLE 10.2

Procedures for Developing a Study Plan *(Continued)*	
Procedures	*Examples*
2. Organize and separate the content into parts	"I have identified six different types of problems I need to learn how to solve in chemistry. I'll work on the problems in three different study sessions."
3. Identify specific study strategies	"I decide which study strategy is most helpful for the different content I must learn. For example, I prefer to use representations for more complex material and note cards for factual content."
4. Estimate the amount of time needed for each strategy	"During my first term in college I underestimated I underestimated how much time I needed to review course content. I now begin to study for exams much earlier because I can't review a large amount of content in a day or two."
5. Allocate time for each study strategy in a weekly schedule	"I try to schedule time during the day and evening when I have an exam so I have time to complete my other assignments."
6. Modify the plan as needed	"I never realized how many unexpected events occur that interfere with my study time. I review my study plan each night and make needed changes."

Key Points

1. The primary activity during study is to predict and answer potential exam questions.
2. A student needs to prepare for different levels of questions on an exam.
3. A study plan should be developed for each exam.
4. Different types of study strategies should be included in a study plan, especially elaboration and organizational strategies.
5. Representations can be a useful method for generating test questions.
6. Time management is an important factor in implementing the activities in a study plan.
7. A student should focus on review material (i.e., note cards, representations, questions, and answers) during the last day(s) before an exam, rather than rereading books and notes.

Follow-up Activities

1. Use the Self-management Process to Improve Exam Preparation

Complete the following self-study during a period of 2 to 3 weeks. Your report should include each of the following processes and should be approximately five to eight typed pages in length. See Appendix A for detailed information on how to conduct a self-management study.

Self-evaluation and monitoring. How effective are my current exam preparation (i.e., study) strategies? Do I need to change the way I plan and study for exams? If yes, what problem do I encounter? What are the symptoms of my problem (i.e., When, where and how often does my problem occur)? How much of an impact does this have on my academic performance? What factors (e.g., beliefs, perceptions, feelings, physiological responses, or behaviors) contribute to this problem? What do I need to change to reduce or eliminate my problem(s)?

Goal setting and strategic planning. What are my goals? What strategies will I implement to improve my exam preparation? When will I use these strategies? How will I record my progress?

Strategy-implementation and monitoring. What strategies did I use to improve my exam preparation? When did I use these strategies? What method(s) did I use to record my progress (e.g., documents, charts, logs, tally sheets, check-lists, or recordings)? When did I use these methods? How and when did I monitor my progress to determine if my new exam preparation plan was working? What changes, if any, did I make along the way?

Strategic-outcome monitoring. Did I attain the goal(s) I set for myself? Have the modifications in my exam preparation improved my academic performance? What strategies were the most and least effective? What changes, if any, do I need to make in the future?

2. Develop a Study Plan

Select a study partner and develop a study plan for an examination on one chapter in this book. Identify the different strategies you used in your plan and compare it with the plan of another pair of students.

3. Develop Questions From a Representation

A student developed the following representation in a physics course. Generate two multiple-choice and two essay questions that an instructor could ask from this representation.

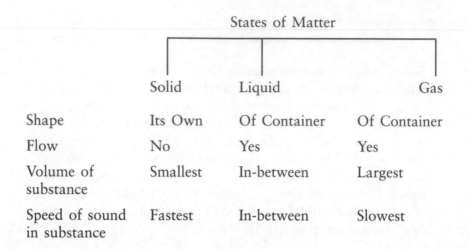

	Solid	Liquid	Gas
Shape	Its Own	Of Container	Of Container
Flow	No	Yes	Yes
Volume of substance	Smallest	In-between	Largest
Speed of sound in substance	Fastest	In-between	Slowest

4. Compare Study Plans

Develop a study plan for a science or math course and compare it with a study plan for a course in the humanities or the social sciences. Discuss how the study plans differ.

11

Taking Exams

Now that you have learned how to prepare for exams, you are ready to improve your test-taking strategies. Although you will learn a number of strategies to help you succeed on exams, it is important to remember that these strategies are most effective when you prepare properly for an exam. Simply stated: *Test-taking strategies cannot substitute for ineffective exam preparation.*

I will focus on two different types of test questions—*objective* and *essay*. Objective tests include true–false, completion, matching, and multiple-choice questions. These questions require students to select correct answers from given choices or to supply an answer limited to a word or phrase. On the other hand, essay questions require students to construct their own responses to questions. Most instructors use combinations of these two major categories of questions.

How many times have you heard the following statements: "I really know the material, but I am a poor test taker," "The test was tricky," "I really knew that question, but I misread it," or " I knew the answer, but I did not organize my response adequately." Although many instructors often will empathize with your predicaments about taking tests, they grade exams on what was checked, circled, underlined, or written. It is your performance that is evaluated, not your intentions, beliefs, or test-taking strategies.

Think about the tests you have taken during your school experience. What type of tests give you some difficulty? Make a list of some of the characteristics of tests that have irritated you at some time during your academic career. What strategies could you use to improve your performance? It is important to learn from exams. The best way to accomplish this goal is to review past exams. Although many instructors will not allow students to keep their exams, they will review them individually with students. Many students do not take the opportunity to review exams, because they incorrectly conclude that they should focus on future rather than past exams. However, by understanding why errors were made in past exams, students can improve strategies for taking future exams.

Finally, all the information in this chapter concerning taking exams also is helpful when writing and answering test questions in preparing for examinations. For example, the more you practice writing good essay responses before an exam, the more likely you will be able to demonstrate the same good responses on actual exams.

After studying this chapter, you will be able to use test-taking strategies to improve performance on objective and essay questions.

EXERCISE 11.1: SELF-OBSERVATION: ASSESSING TEST-TAKING STRATEGIES

Directions: Assess your current test-taking strategies by checking the appropriate responses to each of the following questions. Think about why each of the questions is relevant to successful performance on exams and write a summary statement about your test-taking strategies in the space provided:

	Always	Sometimes	Never
1. Do you preview your entire exams before beginning?			
2. Do you allocate time for each section of your exams before beginning?			
3. Do you carefully read the directions before beginning?			

	Always	Sometimes	Never
4. Do you carefully read all of the response options in multiple-choice questions before selecting the best response?			
5. Do you outline or represent content for essay questions before you begin writing?			
6. Does test anxiety influence your performance on exams?			
7. Do you change a large number of correct answers to incorrect responses?			
8. Do you proofread your responses to essay questions?			
9. Do you review your responses to the exam before turning it in?			
10. Do you review past exams whenever possible to identify test-taking errors and correct them prior to your next test situation?			

Summary Statement:

_____

_____

_____

_____

_____

WHAT STRATEGIES CAN I USE TO ANSWER OBJECTIVE TEST QUESTIONS?

Before I review specific test-taking strategies for different types of objective questions, it is important to review some general strategies to use for all objective questions (Urman 1982):

How Should You Manage Your Time?

To properly manage your time, adhere to the following guidelines:

- Always know how much time you have for the test.
- During the test, check the clock once in a while so that you will know how much time is left.
- When you begin the test:
  a. Answer questions you know first.
  b. Do *not* spend too much time on hard questions. Try not to get upset when you cannot answer a hard question.
  c. Skip hard questions and go back to them at the end of the test.
- When you have answered all the questions, go back and check your work.

How Should You Approach Each Question?

Use the following guidelines to approach each questions:

- If you do not know the answer to a question, read the question again.
- Read each of the answers.
- Mark the best answer only after you have read all of the answers.
- If you cannot figure out the answer to a question, guess.
- Be sure you mark *one answer for each question. Do not leave a question blank.*

When Should You Change an Answer?

You should change an answer:

- When you make a mistake.
- When you think another answer is better. A few minutes after you start taking a test, you sometimes get into the swing of the test and see things in the questions that you did not notice at first. After you finish the test and start going back over the questions, if a different answer seems better, *you should change your answer.*

Let's now review specific strategies for improving performance on true–false, matching, completion, and multiple-choice questions.

Strategies for True–False Questions

True–false questions are statements that you must decide are correct (true) or incorrect (false). Answer the following true–false questions by writing True or False in the space provided:

> Efficacy beliefs refer to a student's attitudes about an academic subject.

The answer to this question is false, because efficacy beliefs refer to the perceptions students' have about their ability to master a specific task.

The following are strategies for answering true–false questions:

- Carefully read key words such as *all, most, some, always, little, none, completely, better,* and *more.* A key word is a single word that can determine the overall meaning of the statement.
- Do not read too much into the statement. Base your response on the information provided in the statement, not additional knowledge you may know about the topic.
- Carefully read questions that have two-part statements. Remember that both parts of a statement must be true for you to correctly mark it "True."

Look at the following statement:

> Working memory is part of the information-processing system and can hold from 7 to 10 units of information at one time.

The first part of the statement is correct, because the working memory is part of the information-processing system. However, the second part of the statement is incorrect, because the capacity is from five to nine units of information. Thus, the response to the statement must be "False."

- Assume a statement is true unless you determine it to be false.
- Do not make decisions regarding a question based on the pattern or number of true and false statements. Incorrect responses to previous questions make such assessments inaccurate.
- If you do not know the answer, guess. You have a 50–50 chance of being correct.

EXERCISE 11.2: IDENTIFYING KEY WORDS

Directions: The following is a list of true–false questions that you might encounter in an introductory psychology course. The list is designed to point to commonly held misconceptions. The answer to each of these true–false questions is "False." Here's a clue: Each statement includes an "absolute" term that makes the statement false. An absolute term implies that there are no exceptions.

What you need to do is to pick out the key words that make them false. When you are finished, check your selections with the answer key at the end of the chapter (adapted from Deese & Deese, 1994, p. 62).

	Key Words
1. Geniuses are always neurotic.	
2. You can accurately tell what someone is thinking from facial expression.	
3. Cats can see in total darkness.	
4. There is a clear distinction between normal people and emotionally disturbed people.	
5. Your IQ is completely determined by heredity.	
6. It has been proven that animals can sense a coming earthquake.	
7. Slow learners remember better what they learn than fast learners.	
8. Darwin was the first person to advocate a theory of evolution.	
9. It is possible to classify everyone as either extroverted or introverted.	
10. Studying mathematics will necessarily make you a better thinker.	

Strategies for Matching Questions

Matching questions require you to associate or match one term or idea with another. A series of items appears in one column and the responses in another. You must select the option that is correctly associated with the item. The following is an example of such a question from a psychology course:

In the lefthand column are terms associated with different psychologists. For each term, choose a name from the righthand column and place the letter identifying it on the line preceding the number of the term. Each letter is used only once.

____ 1.	Self-actualization	a. Binet
____ 2.	Mastery learning	b. Bloom
____ 3.	Operant conditioning	c. Gagné
____ 4.	Assimilation	d. Maslow
____ 5.	Learning hierarchy	e. Piaget
		f. Skinner

The following are strategies for answering matching questions:

- Make sure you understand the directions for matching the items on the two lists. For example, determine whether you can use an answer more than once.
- First match the terms you know and cross them off the list before considering other terms on the list.
- Work from one side only. Crossing off items in both columns can be confusing.
- Eliminate any items on the answer list that clearly are not related to any of the terms.
- Draw a line through all terms that you have matched so you do not use any term more than once.

Strategies for Fill-in-the-Blank Questions

A completion, or fill-in-the-blank, item confronts students with a statement for which they must supply the missing word or phrase. This type of item emphasizes recall of previously learned material rather than recognition. An example of this type of item follows:

The Civil War began in _____.

The following are strategies for responding to fill-in-the-blank test items:

- Read the questions carefully and look for clue words (e.g., *as, an, the, and, these*), especially just before the blanks. Make your response grammatically correct.
- Be sure the answer makes sense.
- Do not leave any blanks. If you cannot think of the exact word, write a synonym for the word or phrase. You might receive partial credit for your response.

Strategies for Multiple-Choice Questions

The multiple-choice item contains a stem, which identifies a problem situation, and several alternatives, or options, which provide possible solutions to the problem. The alternatives include a correct answer and several plausible wrong answers, or distracters. The stem may be stated as a direct question or as an incomplete statement. An example of the two different types of multiple-choice questions follow. Circle the correct answer as you read each question:

Stem	1. Research has indicated that the students who are most successful in school tend to be
Alternatives	a. careful learners
	b. sincere learners
	c. passive learners
	d. active learners
Stem	2. Which of the following behaviors is not a rehearsal strategy?
Alternatives	a. underlining
	b. copying
	c. representing
	d. repeating

The answers to Questions 1 and 2 are d and c, respectively.

The following are strategies for answering multiple-choice test questions:

- Follow the directions to determine if there is any special information for answering the questions, such as a choice in the number of questions to be answered.
- Determine how much time you will allot for answering the questions. Use the rule: Percentage of total points = percentage of total time. This means that a question worth 20% of the exam would be allotted 20% of your test time.
- Read the stem and all of the choices before determining the best answer. Many students quickly select an answer without reading all the alternatives. In most multiple-choice tests, you are often asked to select the best answer. Therefore, you may conclude that there is more than one correct answer, but that one choice is the best answer.
- Skip difficult questions at the beginning of the exam.
- Review choices that are very similar. Many students complain that multiple-choice questions are "tricky," because two items

appear to be similar. Try the following strategy: Translate the similar choices into your own words and then analyze how the choices differ.

- Use caution when "all of the above" and "none of the above" are included as choices. Look carefully at each choice. If you can eliminate one choice, you can eliminate "all of the above" as a response. Likewise, if you are certain that one choice is correct, you can eliminate "none of the above" as a response.
- Review difficult questions before you hand in the exam.
- When in doubt, guess. If there is a penalty for guessing, still guess if you can omit at least two of the alternatives.
- Whenever possible, review exam results.

EXERCISE 11.3: TAKING A MULTIPLE-CHOICE EXAM

Directions: Use the strategies for taking multiple-choice exams by answering the following questions. Circle the letter representing the best response for each question.

1. The 5-minute plan is useful in dealing with
   a. test preparation.
   b. reading comprehension.
   c. note taking.
   d. procrastination.

2. The best study method involves
   a. reading over the assigned material many times.
   b. creating and answering questions about the material.
   c. spending at least 3 hours preparing for each exam.
   d. outlining as much of the material as possible.

3. One of the most important methods in time management is to
   a. wait for your parents to tell you when to study.
   b. listen carefully in class.
   c. spend an equal amount of time on all courses.
   d. prioritize tasks.

4. Improving your reading and note taking involves certain activities that must be completed
   a. before, during, and after reading and note taking.
   b. after learning.
   c. before exams.
   d. before quizzes and exams.

5. To improve your concentration, you need to analyze distractions in terms of
   a. school and home.
   b. internal and external.
   c. independent and dependent.
   d. simple and complex.

6. One of the major mistakes students make while reading is that they
   a. think of questions to answer as they read.
   b. underline as they read.
   c. try to determine what is important.
   d. constantly check on their understanding.

7. All of the following are related to good test preparation except
   a. identifying what must be learned.
   b. deciding how to study.
   c. rewriting notes so they are better understood.
   d. planning and organizing study time.

8. Good note taking involves
   a. writing down everything the teacher says.
   b. separating main ideas from supporting details.
   c. writing down only what the teacher says is important.
   d. recording only information that interests you.

9. One of the most important factors in becoming a more successful student is
   a. being liked by your teachers.
   b. having parents who remind you when to study.
   c. taking charge of your own learning and motivation.
   d. having smart parents.

10. When groups spend time encouraging members to summarize information on what was covered and discuss strategies for remembering the information, they are demonstrating the use of
    a. forming skills.
    b. functioning skills.
    c. formulating skills.
    d. fermenting skills.

WHAT STRATEGIES CAN I USE FOR ANSWERING ESSAY QUESTIONS?

The following strategies are helpful in answering essay questions.

Read the Directions Carefully and Do Exactly What Is Asked

Often students are given a choice of questions to answer, such as three out of four. If a student answers all the questions, only the first three would count. The following is an example of a question that needs to be carefully read:

Explain one effect of the Industrial Revolution on each of three of the following:

a. Transportation
b. Capitalism
c. Socialism
d. Population growth
e. Scientific research

Read Each Question Carefully to Determine What Is Expected in the Response

Circle key words (i.e., *list, describe, compare*, etc.) in each question and take notes as you read. Many questions require more than one type of response, and to receive full credit, the complete question must be answered. Observe the multiple responses required in each of the following questions:

List several categories of speeches and *describe* their primary functions and uses.

For the U.S. invasion of Panama, *discuss* the (a) *causes*, (b) *immediate effects*, and (c) long-term political *implications*.

Discuss how the Equal Rights Amendment was developed and explain why its passage has aroused controversy.

Another difficulty is that some students do not understand key terms in essay questions, and as a result, fail to do what is asked for in the question. The following list of key words and their meaning will be helpful in responding to essay questions (adapted from Jefferson County Schools, Colorado, 1983). Also, when you predict essay questions before exams, use the list to write different type of questions:

If you are asked to:	You should do the following:
Analyze	Break down or separate a problem or situation into separate factors or relationships.
Categorize	Place items under headings.
Classify	Place items in related groups, then name or title each group.
Compare	Tell how things are alike; use concrete examples.
Contrast	Tell how things are different; use supporting concrete examples.
Criticize	Make a judgment of the reading, work of art, or literature, and support your opinion.
Define	Give the meaning.
Describe	State the particulars in detail.
Diagram	Use pictures, graphs, or charts to show relationships of details to main ideas.
Discuss	Consider the various points of view by presenting all sides of the issue.
Distinguish	Tell how something is different from others similar to it.
Enumerate	List all possible items.
Evaluate	Make a judgment based on the evidence and support it; give the good and bad points.
Explain	Make clear and plain; give the reason or cause.
Illustrate	Give examples, pictures, charts, diagrams, or concrete examples to clarify your answer.
Interpret	Express your thinking by giving the meaning as you see it.
Justify	Give some evidence by supporting your statement with facts.
List	Present information in a numbered fashion.
Outline	Use a specific and shortened form to organize main ideas, supporting details, and examples.
Paraphrase	Put ideas in your own words.

If you are asked to:	You should do the following:
Predict	Present solutions that could happen if certain variables were present.
Prove	Provide factual evidence to back up the truth of the statement.
Relate	Show the relationship among concepts.
State	Establish by specifying. Write what you believe and back it with evidence.
Summarize	Condense the main points in the fewest words possible.
Support	Back up a statement with facts and proof.
Trace	Describe in steps the progression of something.
Verify	Confirm or establish the truth or accuracy of a point of view with supporting examples, evidence, and facts.

Determine How You Will Use Your Time

Read all the questions on the exam before responding to a single question. If all the questions are of equal difficulty and value (in terms of the number of points), you should divide your time equally for all the questions. For example, you should allot 30 minutes for three questions each worth 10 points on a 90-minute exam.

Budgeting time does not necessarily mean giving an equal amount of time to each question. You need to consider both the difficulty level and value of the question, in terms of the number of points. Determine how much time you need to spend and actually write down the time you began writing your response. If you finish a question early, you can use the extra time with another question.

Determine the Order in Which You Will Respond to the Questions

Individuals differ on the strategy they use to respond to questions. Some individuals like to begin with the easiest question first to build their confidence and reduce test anxiety. Other individuals prefer to begin with a more difficult question to get the worst part of the exam over. Still other individuals start with the question worth the most points to ensure they spend sufficient time on a question with the greatest payoff.

Organize Your Response by Making an Outline or Representation (Map)

Identify main ideas and supporting details or examples. When you begin writing, you can organize your essay by paragraphs, each with one main idea and several details or examples. This format makes it easy for the grader to follow your response.

Write Your Answer Following Specific Procedures

- Begin with an introductory paragraph that defines terms or describes how you will respond to the question.
- After the introductory paragraph, state your first main idea and back it up with supporting details (i.e., facts, dates, and examples). Go to the next main idea and do the same. Use the ideas, facts, and theories discussed in the course in your response to questions and be sure to support your arguments or point of view with factual information.
- Add transitional words such as first, second, third, moreover, in addition, also, however, finally, therefore, on the other hand, nevertheless.
- Add a summary.
- Proofread and revise your answer.

If Given an Opportunity, Review Your Exam Results

It is important that you analyze test errors, often called an error analysis, to improve future test performance. The answer to the following questions will help in your analysis: Why were points deducted from my answer? Did I answer all parts of the question? Can I easily identify my main ideas? Did I omit examples or supporting details? How well did I answer lower and higher level questions? What were the sources of my errors (e.g., lecture notes, textbooks, or handouts)? How will I adjust my study plan for the next exam? What study strategies were the most and least effective?

The student reporting the following experience indicates that analyzing test results can be beneficial.

Student Reflections

A couple of weeks ago I took a history exam. I used a number of new study strategies and went into the exam with the confidence that I was going to do well. I had studied hard and thought I knew all the important information to be covered. In fact, I came out of the exam with a smile on my face, thinking I had done a good job.

When I got the test back, I scored much lower than I expected and was very upset and disappointed. I went back to my dorm and complained to my roommate. He suggested that I speak to the instructor. After some resistance, I agreed to make an appointment with him to talk about my exam.

We went through each question on the exam. I received a very high score on the multiple-choice section, but missed points on the short essay questions. The answers I gave were correct, but they did not answer the specific questions. My instructor came to the conclusion that it wasn't that I didn't know the material, but that I didn't understand the depth that he expected in the responses to the questions. He gave me some hints for studying for my next exam. I left the meeting feeling much better about myself and the effort I put in studying for the exam.

EXERCISE 11.4: EVALUATING RESPONSES TO AN ESSAY QUESTION

Directions: Review the strategies for writing a response to an essay question and then read the responses to the following two essay questions. Take notes as your read and determine the strengths and weaknesses of each response.

> Discuss the proposed flat tax and describe what effects it might have on the U.S. economy.

Response 1

In light of the public's dissatisfaction with the size and scope of the tax code and the government's reach into the purses of individuals, families, and businesses, a growing number of economists and politicians are calling for the elimination of the present tax system and the institution of a flat tax. Such a tax would apply a single rate (15%, for example) to all taxpayers and would eliminate most or all deductions, exemptions, and the like. A state sales tax would be an example.

Proponents believe that most people would save money, because the effective tax rate would be lower than what it presently is, citizens would appreciate the ease of the new system (the tax form would be no larger than a postcard), and it would be fairer, as everyone would pay the same rate and the rich would be prevented from circumventing their responsibility of paying their fair share by taking advantage of loopholes in the present tax code.

Opponents claim that a single rate would be an undue burden on lower income citizens as they are ill prepared to pay a percentage of their income that could go to food or rent. In addition, they argue that if allowances are made for poverty status, medical and home mortgage interest deductions, and other kinds of exceptions, it will not take very long for the new system to resemble the old one.

The proposed flat tax would immediately change the nature and operation of tax accounting in this country. With deductions and exemptions eliminated, there would be no need for tax specialists looking for ways to save people and businesses money. On a larger scale, people may or may not become more honest in reporting their income. If they stand to pay less in taxes with a flat tax than they had in years past, then citizens probably will report their income. If, however, they stand to lose money because of the elimination of loopholes, then much of the nation's business transactions and economy may go underground.

In conclusion, the flat tax, although clearly simpler, is not considered by all to be fairer or an improvement on the present system. Although it may solve some problems (greatly simplifying the code, for example), other problems may arise and might even make things worse (loss of needed deductions, regressive effect on the poor). Ultimately, a flat tax will only succeed if people believe that they are keeping more of their income, that governmental services are not being curtailed, and that everyone is paying their fair share. Defining *fair share* is at the heart of the issue.

Response 2

The flat tax means that people will no longer have to spend long hours and lots of money trying to figure out how much they owe (or how much they should get back from) the government each year. Instead of some people paying nothing, others paying 28%, and still others paying 39% of their income, the flat tax would have everyone pay the same rate. Many people feel this is the best way of dealing with the problem of paying for the government. Because all citizens, rich and poor, receives the benefit of paved streets, the protection of the armed forces, and public schooling, it seems logical that everyone should have to pay, no matter how little they might be able to afford. Perhaps, for some people, any amount of taxation would prove to be a severe burden; in these rare instances, it would be wise to exempt such individuals from paying taxes until such time as they are financially better off. Still, what drives this whole issue is the population's perception that things are not fair as they are. People feel that they are paying too much money and are receiving too little in return. The rich seem to have ways to hide or shelter their income, and the poor see what little they earn shrink under an ever increasing tax burden. The flat tax will not solve the whole tax problem in one step, but it will help to create more fairness for everyone who has to pay taxes. An example of a flat tax is state sales taxes; rich and poor pay the same percentage, but not the same amount. The rich pay more in total dollars because the items they buy cost more.

It is not possible to totally eliminate problems associated with taxes, money, fairness, and poverty, but the flat tax can help bring the country one step closer to the realization of an equitable society.

Evaluating the Two Essay Responses

Read this section only after you have evaluated the two essay responses. The response to the essay on the proposed flat tax requires the student to discuss and describe. If you refer to the list of key terms presented earlier, you will see that *discuss* requires the student to consider the various points of view by presenting all sides of the issue, whereas *describe* requires the students to state the particulars in detail.

The following guidelines were presented for writing an essay: Begin with an introductory paragraph to define terms or describe your approach to answering the question; state each main idea and back it up with supporting details or examples; add transitional words such as *first, second, third, moreover, in addition, in conclusion,* and *therefore*; add a summary or conclusion; and proofread and revise your answer.

In Response 1, the student's introduction describes why some individuals are interested in the flat tax and defines what it would accomplish. In the next two paragraphs, the student presents the pros and cons of the flat tax (i.e., satisfying the "discuss" aspect of the question). In the third paragraph, the student describes the effects it may have on the U.S. economy, the second part of the question. In the fifth paragraph, the student uses the information presented in the earlier paragraphs to reach some important conclusions regarding the flat tax. The response is well organized, with each paragraph serving an important function in answering all parts of the question. The essay is well written and does not include any serious grammatical or spelling errors.

In Response 2, the student fails to organize his or her response to the question. The response is essentially one paragraph without attention to the two parts of the question. The single paragraph includes many ideas that could have been subdivided. The discussion aspect only includes the writer's point of view, omitting any reference to the oppositional arguments. The example of the flat tax is placed at the end of the first paragraph instead of the beginning. In addition, the preachy or narrow point of view does little to support a balanced response to the question. This point is clearly seen in the conclusion in the final paragraph. Finally, the student should have changed *receives* to *receive* in the ninth line of the essay.

Did you have any other comments regarding the two essays? If the essay was worth 10 points, how would you score each essay?

Table 11.1 reviews the procedures for answering multiple-choice questions, the most common objective question format, followed by procedures for answering essay questions.

TABLE 11.1

Procedures For Answering Multiple-Choice and Essay Exam Questions	
Procedures for Answering Multiple-Choice Questions	*Examples*
1. Carefully read the directions to determine if there is any special information for answering the questions.	Directions: Answer all questions. There is no partial reduction for incorrect answers.
2. Determine how much time you will allot for answering the questions by following the rule: Percentage of total points × Percentage of total time.	"Let's see, I have 50 multiple-choice and 2 essays to answer in 120 minutes. The multiple-choice questions are worth one point each and the essays are each worth 10 points—that's 70 points. The multiple-choice questions are worth 50/70 or .71 of the exam. I better allot about (120 ×.71) 85 minutes for the multiple-choice and about 17 minutes each for the two short essays."
3. Read the stem and all the choices first before determining the best answer.	"I was about to choose 'careful learners' until I read the better choice 'active learners'."
4. Skip difficult questions.	
5. Review choices that are very similar.	"I'm going to read the stem and each alternative before I make a choice. I will cross out each alternative that I know is incorrect and focus only on the alternatives that are left. If necessary, I will redefine terms in my own words to help me make my final choice."

Procedures for Answering Multiple-Choice Questions	*Examples*
6. Go back over difficult questions.	
7. When in doubt, guess. If there is a penalty for guessing, still guess if you can omit at least two of the alternatives.	"I know the meaning of decoding and encoding, but I am not sure of the other two terms. What is my best choice of the remaining terms?"
8. If given an opportunity, review your exam results (error analysis).	"Most of the questions I missed were higher-level questions and came from the lecture notes."

Procedures for Answering Essay Exams	*Examples*
1. Read the directions carefully and do exactly what is asked. If given a choice, determine what questions you will answer.	Directions: Answer questions 1 and 2 and *either* 3 or 4.
2. Read each question carefully to determine what is expected in the response. • Circle key words in each question. • Make notes as you read.	Describe the functions of the Speaker of the House of Representatives and evaluate his performance. Be sure to provide support for your evaluative comments.
3. Determine how you will use your time.	"I have 90 minutes to answer three essays each worth 10 points. This means that I should spend about 30 minutes per essay. If I finished a question in less time, I will have more time for the other two essays. I will also leave some time for outlining and editing each question."
4. Determine the order you will respond to the questions.	"I like to begin with the easiest question. It builds my confidence."
5. Organize your response by making an outline or representation (map).	"I want to present three main ideas."
6. Write your answer in the following manner: • Begin with an introductory paragraph. • State your first main idea and back it up with supporting details or examples. Go to the next main idea and do the same. • Add transitional words. • Add a summary. • Proofread and revise your answer.	
7. If given an opportunity, review your exam results.	"My major problem was that I failed to provide supporting evidence for the ideas I discussed."

Key Points

1. Test-taking strategies cannot substitute for poor exam preparation.
2. Carefully read the directions before beginning an exam.
3. Plan how you will use your time before beginning an exam.
4. Look for key terms to determine how you will answer the question.
5. Be aware that some essay questions may include more than one question.
6. Carefully organize responses to essay exam questions.
7. Conduct an error analysis after each exam to determine how you can improve your performance on future exams.

Follow–up Activities

1. Use the Self-management Process to Improve Test-Taking Strategies

Complete the following self-study during a period of 2 to 3 weeks. Your report should include each of the following processes and should be approximately five to eight typed pages in length. See Appendix A for detailed information on how to conduct a self-management study.

Self-evaluation and monitoring. How effective are my current test-taking strategies? Do I need to change the way I take tests? If yes, what problem do I encounter? What are the symptoms of my problem (i.e., when, where and how often does my problem occur)? How much of an impact does this problem have on my academic performance? What factors (e.g., beliefs, perceptions, feelings, physiological responses, or behaviors) contribute to this problem? What do I need to change to reduce or eliminate my problem(s)?

Goal setting and strategic planning. What are my goals? What strategies will I implement to improve my test-taking strategies? When will I use these strategies? How will I record my progress?

Strategy implementation and monitoring. What strategies did I use to improve my test taking? When did I use these strategies? What method(s) did I use to record my progress (e.g., documents, charts, logs, tally sheets, checklists, or recordings)? When did I use these methods? How and when did I monitor my progress to determine if my new test-taking strategies were working? What changes, if any, did I make along the way?

Strategic-Outcome Monitoring. Did I attain the goal(s) I set for myself? Have the modifications in my test-taking strategies improved my academic performance? What strategies were the most and least effective? What changes, if any, do I need to make in the future?

2. Analyze a Response to an Essay Question

Directions: Using the criteria for writing an essay exam, review the following question and evaluate the quality of the student's response.

> Question: Identify and explain the factors that distinguish successful from less successful learners.

Successful learners can be distinguished from unsuccessful learners in three ways. The first difference is goal setting. The second difference is how they plan and organize their studying. The third difference is how they prepare for and take exams.

Successful learners establish long-term and short-term goals that direct their behavior. This helps them maintain their motivation as they attempt to reach their goals.

Successful learners realize that learning is best accomplished by planning and using different study skills. Rather than leaving things to the last minute, successful learners allocate sufficient time each day to read chapters, answer questions, and work on large projects. For example, if the assignment is to write a history term paper, successful learners dedicate time to obtaining the materials, allowing enough time to read and understand them, and writing the report early enough to allow enough time to edit the report.

Successful learners also plan for and take tests in a systematic manner. They allocate time for study. They realize that tests that are very important or difficult require more time and effort than easier exams. Therefore, they use different study methods to learn the material. Also, before they begin answering exam questions, they carefully determine what specific information is asked for in each question.

In summary, successful learners take charge of their own learning. They set goals, plan and organize their daily tasks, and prepare for and take exams in an orderly manner. Successful learners are not born, they learn to be successful.

Evaluation:

_____

_____

_____

_____

_____

3. Conduct an Error Analysis on an Exam

Select an exam you recently took and use the criteria presented in the chapter for conducting an error analysis for objective and essay questions. Use the format in the following chart to categorize your errors, write a brief analysis of the data you collected, explain what you learned from the analysis, and describe what steps you can take to improve your exam performance. The actual number of rows in your chart will depend on the number of questions missed on your exam.

Question missed	Type of item (higher or lower level)	Topic or Chapter	Error source (textbook or lecture)

4. Practice Writing Responses to Essay Questions

Use the information presented in this chapter to generate and answer essay questions in this course. Select a partner and together write an essay question that could be asked on an exam. Next, write your response to the question independently using the following criteria: Begin with an introductory paragraph, state your first main idea and back it up with supporting details or examples, go to the next main idea and do the same, add transitional words, add a summary, and proofread and revise your answer. Finally, read each other's response and provide feedback. Discuss how each essay could be improved.

Answers to Exercises:

Exercise 11.2

The key words for each question are as follows: (1) always, (2) accurately, (3) total, (4) clear, (5) completely, (6) proven, (7) better, (8) first, (9) everyone, and (10) necessarily.

Exercise 11.3

1. d   2. b   3. d   4. a   5. b   6. b   7. c   8, b   9. c   10. c

GLOSSARY

Academic self-management: The strategies students use to control the factors influencing their learning.

Acronyms: Mnemonics that use the first letter in each word of a list to form a word (e.g. SMART goals).

Active listening: A type of communication in which the listener summarizes and paraphrases what he or she has heard from another individual so the individual feels that he or she has been understood.

Attention: A selective process that controls awareness of events in the environment.

Attribution: An individual's perception of the causes of his or her own success or failure.

Chunking: Grouping of data so that a greater amount of information may be retained in working memory.

Cognitive: Explanations of learning and motivation that focus on the role of the learner's mental processes.

Concentration: The process of continual refocusing on a perceived stimulus or message.

Diagrams: A visual description of the parts of something.

Distributed practice: Learning trials divided among short and frequent periods.

Elaboration strategies: Integration of meaningful knowledge into long-term memory through adding detail, summarizing, creating examples, and analogies.

Encoding: The process of transferring information from short-term memory to long-term memory.

Fermenting skills: Group skills used to stimulate academic controversy so that group members will challenge each other's positions, ideas, and reasoning.

Forming skills: Group skills needed for organizing the group and establishing norms of appropriate behavior.

Formulating skills: Group skills directed at helping members understand and remember the material being studied.

Functioning skills: Group skills that involve managing and implementing the group's efforts to achieve tasks and maintain effective working relationships.

Hierarchies: An organization of ideas into levels and groups.

Information processing system: The cognitive structure through which information flows, is controlled, and is transformed during the process of learning.

279

Key word method: A method of associating new words to ideas with similar-sounding cue words through the use of visual imagery.

Learning strategies: Techniques or methods that students use to acquire information.

Long-term memory (LTM): The part of the information processing system that holds information for long periods.

Maintenance rehearsal: A strategy to keep information activated in the working memory by repeating the information mentally.

Massed practice: Practice that is grouped into extended periods.

Mastery goal: Learning as much as possible for the purpose of self-improvement, irrespective of the performance of others.

Matrices: An organization that displays the comparative relations existing within topics and across topics.

Meaningful learning: A process of learning whereby the student attempts to make sense of the material so it will be stored in the long-term memory and retrieved when needed.

Mirror question: A question that reflects the information in notes.

Mnemonic: A memory technique that makes the task of remembering easier.

Organizational strategies: Learning strategies that impose structure on material via hierarchical or other relationships among the material's parts.

Performance goal: An orientation toward learning in which outperforming others is a major concern.

Rational emotive therapy: A process of dealing with irrational ideas and beliefs and replacing them with realistic statements.

Rehearsal strategies: The process of repeating information over and over in working memory to retain it.

Retrieval: The process of remembering or finding previously stored information in the long-term memory.

Rote learning: A process of learning whereby the student learns through repetition without trying to make any sense of the material.

Self-efficacy: The belief that one can successfully complete a specific task.

Self-talk: The inner speech we use to make evaluative statements about our behavior.

Self-worth: The need for students to maintain a positive image of their ability.

Sequences: An organization that shows the order of steps, events, stages, or phases.

Short-term memory (STM): The part of the information processing system that briefly stores information from the senses.

SMART goals: An acronym identifying the criteria for setting goals—specific, measurable, action-oriented, realistic, and timely.

Stereotype threat: The fear of doing something that would inadvertently confirm a stereotype. An example is an older person who takes an exam after being told that elderly individuals forget much of what they learn.

Summary question: A question that reflects the major theme or main ideas of the total lecture.

Transcendental meditation: A form of mental relaxation whereby an individual assumes a comfortable position and repeats a mantra, or key word.

Working memory (WM): The part of the information-processing system in which the active processing of information takes place.

APPENDICES

The following appendices are designed to help you plan, develop, and implement a self-management study so you can become a more successful learner. Appendix A provides you with the tools and assistance needed to apply the steps of the self-management process introduced in chapter 1. Appendix B includes 3 self-management studies completed over a 2- to 3-week period by students in an educational psychology course on study strategies. Some of the material provided by students was slightly edited to reduce the length of the report. Therefore, as you read these studies, you will be told when additional information was provided by the students, but not reported here. The topics of the self-management studies are listed below:

Self-Management Study 1: Motivation (persistence and management of effort)—written by Mark Flowers

Self-Management Study 2: Methods of learning (improving quiz scores)—written by Fernando Barba

Self-Management Study 3: Motivation (reducing anxiety)—written by Catherine Dizon

At the end of each case study you will find a brief analysis of strengths and areas that need improvement. Remember, there is no one way to complete a self-management study. Be creative in developing your own instruments to assess your behavior and developing strategies for change.

A Guide for Completing a Self-Management Study

by

Amy Gimino

You have been asked throughout this book to reflect on your academic behavior and determine what action you need to take to become a more successful learner. The four-step self-management process was introduced in chapter 1 to help address academic problems. The process includes self-observation and evaluation, goal setting and strategic planning, strategy implementation and monitoring, and strategic-outcome monitoring. The first Follow-up Activities in chapters 5 through 11 provide a series of questions for each of the steps to guide you in your self-study.

The purpose of this appendix is to provide tools and assistance to help you either (a) complete a follow-up study focused on the content in one of the chapters you have read or (b) design a study in an area of interest or concern. You will need to answer a series of questions to complete the four steps in the self-management process. The information under the next four headings will help you answer these questions so you will be able to reduce or eliminate a problem to improve your academic performance. You can refer to Appendix B at any time to view examples of self-management studies that were completed by students in a similar class over a 2- to 3-week period.

SELF-OBSERVATION AND EVALUATION

The first step of a self-management study requires you to observe and evaluate your behavior to select an academic problem you want to solve. An academic problem is defined as any behavior, belief, or perception that has a detrimental impact on your academic performance and is preventing you from attaining your academic potential or goals.

You have learned that your ability to manage or control factors associated with your motivation, methods of learning, use of time, and physical and social environment will enhance your academic performance. These factors include your beliefs, perceptions, physiological responses (e.g., in the case of anxiety), feelings, and behaviors.

There are a number of ways you can determine what aspect of your behavior to study and modify. First, you may have come into this course with an understanding of some aspect of your academic behavior that needs to be modified. Second, you can take a diagnostic test such as the Learning and Study Strategies Inventory (LASSI; Weinstein, Schulte, & Palmer, 1987) to identify your strengths and weaknesses. Your instructor may have used this instrument or some other study skills assessment in your course. Third, you can identify one of the self-management components—motivation, methods of learning, use of time, or physical and social environment—you are concerned about, and then complete the related self-observation exercises in this book. Table A.1 provides a list of these exercises according to the self-management component addressed.

By completing some or all of these exercises, you will learn about (a) behaviors that you never, sometimes, or always engage in that

TABLE A.1
SELF-OBSERVATION EXERCISES

Self-Management Components	Self-Observation Exercises	Chapter and Exercise #
Motivation	Analyzing my personal and sociocultural background	3.1
	Analyzing classroom experiences	3.2
	Identifying your values	4.1
	Assessing emotions	Chapter and 5.1
	Assessing self-talk	Follow-up 5-4
	Exploring anxiety-producing situations in school	Follow-up 5-5
Method of learning	Assessing reading strategies	8.1
	Assessing note-taking strategies	9.1
	Assessing exam preparation	10.1
Use of time	Assessing time wasters	6.1
	Assessing use of time	6.2
	Identifying your escapist techniques	Follow-up 6-3
	Identifying your favorite procrastination beliefs	Follow-up 6-4
Physical and social environment	Evaluating study environments	7.1

could benefit your academic performance or (b) behaviors that you always engage in that have a detrimental effect on your performance.

Once you identify these problems, you will need to select one problem for your study that you *need* and *want* to solve. Notice that the terms *need* and *want* are included in this statement. Changing behavior is a difficult thing to do. It requires you to invest a significant amount of time and effort in the four-step self-management process. Therefore, it is important for you to take the time to select a problem that you need and want to change so that you will be committed to solving it (Martin & Pear, 1988; Watson & Tharpe, 1992). Table A.2 provides examples of academic problems by chapter that you may wish to consider for your study.

TABLE A.2
EXAMPLES OF ACADEMIC PROBLEMS

Self-Management Components	Academic Problems	Chapter
	"I have a problem because I never, or only sometimes . . ." (Insert response [a]) or *"I have a problem because I usually . . ."* (Insert response [b])	
Motivation	[a] choose to complete academic tasks	2
	[a] put forth the effort needed to do well on certain academic tasks	3
	[a] persist when tasks are difficult, boring, or unchallenging	3
	[b] worry or experience anxiety as I study, attend class, or take exams	5
Methods of Learning	[a] take notes in class	9
	[b] experience difficulty with lecture material	9
	[a] read my textbooks or articles	8
	[a] prepare for quizzes and exams	10
	[a] remember the information I studied	2
	[b] have difficulty taking exams	11
Use of Time	[a] have time to do the things I value	6
	[a] have time to complete my academic tasks as well as I would like	6
	[a] have time to review my work before handing it in	6
	[a] have time to test myself before quizzes and exams	6
	[b] miss important events such as classes, review sessions, appointments, meetings	6
	[b] escape from academic events and tasks	3, 5, 6

continued

TABLE A.2 (Continued)
EXAMPLES OF ACADEMIC PROBLEMS

Self-Management Components	Academic Problems	Chapter
Physical and Social Environment	[a] select or arrange the physical setting to make my learning easier	7
	[a] seek assistance from peers, tutors, teaching assistants, and professors when I need help	7
	[a] seek help from non-social resources (e.g., study aids, books) when I need it	7
	[b] have difficulty attending to or concentrating on academic tasks	7
	[b] encounter internal or external distractions that interrupt my studying	7

Once you select a problem, you will need to observe and evaluate your problem in the same manner as a doctor observes a patient to prescribe treatment. That is, you will need to start by providing information (e.g., diagnostic test scores, answers to self-observation exercises, etc.) that supports the fact that your problem exists, as well as information (e.g., grades) that demonstrates the type of impact it has had on your academic performance. Then you will need to gather information on the history of your academic problem (e.g., How long have you had the problem? Under what circumstances have you experienced it?). Finally, you will need to spend time collecting additional information (data) on your problem so you can discover and appropriately diagnose all of the internal factors, such as beliefs, perceptions, physiological responses (e.g., anxiety), and behaviors that are contributing to it. Like a doctor, you will be more likely to prescribe the appropriate treatment (i.e., strategies) if you take the time at the beginning of your study to collect data that will enable you to determine all of the factors that are contributing to your problem. If you choose to guess which factors are contributing to your problem, you will most likely have to prescribe several treatments (strategies) before you find one that will effectively reduce or eliminate your problem. As a result, you will save time by thoroughly investigating your problem at the start of your study.

There are two ways you can gather information (data) on the symptoms of your problem and the internal factors and behaviors that contribute to it. The first way is to look at documents to which you already have access. Table A.3 provides a list of documents that you may wish to consult. The second way is to set aside a period of time

TABLE A.3
DOCUMENTS

Self-Management Components	Documents
Motivation	Written goals Diaries or journals (e.g., to evaluate: self-efficacy, attributions, and self-talk)
Methods of Learning	Class notes Notes from readings Study plans Study aids (i.e., flashcards, outlines, and representations) Practice tests
Use of Time	Attendance sheets Course syllabi Semester calendars Weekly priority tasks lists Weekly schedules
Physical and Social Environment	Notes from meetings with instructors, teaching assistants, tutors, and classmates Nonsocial resources (i.e., articles, books, study guides)
Performance	Scores on assignments, quizzes, exams, papers, and presentations
All Components	The self-observation checklists in this book Results from any learning and study skills assessments

(preferably 1 to 2 weeks) to study your problem. During this time, you can collect documents listed in Table A.3. In addition, you can use instruments such as charts, journals, tally sheets, and checklists to collect data on the symptoms of your problem and the internal factors and behaviors that contribute to it. Each of these instruments is described in the following section.

Charts

Charts are tools you can use to diagnose the internal beliefs, perceptions, physiological responses, feelings, or behaviors that contribute to your academic problem. Charts include topics that are placed across the top row and details that are placed underneath each topic. For example, if your problem is that you never or only sometimes remember the information you study, you may wish to use a chart like the following one to record the strategies you use as you study.

Class: Motivation and Learning
                    Strategies   From: 10/26 to 11/3

Date	Task	Strategy Use	Physical /Social Environment (including course procedures and requirements)	Motivation
10/26	Read Ch.3	None	Roommate wanted to go out for pizza	Was not interested in this content
10/27	Study for quiz	Reread and underlined	Quiz this morning	Didn't feel like studying
10/27	Take quiz	Wrote answers	Sat next to a friend who felt confident before the quiz and completed the quiz early	Was anxious and didn't have enough time to complete my thoughts
10/28	Read Ch. 7	Underlined text, turned headings into questions, came up with a few examples from my own experience		Believed I could relate to this content and was confident about it
11/1	Read article	Turned headings into questions, underlined answers, and developed a matrix	Read article in library	Was disappointed in my last quiz score (+6/10), wanted to get at least a +8 on my quiz and believed the material was interesting
11/2	Study for quiz	Asked the questions I developed to test myself, reviewed the matrix	Discussed my thoughts about the article with a classmate	Answered all of the questions I asked myself and was confident after studying
11/3	Take quiz	Made a brief outline of each answer before starting	Compared my summary with a classmate's summary and saw that mine was more detailed	Was confident about the quiz because I was able to predict the questions and was able to finish early

The advantage of using this type of chart is that it will help you see the relationship between: (a) environmental factors (i.e., where you studied, when you studied, and with whom you studied), (b) motivation (i.e., your interest level, confidence level, and goals), (c) learning strategies (e.g., rehearsal, elaboration, and organization), and (d) your performance outcomes. As a result, it should become easier for you to identify beliefs, perceptions, physiological responses, feelings, and behaviors you need to change.

There are several examples of charts that you may wish to use or model including:

- A chart for analyzing efficacy scores (chapter 3)
- A weekly priority task list (chapter 6)
- A chart for becoming aware of misdirected attention (chapter 5)

You may also find it is helpful to design you own chart(s) for your study. The following list provides a number of topics you may wish to include on a chart:

- Environmental factors (e.g., dates, times, locations, and people)
- Internal or personal factors–beliefs and perceptions (demonstrated by your self-efficacy, attributions, and self-talk), physiological responses (e.g., anxiety), and your mood (e.g., whether you are interested or bored)
- Behaviors—(a) motivation (e.g., goals, choices, levels of involvement [effort] and persistence), (b) methods of learning (e.g., use of rehearsal, elaboration, and organizational strategies), (c) use of time (e.g., planning, prioritizing, and scheduling; the times when tasks are assigned, started, and completed), and (d) physical and social environment (types of internal and external distractions, the amount of time spent attending to or concentrating on tasks) and the use of social resources.

Journals

Daily journals (or diaries) provide an effective means of collecting information about your internal beliefs, perceptions, and feelings. For example, the Follow-up Activity in chapter 5, titled "Assessing Self-Talk," asks you to keep a journal to help you identify the type(s) of self-talk you exhibit. Journals may also help you to keep track of the strategies you use and the behaviors you exhibit throughout your study.

Tally Sheets

Tally sheets are tools you can use to count the number of times a particular belief, perception, physiological response, feeling, or behavior occurs within the time frame you establish for your study (Cartwright & Cartwright, 1984). You may design tally sheets a number of ways based on what you would like to learn about your problem. For example, if your problem is that you always encounter distractions that interrupt your studying, you may find either of these tally sheets helpful.

From: <u>10/1</u> To: <u>10/5</u> Distractions During Studying

Location	Tally	Total
Room	⦀⦀ ⦀⦀⦀	8
Library	⦀⦀	2
Lounge	⦀⦀⦀⦀ ⦀⦀⦀⦀	10
Friend's room	⦀⦀⦀⦀	5
Total		25

Distractions During Studying

Date	From:	To:	Task & Number of Distractions	Total	
				Time	Distractions
10/1	7:30 p.m.	8:30 p.m.	⦀⦀⦀⦀	60 m	5
10/2	9:00 a.m.	9:45 a.m.	⦀⦀⦀	45 m	3
10/2	1:00 p.m.	2:00 p.m.	⦀⦀⦀⦀	60 m	4
Total				165 m	12

Adapted from Alberto & Troutman (1986).

The advantage of using these tally sheets is that they will enable you to determine the number of times you were distracted (i.e., 25 vs. 12) within the time frame you selected. The first tally sheet will help you learn where your distractions most frequently occur, whereas the second tally sheet will enable you to determine your *rate* of distraction. You can calculate this rate by dividing the number of minutes you spend studying by the number of distractions you encounter. For example, if you calculate the rate for each of the rows in the sample tally sheet, you will find that you were distracted once every 12 minutes in the evening, once every 15 minutes in the morning, and once every 20 minutes in the afternoon. Thus, the afternoon appears to be the best time for you to study.

The disadvantage of using the tally sheets is that they limit the amount of information you can gain from using them. For example, the tally sheets only provide you with information about the location where, or time periods when, the student experienced distractions. However, they do not provide you with information about the types of internal and external distractions experienced. Therefore, if you decide to use tally sheets in your study, your instructor will most likely require that you keep a journal that describes what you learn each day from your tally sheets.

Checklists

Checklists are similar to tally sheets. The only difference is that checklists use checkmarks to monitor whether or not a particular behavior on a list has or has not occurred. For example, you may wish to use a checklist to keep track of such things as: your class attendance, the criterion for an assignment that you have met, the assignments listed on your course syllabus that you have finished, and the items on your weekly priority task list that you have completed.

Once you complete a thorough investigation of your problem using one or more of the previously described methods, you will need to provide a brief narrative description of what you learned from each document, chart, journal, tally sheet, or checklist you use (i.e., just like a doctor makes notes of what he or she learns in a patient's chart). For example, if you were to collect the data displayed in the first chart (Motivation and Learning Strategies class), you might describe the fact that you were not confident about your study techniques and received a low quiz grade when you: (a) were not interested in the content, (b) used rehearsal strategies (e.g., underlining and rereading), or (c) were anxious during the exam. However, when you were confident and received a high quiz score, you: (a) could relate to the material, (b) used elaboration and organization strategies (e.g., turned headings into questions, came up with your own examples, and developed a matrix), (c) studied at the library, (d) discussed your thoughts with a classmate, (e) tested yourself before the exam, and (f) made a brief outline before answering each question. This narrative description serves two purposes. First, it helps identify the changes you need to make to reduce or eliminate your problem. In addition, it helps you and your instructor keep track of your reasoning throughout the course of your study.

GOAL SETTING AND STRATEGIC PLANNING

By now, you should have established a SMART goal such as: "I want to obtain a 3.0 GPA. this semester" or "I want to get a B in my Psychology class this semester." Chapter 4 describes the steps you need to take to make sure you set a specific, measurable, action-oriented, realistic, and timely (SMART) goal (Smith, 1994). Once you establish a SMART long-tem goal, you need to set a SMART intermediate goal related to your self-management problem. For example, if your problem is that "you only sometimes remember the information you studied in your biology course" and, as a result, have low quiz and exam scores (i.e., Cs or below), you may wish to set a SMART intermediate goal such as: earning at least a B on the rest of your quizzes and exams this semester. Your long-term and intermediate goals will provide the direction for what you hope to accomplish in your self-study.

Once you establish your SMART long-term and intermediate goals, you will need to identify strategies to help you reduce or eliminate your problem and reach your goal(s). Table A.4 provides a list of the strategies found in each chapter. To reduce or eliminate your problem, you will need to select a strategy (or set of strategies) that you know you will feel comfortable using. For example, one solution (or strategy) may be sufficient for solving certain problems, whereas other problems may require the use of many strategies. For instance, if your problem is that you only sometimes remember the information you studied in your biology course, you may need to choose strategies to improve your motivation, time management, and social and physical environment in addition to your methods of learning. The strategies you choose should be based on the factors that you found were contributing to your problem in the self-observation and evaluation stage of your study.

TABLE A.4
STRATEGIES TO SOLVE ACADEMIC PROBLEMS

Components of Academic Behavior	Strategies	Chapter
Motivation		
Goal-setting	Align values, goals, and daily tasks	4
	Set long-term and short-term SMART goals	4
Self-rewards	Arrange or imagine rewards for positive behaviors or successes, for example: "If I do well on my homework, I will treat myself to my favorite TV show."	3
	Arrange or imagine punishments for negative behaviors or failures, for example: "If I don't do well on my homework, I won't be able to watch my favorite TV show."	

STRATEGIES TO SOLVE ACADEMIC PROBLEMS

Self-talk	Use rational emotive therapy and positive self-talk to combat irrational beliefs and perceptions; attribute successes and failure to effort	3 3
Relaxation techniques	Use diaphragmatic breathing Use transcendental meditation	5 5

Methods of Learning

Elaborating and organizing	Use elaboration strategies such as: • Asking and answering questions as you read, take notes, and study • Paraphrasing and summarizing • Creating analogies • Creating acronyms Use organizational strategies such as: • Outlining • Representations	 2, 8, 9 2 2 2 8 8
Reviewing records	Review class notes and handouts before and after each lecture Review your course syllabus, class notes, handouts, course books and previous quizzes and exams as you prepare for further testing.	10 10, 11
Planning	Determine how you will prepare for exams Determine how to approach different types of exam questions	10 11
Self-testing	Test yourself to see if you recall information	10

Use of Time

Planning	Make sure your daily tasks are aligned with your values and goals Break down your tasks into smaller more manageable parts Set goals for you daily tasks Determine how you will eliminate your escapist techniques Determine how you will eliminate your procrastination beliefs	6 6 6 6 3, 6
Scheduling	Maintain a monthly calendar Maintain a weekly priority tasks list Maintain a weekly schedule	6 6 6

Physical and Social Environment

Seeking social assistance	Seek help from peers, tutors, or instructors when you need it	7
Seeking information	Use campus resources Locate additional study aids and books in areas that are difficult for you	7 7

Once you select the strategies you will use to reduce you problem and meet your intermediate goal, you will need to develop an action plan. This action plan should include the time frame for your study and should discuss (a) the strategies you plan to use, (b) when you plan to use each strategy, and (c) the method(s) you plan to use to record your progress. For example, if your intermediate goal is "to obtain at least a B on the rest of the quizzes in your biology course," you may develop a strategic action plan similar to the following:

An Example of a Strategic Action Plan

Time Line: From: <u>February 1</u> to <u>February 21</u>.

Self-management strategies	When will I use the strategy?	What method will I use to record or indicate my progress?
Change headings to questions and answer question	Each time I read	Markings in textbooks
Develop at least one representation per chapter	When I review chapter	Notes
Test myself on mirror and summary questions in notes	After each lecture	Notes
Complete study for each quiz 2 days before exam	For each quiz	Check off on weekly calendar
Attend office hours or get help from a classmate	Each time I have a question or do not get 80% on my practice quiz in my textbook	Practice quiz score and notes from meeting
Put a note on my door and turn on answering machine	Each time I study for a quiz	Develop a checklist for number of distractions per study session

As you develop your plan, ask yourself the following question: "Why should I use each of these strategies?" If you cannot justify your answer based on the information you learned from the self-observation and evaluation stage of your study, you need to find an alternative strategy (or set of strategies) to use. Please keep in mind that the number or type of strategies used to modify behavior will vary according to the nature of the problem. This means that you will not necessarily use strategies in all of the components of academic self-management.

STRATEGY IMPLEMENTATION AND MONITORING

Now is the time for you to try to reduce or eliminate your problem by implementing each of the strategies specified in your action plan. During this time you will need to do three things. First, you will need to keep track of all of the strategies you use in an attempt to change you behavior, as well as the date and time when you use each strategy. This information will enable you to determine the extent to which you follow your strategic plan. Second, you will need to keep track of the methods you use to record your progress (e.g., documents, charts, journals, tally sheets, or checklists). Finally, you will need to evaluate your progress by asking the following questions:

- "Are the data collection methods I am using working?"
- "Are the strategies I am using working?"

To answer the first question, "Are the data collection methods I am using working?" You will need to check to see if: (a) you have followed the data recording methods specified in your plan, (b) you are comfortable with these methods, and (c) you have enough data to objectively evaluate your progress. If you fail to meet any of these criteria, you will need to change your data collection methods.

To answer the second question, "Are the strategies I am using working?" you will need to see if (a) you are comfortable using these strategies and (b) you are meeting the criterion you set in both your SMART goal and strategic action plan. For example, if your intermediate SMART goal is to obtain at least a B on the rest of your quizzes and exams in your biology course this semester, you will need to record and evaluate all of your weekly quiz scores. If you meet your goal and are comfortable with the strategies you are using, you do not need to modify your action plan. However, if you find that you are uncomfortable with the strategies or that the strategies you are using are not helping you meet your goal (e.g., you are not earning at least a B on your quizzes and exams), you will need to adjust your strategies in your strategic action plan.

Once you evaluate the effectiveness of your data collection methods and strategies, you will need to ask: "What changes, if any, do I need to make?" You may wish to change (a) the instruments you use to record your data or (b) the strategies you use as you attempt to reduce or eliminate your problem. In addition, you may wish to change the time frame in which you plan to implement different strategies. During this strategy implementation and monitoring stage, it is extremely important for you to make a note of all of the changes you make to your study along the way.

STRATEGIC-OUTCOME MONITORING

Strategic-outcome monitoring is the last step in the self-management process. At the end of the time frame specified in your strategic action plan, you will need to refer to your intermediate SMART goal to answer the following questions: "Did I attain each of the goals I set for myself?" and "How do I know?" In addition, you will need to ask yourself: "What did I learn from my self-study?" To answer this question, you will need to review every document, chart, journal, tally sheet, or checklist you collect and describe what each piece of evidence tells you. This evidence should help you determine which strategies were the most and least effective in helping you reduce or eliminate your problem. In addition, this information should help you determine if there are any changes you need to make to improve your academic performance in the future.

Once you complete all four steps of your self-management study, your instructor will most likely ask for you to write a report describing the process you used and the extent to which you were able to modify or change your behavior. You will find the questions in the Follow-up Activities provide a structure for writing the paper. The following are the questions for a self-management study in time management:

> **Self-observation and evaluation.** How do I manage my time? Do I need to change the way I plan and manage my study schedule? If yes, what problem(s) do I encounter? What are the symptoms of my problem (i.e., when, where, and how often does my problem occur)? How much of an impact does this problem have on my academic performance? What factors (e.g., beliefs, perceptions, physiological responses, feelings or behaviors) contribute to this problem? What do I need to change to reduce or eliminate my problem(s)?
>
> **Goal setting and strategic planning.** What are my goals? What strategies will I use to improve my time management?

When will I use these strategies? How will I record my progress?

Strategy implementation and monitoring. What strategies did I use to improve my time management? When did I use these strategies? What method(s) did I use to record my progress (e.g., documents, charts, journals, tally sheets, and checklists)? When did I use these methods? How and when did I monitor my progress to determine if my new time-management plan was working? What changes, if any, did I make along the way?

Strategic-outcome monitoring. Did I attain the goal(s) I set for myself? Have the modifications in my time management improved my academic performance and personal life? What strategies were the most and least effective? What additional changes, if any, do I need to make in the future?

APPENDIX B

Examples of Self-Management Studies

SELF-MANAGEMENT STUDY #1: MOTIVATION (I.E., PERSISTENCE AND MANAGEMENT OF EFFORT), SELF-OBSERVATION AND EVALUATION

Problem Identification

I identified my problem through my laziness and procrastination of tasks. As I looked back at my work in this course, I realized that I wrote about this problem in my first journal entry (see Attachment 1). My scores on the Learning and Study Strategies Inventory also reflect this problem. For example, my scores were below average on the Motivation scale, which assesses motivation, diligence, self-discipline, and willingness to work hard, and on the Concentration scale, which assesses concentration and attention to academic tasks. Furthermore, my grades in this course reflect a lack of motivation. (Student attached homework and quiz scores indicating a low performance). So far, I have turned in three of the five homework assignments late and have received partial or no credit for my work. My quiz scores, which range from 2 to 10 on a scale of 10, also reflect an inconsistent pattern of motivation.

History of My Problem

When I was in junior high, I achieved good grades because I was motivated by my mom's constant supervision. She would sit me down every night at the kitchen table and make sure I did not get up until my homework was finished. By the time I reached high school, however, my grades reflected the fact that I monitored my own schoolwork. My grades, especially in courses that required daily assignments, dropped significantly. For example, I earned a C in my 9th-grade geometry class and an F during the first semester of my 11th-grade trigonometry class. Thus my grade point average, which was excellent in junior high, was only mediocre in high school.

Current Symptoms of My Problem

Unfortunately, as demonstrated by my past semester's grades (a GPA of 2.9 out of 4), my problem still exists in college. I have earned mediocre grades, because I am not disciplined and I procrastinate on important tasks. I believe that my lack of discipline is a direct result of my motivation. It is difficult for me to stay motivated, no matter where I study. I get bored and often fall asleep studying at the library or at home. The classes that I seem to have the most difficulty in are those that require daily attention. For example, because math classes have such requirements, my grades reflect my disinterest.

Although motivation tends to be a constant problem, there are times when I am focused on my assignments. Unlike A students, I cannot keep myself highly motivated throughout the semester. Instead, I tend to be more motivated at the beginning and end of each semester than I am during the middle of the semester. When I am motivated, I notice that I am more persistent and less inclined to wait until the night before an assignment is due to begin working. As a result, I tend to earn higher grades. This is evident in my quiz scores for this class. However, during the middle of the semester, when I am less motivated, I tend to procrastinate on my assignments. This behavior is not good, because my lack of motivation stops me from achieving the grades I am capable of earning in school.

Diagnosis of My Problem

The internal beliefs that contribute to my problem are irrationality and pride. I believe that because I've done well in the past with little effort, I can do the same thing in college. A key difference is that in college I can't simply memorize and regurgitate information. Professors expect me to think and analyze the information they give me. My stubborn and irrational pride, however, tells me that I can put in the same amount of time and effort and do well. The problem is that I've been telling myself the same thing since junior high. Thus, I believe that if I can reduce my irrational thinking and pride, I will start my assignments earlier and I will be more motivated to see my assignments through to completion. This should help me reach my long-term goal of earning all As in my courses.

GOAL SETTING AND STRATEGIC PLANNING

Because I have an important research paper due in my international relations class, my short-term goal is to finish this paper in 5 days. I will accomplish this goal by breaking this paper into manageable parts according to the following schedule:

Day	Task
Thursday	I want to gather all the information I need for my paper from the library and Internet.
Friday	I want to write five pages.
Saturday	I want to write five pages.
Sunday	I want to write the last two pages.
	I want to complete the bibliography section.
	I want to revise my paper.
Monday	I want to read my paper and make final revisions. I want to print out my paper.

My Strategic Plan to Reach My Goal

Strategies	When	Method of Recording
Break the paper down into manageable parts.	Complete the paper over a 5-day period rather than the night before it is due.	Develop a 5-day plan and check off the activities that I successfully complete each day.
Work on my paper in the library so that I won't be distracted. Use television shows and playing basketball as self-rewards. Use positive self-talk.	Each day if I accomplish my goal in the library I will reward myself. Whenever I get down on myself.	I will monitor these strategies by including a journal entry that will record what I think I've done well or what I need to work on. In essence, this journal will monitor the progress I hope to make.

STRATEGY IMPLEMENTATION AND MONITORING

Along the way, I noticed that as the days drew closer to the end, I began to procrastinate on my daily assignments (see Attachment 2). What I realized on Sunday was that I wasn't specific enough with my goal. I needed to schedule a specific time to complete my paper each day. In addition, I noticed that I needed to find ways to manage distractions that contributed to my procrastinating, such as being tired, taking long study breaks (e.g., Saturday), and working on assignments from other courses.

STRATEGIC-OUTCOME MONITORING

I only completed some of the daily goals I set for myself at the beginning of the study. My strategic planning checklist (see Attachment 2) and journal entries (see Attachment 3) show what I did and did not accomplish according to my initial plan. Furthermore, because I didn't meet my goal of completing 10 pages of my paper by Saturday, I set a new goal to write the final 3 pages of my paper in a 5-hour block of time on Sunday evening. I successfully accomplished this goal. In fact, I was able to complete all 3 pages with an hour to spare.

FINAL THOUGHTS

Because the paper I turned in was of much higher quality than I am accustomed to, I see the value of breaking down a large assignment into smaller pieces. This way I am much more likely to sustain my motivation through the course of a project. Furthermore, I have learned that I can find other ways to motivate myself (besides having my mom as the primary motivator), which will help me earn As rather than Bs in my classes.

In conclusion, although I already knew some of the reasons I could not sustain motivation, I discovered some interesting things about myself. For example, I didn't realize that I wasted so much time. I must admit that although I found this assignment extremely helpful, I will most likely monitor my progress in my head rather than writing everything out in the future.

ATTACHMENT 1: JOURNAL 1

Another Year

Here we are at the beginning of a new academic year. It's funny, because at the beginning, everybody looks nice and acts smart. Students are wearing their brand new clothes—everyone looks prepared—and there is a genuine sense of happiness. The problem is that we haven't done anything yet. But as we do, some students will fly high, some will drift along, and others will simply sink. Unfortunately, I've visited all parts of this spectrum in my short college career.

When I came to school as a freshman, I had unrealistic hopes that I would do well. College would soon teach me that this was not high school and that students actually had to work for their grades. In high school, I got by with poor study habits. In college, however, I initially fared poorly and had to learn how to become an effective student.

Part of my problem was that I didn't value education. Freshman year taught me that my mom loved education and that I shunned hard work. I was simply trying to get by in life. Sadly enough, I don't know if I ever would have made it to college if my mom didn't push me. After a tough year and a half, however, I pulled my grades up, and now I expect to achieve straight As.

This confidence is the result of hard work and seeing my character strengthen. I now have the discipline to go home and study every night. It will be interesting to see if I can maintain this high level of motivation throughout the semester.

ATTACHMENT 2: STRATEGIC PLANNING CHECKLIST

Day	Task	Accomplished
Thursday	I want to gather all the information I need for my paper from the library and Internet.	Yes
Friday	I want to write five pages.	No
Saturday	I want to write five pages.	No
Sunday	I want to write the last two (or three) pages. I want to complete the bibliography section. I want to revise my paper.	Yes Yes Yes
Monday	I want to read my paper and make final revisions. I want to print out my paper.	Yes Yes

ATTACHMENT 3: JOURNAL ENTRIES

Thursday

I delayed going to the library. Right after class I went home, ate, and listened to music in my room. When I was in my room I started cleaning it and made some phone calls. Two and a half hours after my class let out, I went to the library and photocopied some materials from three different sources. After that, I jumped on a computer and looked through this cool Web site my teacher suggested. In conclusion, I finished my goal but need to be better disciplined.

Friday

Today I got started right after my class let out at noon. (I don't want a repeat of yesterday.) Although it was difficult starting the paper, I encouraged myself through positive self-talk to get started, and I did. I did not finish my goal tonight. I had an engagement at 7:30 p.m. and decided to leave the library at 6 p.m. to ensure that I would make it on time. After the engagement, I decided to go to sleep early. Tomorrow I will get an early start.

Saturday

Although I was lazy, my roommate woke me up around 8 a.m. I ate breakfast, did my household chores, and watched some football with one of my housemates. I finally got to the library at 12:15 p.m. Where did all the time go? Anyhow, once I got started, I got into a pretty good rhythm. I cranked until 4:30 p.m., when I decided to reward myself by playing basketball on the outside courts on campus. Although I only played an hour and fifteen minutes, by the time I got back to the library, it was 7:25 p.m. By the end of the evening I was up to nine pages. A good accomplishment, considering I wrote six pages today. I still feel short, however. What I will do is plan out how long it should take me to complete each task and use that as a deadline. I have to be more focused tomorrow.

Sunday

After church I did other homework, as well as other stuff, including eating, relaxing, going to a meeting, and talking to my mom on the phone. I estimated that it would take me 5 hours to write three pages, complete my bibliography section, and make slight revisions. In the evening, I allotted 5 hours to complete these tasks. The time frame and deadline helped tremendously. In fact, it only took me 4 hours to finish everything, because I wrote the conclusion pages quicker than I thought. This is great, because I cannot afford to miss another deadline and I have class tomorrow.

Monday

Today's goal: although I delayed getting started, my homework only took an hour and a half. This was within my estimated time frame. This is good because I have other assignments to do.

ANALYSIS OF SELF-MANAGEMENT STUDY #1

Self-Observation and Evaluation

Strengths. The student did an excellent job organizing this section of his paper. The headings he provides makes it easy to follow how he identified and ultimately diagnosed his problem. Furthermore, the evidence he provided support his claim that he has difficulty persisting at tasks and managing his effort. Finally, unlike the other case studies printed in this appendix, this student provides a historical analysis of how his problem developed, starting in junior high.

Areas for Improvement. The student discusses the fact that he identified his problem through his procrastination of tasks. Unfortunately, we do not know the extent of his procrastination. Here he could have improved his study by adding an analysis of his use of time that includes when he starts and completes assignments in relation to when assignments are due.

Goal Setting and Strategic Planning

Strengths. The student sets a SMART goal to complete a term paper in five days and effectively breaks this goal down into a series of manageable daily tasks. Both the strategies he plans to implement and the methods he plans to use to record his progress are logical.

Areas for Improvement. The student originally discussed the fact that he tends to procrastinate on tasks. Although he did a good job selecting strategies that will help him combat this problem, he did not include a method for monitoring his procrastination throughout the course of his study. In addition, he could have improved his study by specifying a date and time when he would check his progress to see if his strategies and data collection methods were working.

Strategy Implementation and Monitoring

Strengths. Through his journals, the student monitors his progress toward his daily goals. When the student fails to meet his goal on Saturday, he decides to modify both his plan (i.e., to estimate the amount of time it will take him to accomplish a task and use this as a deadline) and his daily goal for the next day (i.e., to complete three pages of the paper in a 5-hour block of time the next day). This enabled him to make up for lost time and successfully accomplish his goal—completing his paper in 5 days.

Areas for Improvement. The student mentions that he needed to find ways to manage distractions (e.g., being tired, taking long study breaks, and working on assignments from other courses) that contributed to his procrastinating.

Although his journal entries discuss some of the distractions he encountered, they do not provide the reader with a clear understanding of how and when he put off working on his paper. He could have improved his study by providing the reader with a detailed account of how he spent his time by using the form provided in chapter 6. In addition, on Saturday the student decided that to avoid procrastinating, he would plan out how long he would give himself to complete each assignment. Therefore, on Sunday he allotted himself 5 hours in the evening to write three pages, complete his bibliography, and make slight revisions. Most likely, the student would have benefited from using the strategies described in chapter 6 to schedule these tasks throughout the course of his day rather than in one large block at the end of the day.

Strategic-Outcome Monitoring

Strengths. The student's strategic planning checklist provides a good analysis of the goals he did and did not accomplish throughout his study.

Areas for Improvement. The student mentions that on Sunday evening he was able to complete his daily tasks with an hour to spare but fails to provide the reader with evidence of this fact. He could have strengthened his study by including a chart of when he hoped to complete his tasks and the time when he actually finished these tasks. In addition, at the end of the study, the student mentions that he met his goal by successfully completing his paper in 5 days. He could have presented a copy of this paper with his self-management study.

SELF-MANAGEMENT STUDY #2: METHODS OF LEARNING (IMPROVING QUIZ SCORES)

Introduction

This semester I decided to take the initiative to set a goal that I am determined to accomplish—to earn a 3.0 grade point average. This goal should motivate me to do all of my work for my classes. At times, I believe that the motivation I had at the start of the semester diminished. I have found this to be especially true in my Policy Planning and Development class.

Self-Observation and Evaluation

I have elected to do my case study for my Policy Planning and Development class. In this class, I want to improve my quiz scores because they will heavily determine my grade at the end of the course. These quizzes are pop quizzes, and the element of surprise is what I find most disturbing, because the quizzes consist of both the readings and the lectures. Thus, I must make sure I really learn the information so that I can recall it at any time.

So far I have taken four quizzes, and all of my scores have been relatively low. I have earned one F, one D, and two Cs. (Note: the student also provided documentation of these quiz scores.) The reason these scores are so low is because I have not kept up with the reading material and my attendance in class has been poor (see Attachment 1). (Note: the student also provided a copy of his syllabus, which indicated the readings he did and did not complete.)

Goal Setting and Strategic Planning

My goal for this self-management study is to improve my scores on the next two quizzes (i.e., Quiz 5 and 6) in my Policy Planning and Development Course. I will start by attaining at least a C on the next quiz. The strategies I plan to use to accomplish this goal are listed in the following chart:

Strategies	When	Method of Recording
Reading I will be on schedule for all of my readings.	During the next week	I will highlight each reading I complete on my syllabus.
I will turn headings into questions and answer these questions.	Each time I read a chapter or article	Textbook
Class Notes I will attend all of my lectures and discussion sections and use the note-taking strategy I learned in chapter 9.	Until the end of the semester	I will use a checklist to keep track of my attendance, and I will provide documentation of my note taking.
Office Hours I will set up appointments with my professor and my teaching assistant.	Before the next quizzes	I will provide my weekly schedule (noting the appointment times) as well as documentation of the notes I take at each appointment.

To earn better quiz scores, I must start with the basics. I will catch up on all of my readings and ask myself questions on what I read. All of these assignments are marked on my syllabus. As I read each assignment, I will use the reading comprehension strategies in chapter 8.

Then, when I finish each assignment, I will highlight it on my syllabus so that I will know I have read it. I also plan to attend all of my lectures and discussion sessions, because my professor often gives hints about the material that will be on our quizzes. At each class, I will take good notes during these lectures using the note-making strategy in chapter 9. These notes should help me predict which questions will show up on the quizzes. Finally, I plan to set several appointments with my professor and teaching assistant. In these meetings, I will ask questions about the content I do not understand.

Strategy Implementation and Monitoring

So far I have used all of the strategies listed in my plan, and my strategies seem to be working. On my fifth quiz (11/5/98), I earned a B, which exceeded my goal [note: the student also provided documentation of this score]. I feel I was able to earn a decent grade on this quiz because I followed the strategies set forth in my plan. I was able to catch up with the readings, and I have used the reading strategies I learned [note: the student provided documentation of the readings he completed using this strategy]. I completed these readings in a tranquil and quiet environment. I also attended every lecture since the start of this study and took notes using to the procedures in chapter 9 (see Attachment 2). [Note: the student also provided documentation of the notes he took using this strategy.] I feel that the most positive step I made was that I scheduled an appointment with my teaching assistant. At this meeting, my teaching assistant gave me plenty of useful information (see Attachment 3). [Note: the student also provided documentation of his notes from this meeting.] Because of my success, I plan to continue to abide by my plan and hope to earn even higher grades.

Strategic-Outcome Monitoring

Quiz 6 took place on November 19, and I earned an A+ [note: the student provided documentation of this score]. I must admit, I felt confident before taking the quiz—it was the first time I had used positive self-talk in this class. I followed all of the steps in my strategic plan, and my results were extremely satisfying. I read all of my reading materials, attended every lecture, and was able to set an appointment with my professor. The appointment was very helpful, so I plan to continue attending office hours.

Overall, my strategic plan had a positive impact on my quiz scores. I have been able to raise my grades significantly. Hopefully, I will continue to maintain this progress on the last two quizzes and final exam in this course.

Evidence Sheet

Attachment 1: Class Attendance Before

9/3	9/8	9/10	9/15	9/17	9/22	9/24	9/29	10/1	10/6
X	X			X	X				X

10/8	10/13	10/15	10/20	10/22	10/27	10/29
	X		X		X	X

Attachment 2: Class Attendance After

11/3	11/5	11/10	11/12	11/17	11/19	11/24
X	X	X	X	X	X	X

Attachment 3: Weekly Schedule

Monday, November 2	Thursday, November 5
	1. Study for quiz PLDV
	2. Work on portfolio for educational
	psychology course
	3. Read for English
Tuesday November 3	Friday, November 6
Election Day (U.S.)	
Wednesday, November 4	Saturday, November 7
1. Study for Eng. quiz	
2. Write journal for educational	Sunday, November 8
psychology course	
3. Meet with TA	
4. Study for quiz	

ANALYSIS OF SELF-MANAGEMENT STUDY #2

Self-Observation and Evaluation

Strengths. The student uses his course quiz grades to identify his problem—not performing as well as he would like to in his Policy Planning and Development class. In addition, he provides evidence of the symptoms of his problem (poor attendance and not keeping up with his reading assignments) by including an attendance chart and by checking off the assignments he has and has not completed on his syllabus.

Area for Improvement.   The student could have improved his study by providing the reader with more information related to the history of his problem (e.g., when he first noticed the problem). In addition, he could have strengthened his study by exploring internal factors (e.g., beliefs, perceptions, physiological responses, and feelings) and other behaviors that may be contributing to his problem.

Goal Setting and Strategic Planning

Strengths.   The student develops a SMART goal to improve his scores on the next two quizzes in his Policy, Planning, and Development Course and to get at least a C on his next quiz. Further, he developed a detailed plan to help him reach his goals, which includes: using the reading comprehension and note-making strategies discussed in chapters 8 and 9, setting up office hours with both his professor and teaching assistant, and studying in a quiet environment. One of the strengths of his plan is that he decided to use more than one method (e.g., his weekly schedule and notes) to record his use of strategies (i.e., attending office hour appointments). Moreover, by displaying this plan in a chart, the student makes it easy for the reader to follow both when and how he plans to implement each strategy.

Areas for Improvement.   Although the student specifies how he will record his use of learning strategies and how he will keep track of his office hour appointments, he does not specify how he will record where he studies. A chart or structured diary would have been an easy means for him to record information related to his physical environment.

Strategic-Implementation Monitoring

Strengths.   The student adhered to his plan and provided concrete evidence of the reading assignments he completed (e.g., by marking them off on his syllabus and documenting his use of reading comprehension strategies), his attendance at class lectures (e.g., through his attendance sheet and notes using the note-making strategy), and his office hour appointments (e.g., by providing his weekly calendar and meeting notes). To determine if his strategies were working, he looked at his fifth quiz score (a B–) and decided that because his score exceeded his goal of attaining at least a C, he would continue with his plan.

Areas for Improvement.   The student could have improved his study by providing the reader with information about his physical environment (e.g., did he study in a quiet place as he had planned?). In addition, in the next section of his paper, the student mentions that he decided to use self-talk midway through his study. He should have addressed this change in this section of the paper.

Strategic-Outcome Monitoring

Strengths. The student demonstrates that he met his goal of improving his scores on the next two quizzes in his Policy, Planning, and Development Course by providing the reader with documentation of his quiz scores both before his study (e.g., one F, one D, and two Cs) and after his study (e.g., a B− and an A+).

Areas for Improvement. The student could have improved his study by discussing what he learned from his self-management study (e.g., what strategies were the most and least effective and what changes, if any, he would make in the future).

SELF-MANAGEMENT STUDY #3: MOTIVATION (I.E., REDUCING ANXIETY)

Self-Observation and Evaluation

Identifying my problem wasn't very difficult. I had an idea of what my problem was before I was given this assignment. I have realized it since the beginning of this class; however, I never took it into full consideration. I really began to notice my problem in the middle of this course when I completed the follow-up activities in chapter 5 (see Attachment 1). My answers to the first exercise, "Assessing Self-talk," indicate that I am full of anxiety and negative self-talk, and my answers to the second exercise, "Exploring Anxiety-Producing Situations in School," display my high test anxiety. My problem with anxiety is also evident on the anxiety scale of the Learning and Study Skills Inventory. My score of 14 in anxiety and worry about school performance is ranked extremely high among other college students.

After identifying my problem, I carefully examined my behavior and the way I handle my learning skills. I found that I display all of the different types of negative self-talk. At times, I find myself being a big worrier, a critic, a victim, and even a perfectionist. It sounds pretty crazy, but it's true. I display negative self-talk in many situations in my life where I undergo pressure and stress. For example, I talk negatively to myself when I prepare for tests, when assignments are due, or just when I'm stressed out with certain tasks and problems in my life. At times, my negative self-talk impacts my sense of self-worth, my self-efficacy, and even my performance (see Attachment 2). For example, in this course, my self-efficacy ratings are always lower than my quiz scores. In addition, my quiz scores in math (a course I am anxious about) are low. Although I am a hard worker who always persists and strives to do my best, I find that my best is never enough for me. I also find that my anxiety affects my self-esteem and views about myself. I seem to never be satisfied with what I accomplish.

I believe that my internal beliefs, perceptions, and behaviors contribute to my anxiety problem. My self-efficacy beliefs are mostly average or below average. This, in turn, causes me to start saying negative things about myself, which has an effect on my performance. I also use failure-avoiding techniques that build my anxiety. For example, I tend to put things off until the last minute, which makes me more stressed and prevents me from being satisfied with my level of performance. Now that I have recognized these factors, I have developed a plan that deals with all of this information.

Goal Setting and Strategic Planning

My goal for this study is to reduce my negative self-talk and procrastination so that I will feel less anxious and more confident in myself, and as a result improve my performance on the exams I take between November 16th and November 20th. To accomplish this goal, I have developed the following plan:

Strategies	*When*	*Method of Recording*
Weekly Schedule Schedule tasks so they are done ahead of time (preferably 1 week in advance).	Make a weekly schedule at the beginning of each week.	I will check off each task I complete on my schedule.
Self-talk Use positive self-talk to improve my confidence.	Each day (mornings and sometime evenings) I will speak to myself through a journal reflection.	Daily journal reflections
Meditation and Relaxation Techniques	Each day I will use one of the meditation and relaxation techniques in this book.	I will mark each time I practice these techniques and the results onto a weekly calendar.
Universal Writing Trick Sheet	Before taking my writing exam.	I will provide documentation of these procedures along with my daily journal reflections.

The first part of my plan entails making a weekly calendar and scheduling assignments early so I will complete them early—maybe even a week in advance. This should prevent me from procrastinating so I can reduce my stress and anxiety. The second part of my plan involves using more positive self-talk. I plan to speak to myself every day (mornings and sometimes evenings) for 1 week through a journal. During this time, I will assure myself that I can successfully accomplish each task I face. This should get me started using positive self-talk in my everyday life and should boost my confidence level. The third part of my plan involves using the meditation and relaxation techniques in this book each day to help reduce my anxiety and stress. This should help me deal with the physical aspect of my anxiety problem. The last part of my plan involves using the Universal Smart Test Taker Trick sheet that my English professor recently gave me. When I take writing exams, I become nervous and uptight. At times, my mind even goes blank. I feel this sheet will help reduce my anxiety as I prepare my next written exam (i.e., my Art of Asia paper).

Strategy Implementation and Monitoring

I implemented all of the strategies as specified on my plan. I started by scheduling time on my weekly schedule so that I would have plenty of time to write my Art of Asia midterm paper and study for my math and educational psychology exams (see Attachment 3). I completed all of my daily tasks as planned, except for reviewing my readings for my educational psychology class on Sunday. Then, during my exam week, I used several meditation and relaxation techniques (see Attachment 4). Each day I described how these strategies made me feel prior to my exams. As you can see, I felt that these techniques really helped me ease my tension and test anxiety. I also used the Universal Writing Tricks sheet that was provided by my professor to help me write my Art of Asia midterm [note: the student provided a list of these strategies in her evidence section]. Finally, I used my self-talk reflection journal to record my self-talk each day throughout the week [see Attachment 5].

Strategic-Outcome Monitoring

My plan was somewhat effective, but not as effective as I hoped it would be. On the one hand, I found that my weekly schedule helped me stay on task and prevented me from procrastinating. I began studying for my math and educational psychology tests, and writing my papers several days in advance (see Attachment 3). I feel that because I was able to stick to this schedule, I was able to reduce my anxiety. In addition, I feel that the meditation and relaxation techniques and universal writing tricks I implemented (see Attachment 4) effectively reduced my anxiety and stress levels [note: the student included the Universal Writing Trick form]. The grades I earned in my math and writing courses improved during this time (see Attachment 6). Furthermore, my self-efficacy ratings and quiz scores in my educational psychology course became more aligned after implementing these strategies (see Attachment 6). On the other hand, the one thing I am still struggling with is my negative self-talk and confidence level (see Attachment 6). My reflection journals demonstrate that although I am beginning to use positive self-talk, I still display a lot of self-doubt. I build a fear of failure, and this fear contributes to my anxiety.

Conclusion

I can't completely say that this case study eliminated my anxiety problem. I also can't say that all of the strategies I used were fully effective. I also can't say that I am a changed person. However, I do know that this case study helped me reduce my anxiety. It also helped me become more aware of my problem. Before this study, I never took notice of my problem. I never really understood how and why it was there.

This case study increased my knowledge of the problem I have within myself. It made me more determined to change my attitude. I used to be in complete fear of failure. I can't say that I am not in fear of failure anymore because I'd be lying. But now I can look at my mistakes as stepping-stones to succeed in life. I can also see my mistakes as a means to enhance my motivation and feel better about myself. As I completed this case study, I explored new ways to expand my learning capabilities. I also applied skills that I can use in the future. I found out that I am capable of changing my behavior to achieve my full potential not only for my education, but also for myself.

Evidence

Attachment 1: Chapter 5 Follow-Up Activities 1 and 2.

Activity 1. Assess Self-Talk

During the next week, monitor your self-talk and evaluate how it affected your motivation and self-confidence. Consider all situations and tasks in which you engage—academic, athletic and recreational, social, occupational, and personal. Include in your report the following information: date, situation (e.g., academic), setting (describe where you were and what you were trying to accomplish), and report the self-talk as specifically as possible. Finally, discuss what strategies you used to deal with any negative self-talk.

Date: Wednesday 11/4
Setting: Computer lab: typing peer review rough draft for English due the next day
Self-talk: Anxiety and Worry—"How am I going to do this?" etc.
Strategy: None.

Date: Thursday 11/5
Setting: Dorm—studying for my math quiz
Self-talk: "I'll never pass this quiz."
Strategy: None.

Date: Monday 11/9
Setting: Class during my Arts of Asia exam
Self-talk: nervous worrier—although I studied well, I was very negative and I worried about my performance.
Strategy: None.

Comments: I find myself full of anxiety and negative self-talk. I do not use positive self-talk.

Activity 2: Explore Anxiety-Producing Situations in School

The following is a list of items the student indicated she identified with:

a. Worry about performance
   I should have reviewed more. I'll never get through.
   My mind is blank, I'll never get the answer. I must really be stupid.
   I knew this stuff yesterday. What is wrong with me?
   I can't remember a thing. This always happens to me.

b. Worry about bodily reactions
   I'm sweating all over—it's really hot in here.
   My stomach is going crazy, churning and jumping all over.
   Here it comes—I'm getting really tense again. Normal people just don't get like this.

c. Worry about how others are doing.
   I know everyone's doing better than I am.
   I must be the dumbest one in the group.
   I am going to be the last one done again. I must be really stupid.
   No one else seems to be having trouble. Am I the only one?

d. Worry about the possible negative consequences
   If I fail this test, I'll never get into the program.
   I'll never graduate.
   I'll think less of myself.
   I'll be embarrassed.

Effective strategies: Try to use positive self-talk to counter my negative statements.

Attachment 2: Previous Performance Educational Psychology

EDPT	1	2	3	4	5	6	7	8	9	Total
Quiz score	10	9	8	7	10	8	9	10	9	80
Efficacy score	8	6	5.5	6	6.5	7	8	8	6	61

Midterm #1: 83%

Math

Math	1	2	3	4
Quiz score	6	6	6	7

Attachment 3: Weekly Schedule

Week of 11/9–11/15

Mon. Nov. 9	Tues. Nov. 10	Wed. Nov. 11	Thurs. Nov. 12	Fri. Nov 13	Sat. Nov. 14	Sun. Nov. 15
		Write Rough draft for assign. #4 Finished at 4:30 p.m.	Writing 8 p.m. Revise rough draft Finished at 9:16 p.m.	2 p.m. write Arts of Asia rough draft Also typed final paper		1. Review math ch. 5 2. Review educ. psych. Did not complete

Week of 11/16–11/20

Mon. Nov. 16	Tues. Nov. 17	Wed. Nov. 18	Thurs. Nov. 19	Fri. Nov. 20
1. Revise Art of Asia rough draft Finished at 5:30 p.m. 2. Review Educ. Psych. Finished at 10:30 p.m.	Math quiz 5.3–5.5	Writing assign. #4 due Review Educ. Psych. Finished at 11:30 p.m.	Exam 2. Educ. Psych.	Math test (5 & 6) Art of Asia paper due

Attachment 4: Chart of My Anxiety-Reducing Techniques

Date	Relaxation and Meditation Techniques	Result
Nov. 17	7:45 Before math quiz I used the diaphragmatic breathing technique for 7 minutes. (math quiz at 8:00 a.m.)	I feel that I had rhythm to perform better. It allowed me to open my feelings and calm down.
Nov. 18	9:30 a.m. I meditated with soft, slow music to relax from my studies and work for 15 minutes.	I feel it eased my tension for my math quiz. I was able to calm down and felt less uptight and nervous.
Nov. 19	7:45 a.m. I relaxed with soft slow music for 15 minutes. (EDPT exam at 9 a.m.)	I relaxed and felt prepared for my test. It reduced my stress and nervousness. Beforehand I was afraid that I might forget the information I had learned. It made me less uptight and more energized to take the test.
Nov. 20	8:45 a.m. I meditated to soft music. (math exam)	It reduced the anxiety I had because of the overwhelming work I did in the past 2 weeks. I feel that it relaxed me for my math test.

Attachment 5: Self-Talk Reflection Journal

Mon. Nov. 16th

Today is the first day I implemented my plan. Today I had nothing due, but this week I have a load of assignments to turn in. Furthermore, I have two papers due, a quiz, and two tests. I've got to believe I can do all of this. I've done it before. It is 9:30 p.m. right now. I guess I can start studying. I can achieve . . . I can achieve . . . I'm trying to think positive. This is hard. I'm saying the words, but do I mean it? I've always been able to keep my head up before. Don't worry, this week will be fine! I know I can do it.

Tues. Nov. 17th

Well, I'm about to head to class. It's 7:45. I've got a quiz in this class. It's only two sections—I can handle it. I didn't study that hard, though, but I kind of know the material. I was worrying about my other assignments. Well, I know it will be easy and just right. Oh, it's 7:50 a.m. Got to go. I'll pass!

Well, I'm back now and it's 3:30. I'm about to go to work. The quiz was okay—I think I did well. I was speaking to myself, trying to think positive. I guess I'll find out Thursday how I did and I'll record it in here. I won't be able to write in here tonight, so I guess this is it.

Wed. Nov. 18th

Well, today is my mom's and cousin's birthday. This should be a good day. I've got to think positive today. It's about 8:35 a.m. and I'm about to go to my 9 a.m. class right now. Today I will turn in my fourth writing assignment for my writing class. I worked hard on it all last week. I think I did pretty well. I always get good grades on my papers. It had better be good! Well, I'll be back later.

Hello, I'm back from the library and it's 11:30 p.m. I just finished reviewing for my educ. psych. 110 test. I feel pretty confident, but I'm worried that I'll forget some information. Do you think I'll forget? I studied pretty well. Well, I'm going to call my mom right now, and then sleep or maybe watch television?

Thurs. Nov. 19th

Gosh, I hate waking up early for this 8 a.m. class. Today I have my EDPT 110 test at 9 a.m. Aaah! I studied, but I don't know. I'm afraid I'll fail. I know I can do it. I did well on Exam 1. Anyhow, I'm getting my math quiz back from Tuesday. That should be cool! Well, it's 7:15 a.m. right now and I'm hungry. I think I'll get some food downstairs—I might get a stomachache before the test. I hope I pass!

Well, I'm back from work. It's 3:30 p.m. I'm about to watch televison right now. Then I'm going to study for my math test tomorrow. It's pretty easy, so I think I can do it. Well, I can't wait until this weekend, when I can relax. My friend is having a party that should be fun and I'm going home Friday afternoon—Yes! Gotta study, Bye

Fri. Nov. 20th

It's 7:30 a.m. I work up early to review for my math test. I'm really scared right now. I'm not very confident. I reviewed a little here and there. I know the material though. I also have a paper due for my Art of Asia class at 2 p.m. today. I finished it a while ago, so at least that stress is gone. I can't wait to go home this weekend. I will soon be able to see my friends again. I guess I'll leave for class now.

I'm back from my math test. It wasn't as hard as I thought it would be. I don't want to be too confident because it might turn out negative. I hope I did well. Well, I'm going to turn in my Art of Asia paper. Then I am going to go home . . . Yeah!

Attachment 6: Grades After Using My Strategies

Future educ. psych. quizzes

Quiz	7	8
Efficacy score	7	8

Educ. psych. midterm: 94%
Math quiz: 10/10
Math exam: 90%
Art of Asia paper: 92%

ANALYSIS OF SELF-MANAGEMENT STUDY #3

Self-Observation and Evaluation

Strengths. The student does a good job identifying her anxiety problem and describing both internal factors (e.g., low confidence, and low self-efficacy) and behaviors (e.g., negative self-talk) that contribute to her problem. Further, she provides the reader with evidence to support her self-evaluation: her scores on the Learning and Study Skills Inventory, answers to the follow-up activities in chapter 5, quiz and self-efficacy scores in this course, and her quiz scores in her math course that support her self-evaluation claims.

Areas for Improvement.   The student could have improved her study by completing a more thorough analysis of her self-talk by listing and classifying each negative statement she made. She mentions that her self-talk can be classified as that of a worrier, critic, victim, and perfectionist, but she does not support this claim with evidence. If she had classified each statement she made, she would have been better able to determine the type of positive self-talk she needs to counteract her beliefs and ultimately change her behavior. In the next section of her paper, the student mentions that her tendency to procrastinate contributes to her anxiety. Here she could have improved her study by providing the reader with information on how she uses her time, as well as the extent of her procrastination.

Goal Setting and Strategic Planning

Strengths.   The student sets a goal to reduce her negative self-talk and procrastination so she will feel less anxious and more confident in herself and ultimately improve scores on the exams she takes between November 16th and 20th. By listing her grades in her math and educational psychology courses, she made it possible to monitor her progress toward this goal. Further, her plan, which includes monitoring her self-talk through a self-reflection journal and monitoring her anxiety though a chart, made it possible for her to monitor her anxiety and confidence levels. The student selects a variety of strategies such as breaking tasks down into manageable parts, scheduling tasks ahead of time, and using positive self-talk, meditation and relaxation techniques, and techniques suggested by her professor to combat her problem. Her strategic-planning chart makes it easy for the reader to follow her use of each of these strategies.

Areas for Improvement.   The student could have improved her study by providing more information about the extent of her negative self-talk and procrastination prior to her study. This would have enabled her to determine if the strategies she implements reduce these behaviors. Likewise, she could have provided information regarding her anxiety confidence levels both prior to and during her study. This information would have made it easier for her to assess whether or not she met her goal. Finally, although the student provided information about her previous academic performance in her educational psychology and math courses, she did not provide any information about her previous performance in her Art of Asia course. Thus, it is not possible to determine if she improved her performance in this class.

Strategic Implementation and Monitoring

Strengths.   The student implemented all of the strategies in her plan and provided the reader with evidence of the fact she scheduled tasks in advance and used both positive self-talk and relaxation and meditation techniques.

Areas for Improvement. The student used her daily reflection journal to record her self-talk once or twice each day. In this journal it is clear that the student encounters many negative beliefs and perceptions, yet does not challenge each negative statement she makes. She would have learned a lot more about herself if she had recorded each negative statement she made throughout the day, each positive counterstatement, and her perceptions of whether each counterstatements worked (e.g., on a chart). This information would have enabled her to determine which types of counterstatements are the most and least effective and adjust her behavior accordingly. In addition, although the student provided documentation of the Universal Writer Tricks Form that she used to help her with her Art of Asia exam, she did not provide the reader with any evidence that she actually used these strategies.

Strategic-Outcome Monitoring

Strengths. The student demonstrates that she met her goal by improving her performance in her math and educational psychology courses. In addition, she provides support for the fact that she felt more confident and less anxious through her self-reflection journal and relaxation and meditation chart.

Thus, her conclusions are consistent with the evidence she provides.

Areas for Improvement. The student could have strengthened her study by comparing both her use of negative self-talk and her tendency to procrastinate before and after her study. This information would have enabled her to determine if her strategies helped her accomplished her goal (i.e., to reduce these behaviors). In addition, the student could have improved her study by providing information on her previous performance in her Art of Asia class. This information would have enabled the reader to determine if the 92% score she earned was an improvement over the previous scores.

REFERENCES

Alberto, P. A., & Troutman, A. C. (1986). *Applied behavior analysis for teachers* (2nd ed.). Columbus, OH: Merrill.

Ames, C. (1992). Classrooms: Goals, structures, and student motivation. *Journal of Educational Psychology, 84,* 261–271.

Ames, C., & Archer, J. (1988). Achievement goals in the classroom: Students' learning strategies and motivation processes. *Journal of Educational Psychology, 80,* 260–267.

Ames, R., & Lau, S. (1982). An attributional analysis of student help-seeking in an academic setting. *Journal of Educational Psychology, 74,* 414–423.

Aronson, J. (2002). Stereotype threat: Contending and coping with unnerving expectations (pp. 279–301). In J. Aronson (Ed.), *Improving academic achievement: Impact of psychological factors on education.* San Diego, CA: Academic Press.

Baker, L. (1989). Metacognition, comprehension monitoring, and the adult reader. *Educational Psychology Review, 1,* 3–38.

Bandura, A. (1982). Self-efficacy mechanism in human agency. *American Psychologist, 37,* 122–147.

Bargh, J. A., & Chartrand, T. L. (1999). The unbearable automaticity of being. *American Psychologist, 54,* 462–479.

Benson, H. (1976). *The relaxation response.* New York: Avon.

Bliss, E. (1983). *Doing it now.* New York: Bantam.

Bourne, E. J. (1995). *The anxiety & phobia workbook* (2nd ed.). Oakland, CA: New Harbinger.

Bower, G. H., Clark, M. C., Lesgold, A., & Winzenz, D. (1969). Hierarchical retrieval schemas in recall of categorized word lists. *Journal of Verbal Learning and Verbal Behavior, 8,* 323–343.

Bransford, J. D. (1979). *Human cognition: Learning, understanding, and remembering.* Belmont, CA: Wadsworth.

Bransford, J. D., & Johnson, M. K. (1972). Contextual prerequisites for understanding: Some investigations of comprehension and recall. *Journal of Verbal Learning and Verbal Behavior, 11,* 717–726.

Britton, B. K., & Glynn, S. M. (1989). Mental management and creativity: A cognitive model of time management for intellectual productivity. In J. A. Glover, R. R. Ronning, & C. R. Reynolds (Eds.), *Handbook of creativity* (pp. 429–440). New York: Plenum.

Britton, B. K., & Tesser, A. (1991). Effects of time management practices on college grades. *Journal of Educational Psychology, 83,* 405–410.

Burka, J. B., & Yuen, L. M. (1983). *Procrastination: Why you do it and what to do about it.* Reading, MA: Addison-Wesley.

Butler, P. E. (1981). *Talking to yourself: Learning the language of self-support.* San Francisco: Harper & Row.

Cartwright, C. A., & Cartwright, G. P. (1984). *Developing observation skills* (2nd ed.). New York: McGraw-Hill.

Chaney, L. H. (1991). Teaching students time management skills. *Business Education Forum, 45,* 8–9.

Cortina, J., Elder, J., & Gonnet, K. (1992). *Comprehending college textbooks* (2nd ed.). New York: McGraw-Hill.

Covington, M. V. (1992). *Making the grade: A self-worth perspective on motivation and school reform.* New York: Cambridge University Press.

Covington, M. V., & Omelich, C. (1979). Effort: The double-edged sword in school achievement. *Journal of Educational Psychology, 71,* 169, 182.

Davis, M., Eshelman, E. R., & McKay, M. (2000). *The relaxation & stress reduction workbook* (5th ed.). Oakland, CA: New Harbinger Publications.

Deese, J., & Deese, E. K. (1994). *How to study* (4th ed.). New York: McGraw-Hill.

Dembo, M. H. (1994). *Applying educational psychology in the classroom* (5th ed.). White Plains, NY: Longman.

Dole, J., Duffy, G., Roehler, L., & Person, P. D. (1991). Moving from the old to the new: Research on reading comprehension instruction. *Review of Educational Research, 61,* 239–264.

Dweck, C. S., & Leggett, E. L. (1988). A social-cognitive approach to motivation and personality. *Journal of Personality and Social Psychology, 95,* 256–273.

Eggen, P., & Kauchak, D. (1997). *Educational psychology: Windows on classrooms* (3rd. ed.). Columbus, OH: Merrill.

Ellis, A. (1962). *Reason and emotion in psychotherapy.* New York: Stuart.

Ellis, A., & Knaus, W. J. (1977). *Overcoming procrastination.* New York: New American Library.

Erikson, E. (1968). *Identity, youth, and crisis.* New York: Norton.

Ferrari, J. R., & Johnson, J. L., & McCown, W. G. (1995). *Procrastination and task avoidance: Theory, research, and treatment.* New York: Plenum.

Ferrari, J. R. (2001). Getting things done on time: Conquering procrastination. In C. R. Snyder (Ed.), *Coping with stress: Effective people and processes* (pp. 30–46). New York: Oxford University Press.

Flett, G. L., Hewitt, P. L., & Martin, T. R. (1995). Dimensions of perfectionism and procrastination. In J. R. Ferrari, J. L. Johnson, & W. G. McCown (Eds.), *Procrastination and task avoidance: Theory, research, and treatment* (pp. 113–136). New York: Plenum.

Frender, G. (1990). *Learning to learn.* Nashville, TN: Incentive.

Gagné, E. D. (1985). *The cognitive psychology of school learning.* Boston: Little, Brown.

Gagné, E. D., Yekovich, C. W., & Yekovich, C. W. (1993). *The cognitive psychology of school learning* (2nd. ed.). New York: HarperCollins.

Gallwey, W. T. (1974). *The inner game of tennis.* New York: Random House.

Garcia, T. (1995). The role of motivational strategies in self-regulated learning. *New Directions in Teaching and Learning, 63,* 29–42.

Garfield, H. Z. (1984). *Peak performance*. New York: Warner.

Gaskins, I., & Elliot, T. (1991). *Implementing cognitive strategy instruction across the school*. Cambridge, MA: Brookline.

Glaser, R. (1996). Changing the agency for learning: Acquiring expert performance. In K. Ericsson (Ed. 1996), *The road to excellence: The acquisition of expert performance in the arts and sciences, sports and games*. Mahwah, NJ: Lawrence Erlbaum Associates.

Goetz, E. T., Alexander, P. A., & Ash, M. J. (1992). *Educational psychology: A classroom perspective*. New York: Macmillan.

Gordon, T. (2001). *Leader effectiveness training: Proven skills for leading today's business into tomorrow*. Berkeley, CA: Berkeley Publishing Group.

Halpern, D. F. (1996). *Thought and knowledge: Introduction to critical thinking* (3rd. ed.). Mahwah, NJ: Lawrence Erlbaum Associates.

Harackiewicz, J. M., Barron, K. E., Tauer, J. M., Carter, S. M., & Elliot, A. J. (2000), Short-term and long-term consequences of achievement goals: Predicting interest and performance over time. *Journal of Educational Psychology, 92,* 316–330.

Harackiewicz, J. M., Barron, K. E., Carter, S. M., Lehto, A. T., & Elliot, A. J. (1997). Predictors and consequences of achievement goals in the college classroom: Maintaining interest and making the grade. *Journal of Educational Psychology, 73,* 1284–1295.

Hattie, J., Biggs, J., & Purdue, N. (1996). Effects of learning skills interventions on student learning: A meta-analysis. *Review of Educational Research, 66,* 99–136.

Heiman, M., & Slomianko, J. (1993). *Success in college and beyond*. Cambridge, MA: Learning to Learn.

Hembree, R. (1988). Correlates, causes, effects, and treatment of test anxiety. *Review of Educational Research, 58,* 47–77.

Holt, J. (1982). *How children fail* (rev. ed.). New York: Delta.

Isaacson, R. M. (2002, April). *Shocking college students into self-regulation: When hand-holding and jump-starting isn't working*. Paper presented at the annual meeting of the American Educational Research Association, New Orleans, LA.

Jalomo, R. (1995). *Latino students in transition: An analysis of the first-year experience in community college*. Unpublished doctoral dissertation, Arizona State University, Tempe.

Jefferson County Schools. (1982). *Senior high study skills booklet*. Jefferson County, Colorado. CO: Author.

Johnson, D. W. (2003). *Reaching out: Interpersonal effectiveness and self-actualization* (8th ed.). Boston: Allyn & Bacon.

Johnson, D. W., & Johnson, R. T. (1987). *Learning together and alone* (2nd ed.). Upper Saddle River, NJ: Prentice Hall.

Johnson, D. W., Johnson, R. T., & Holubec, E. (1994). *The new circles of learning*. Alexandria, VA: Association for Supervision and Curriculum Development.

Jones, G., & Hardy, L. (1990). *Stress and performance in sport*. Chichester, England: Wiley.

Kanfer, F. H., & Goldstein, A. P. (Eds.) (1991). *Helping people change: A textbook of methods* (4th ed.). New York: Pergamon Press.

Kiewra, K. A. (1989). A review of note-taking: The encoding-storage paradigm and beyond. *Educational Psychology Review, 1,* 147–172.

Kiewra, K. A., & DuBois, N. F. (1998). *Learning to learn.* Boston: Allyn & Bacon.

Knauss, W. (2002). Procrastination, blame, and change, *Journal of Social Behavior and Personality, 15,* 153–166.

Kuhl, J., & Beckman, J. (1985). Historical perspectives in the study of action control. In J. Kuhl & J. Beckman (Eds.), *Action control: From cognition to behavior* (pp. 89–100). New York: Springer-Verlag.

Larson, R., & Richard, M. (1991). Boredom in the middle school years: Blaming schools versus students. *American Journal of Education, 99,* 418–443.

Levin, J. R. (1986). Four cognitive principles of learning-strategy instruction. *Educational Psychologist, 21*(1/2), 3–17.

Levy, B. (1996). Improving memory in old age through implicit self-stereotyping. *Journal of Personality and Social Psychology, 71,* 1092–1107.

Light, R. J. (2001). *Making the most of college: Students speak their minds.* Cambridge, MA: Harvard University Press.

Locke, E. A. (1968). Toward a theory of task motivation and incentives. *Organizational Behavior and Human Performance, 3,* 157–189.

Locke, E. A., & Latham, G. P. (1990). *A theory of goal setting and task performance.* Englewood Cliffs, NJ: Prentice Hall.

Loftus, E. F. (1980). *Memory: Surprising new insights into how we remember and why we forget.* Reading, MA: Addison-Wesley.

Marcia, J. E. (1967). Ego identity status: Relationship to change in self-esteem, "general maladjustment," and authoritarianism. *Journal of Personality, 35,* 118–133.

Marcia, J. E. (1980). Identity in adolescence. In J. Adelson (Ed.), *Handbook of adolescent psychology.* New York: Wiley.

Martin, G., & Pear, J. (1988). *What it is and how to do it* (3rd Ed.). Englewood Cliffs, NJ: Prentice Hall.

McCombs, B., & Encinias, P. (1987). *Goal setting. Coping strategies program.* Unpublished manuscript, University of Colorado at Denver.

McKay, M., Davis, M., & Fanning, P. (1997). *Thought & feelings: Taking control of your moods and your life.* Oakland, CA: New Harbinger.

McWhorter, K. T. (1995). *College reading & study skills* (6th ed.). New York: HarperCollins.

McWhorter, K. T. (1996). *Study and critical thinking skills in college* (3rd ed.). New York: HarperCollins.

Meichenbaum, D. (1977). *Cognitive behavior modification.* New York: Plenum.

Merrell, K. W. (2001). *Helping students overcome depression and anxiety.* New York: Guilford.

Midgley, C., Kaplan, A., & Middleton, M. (2001). Performance-approach goals: Good for what, for whom, under what circumstances, and what cost? *Journal of Educational Psychology, 93,* 77–86.

Miller, G. A. (1956). The magical number seven, plus or minus two: Some limits on our capacity to process information. *Psychological Review, 63,* 81–97.

National Center for Education Statistics. Washington, DC. (1998). *Trends in academic progress* (NCES 97–985).

Naveh-Benjamin, M., McKeachie, W., & Lin, Y. G. (1987). Two types of test-anxious students: Support for an information processing model. *Journal of Educational Psychology, 19,* 131–136.

Newman, R. S. (1991). Goals and self-regulated learning: What motivates children to seek academic help. In M. L. Maehr & P. L. Pintrich (Eds.), *Advances in motivation and achievement* (Vol. 7, pp. 151–183). Greenwich, CT: JAI.

Newman, R. S., & Goldin, L. (1990). Children's reluctance to seek help with schoolwork. *Journal of Educational Psychology, 82,* 92–100.

Newman, R. S., & Schwager, M. T. (1992). Student perceptions and academic help-seeking. In D. H. Schunk & M. T. Meece (Eds.), *Student perceptions in the classroom (*pp. 123–146). Hillsdale, NJ: Lawrence Erlbaum Associates.

Ormrod, J, E. (1995). *Human learning* (2nd ed.). Englewood Cliffs, NJ: Prentice Hall.

Ormrod, J. E. (1998). *Educational psychology: Principles and applications* (2nd ed.). Englewood Cliffs, NJ: Prentice Hall.

Ottens, A. J. (1991). *Coping with academic anxiety* (2nd ed.). New York: Rosen.

Paris, S. G. (1988, April). *Fusing skill and will in children's learning and schooling.* Paper presented at the annual meeting of the American Educational Research Association, New Orleans.

Pauk, W. (1993). *How to study in college.* Boston: Houghton-Mifflin.

Pekrun, R., Goetz, T., & Titz, W., & Perry, R. P. (2002). Academic emotions in students' self-regulated learning and achievement: A program of qualitative and quantitative research. *Educational Psychologist, 37,* 91–105.

Peterson, K. (2002, May, 30). College weighs on minds: Depression rates soaring for students. *USA Today,* p. 7D

Peurifoy, R. Z. (1995). *Anxiety, phobias, and panic.* New York: Warner.

Pintrich, P. R. (1994). Student motivation in the college classroom. In K. W. Prichard & R. M. Sawywer (Eds.), *Handbook of college teaching: Theory and applications* (pp. 23–43). Westport, CT: Greenwood.

Prochaska, J. O., & Prochaska, J. M. (1999). Why don't continents move? Why don't people change? *Journal of Psychotherapy Integration, 9,* 83–102.

Ratcliff, J. L. (1995). *Realizing the potential: Improving postsecondary teaching, learning, and assessment* (National report of the National Center on Postsecondary Teaching, Learning, and Assessment). University Park, PA: National Center on Postsecondary Teaching, Learning, and Assessment.

Reeve, J. (1996). *Motivating others: Nurturing inner motivational resources.* Boston: Allyn & Bacon.

Reglin, G. L., & Adams, D. R. (1990). Why Asian American high school students have higher grade point averages and SAT scores than other high school students. *The High School, Journal, 73,* 143–149.

Reisberg, L. (2000, January 28). Students stress is rising, especially among women. *Chronicle of Higher Education, 46*(21), A49.

Rosenberg, E. L. (1998). Levels of analysis and the organization of affect. *Review of General Psychology, 2,* 247–270.

Schacter, D. L. (2001). *The seven sins of memory: How the mind forgets and remembers.* Boston: Houghton Mifflin.

Scharf, D. (1985). *Studying smart: Time management for college students.* New York: Barnes & Noble.

Schunk, D. H. (1982). Verbal self-regulation as a facilitator of children's achievement and self-efficacy. *Human Learning, 1,* 265–277.

Schunk, D. H. (1989). Self-efficacy and cognitive skill learning. In C. Ames & R. Ames (Eds.), *Research on motivation in education: Goals and cognition* (Vol. 3, pp. 13–44). San Diego, CA: Academic Press.

Schunk, D. H. (1991). Goal setting and self-evaluation: A social cognitive perspective on self-regulation. In M. L. Maehr & P. R. Pintrich (Eds.), *Advances in motivation and achievement* (Vol. 7, pp. 85–113). Greenwich, CT: JAI.

Schunk, D. H., & Zimmerman, B. J. (Eds.). (1994). *Self-regulation of learning and performance: Issues and educational applications.* Hillsdale, NJ: Lawrence Erlbaum Associates.

Semb, G., Glick, D. M., & Spencer, R. E. (1979). Student withdrawals and delayed work patterns in self-paced psychology courses. *Teaching of Psychology, 6,* 23–26.

Simon, S. B., Howe, L. W., & Kirschenbaum, H. (1972). *Values clarification: A handbook of practical strategies for teachers and students.* New York: Hart.

Smith, H. (1994). *The 10 natural laws of successful time and life management.* New York: Warner.

Smith, R. M. (1982). *Learning how to learn: Applied theory for adults.* New York: Cambridge University Press.

Spencer, S. J., Steele, C. M., & Quinn, D. M. (1999). Stereotype threat and women's math performance. *Journal of Experimental Social Psychology, 35,* 4–28.

Steele, C. M. (1999, August). *Thin ice: "Stereotype threat" and Black college students.* Retrieved from The Atlantic Monthly online (www.theatlantic.com/issues/99aug/9908stereotype.htm).

Steele, C. M., & Aronson, J. (1995). Stereotype threat and the intellectual test performance of African-Americans. *Journal of Personality and Social Psychology, 69,* 797–811.

Steele, C. M., Spencer, S. J., Hummel, M., Carter, K., Harber, K., Schoem, D., & Nisbett, R. (1997). *African-American college achievement: A "wise" intervention.* Unpublished manuscript, Stanford University.

Stepich, D. A., & Newby, T. J. (1988). Anological instruction within the information processing paradigm: Effective means to facilitate learning. *Instructional Science, 17,* 129–144.

Stipek, D. (1998). *Motivation to learn: From theory to practice* (3rd ed.). Boston: Allyn & Bacon.

Tobias, S., & Everson, H. (2000). Assessing metacognitive knowledge monitoring. In G. Schraw & J. Impara (Eds.), *Issues in measurement of metacognition* (pp. 147–222). Lincoln, NE: Buros Institude of Mental Measurement.

Turner, J. E., Husman, J., & Schallert, D. L. (2002). The importance of students' goals in their emotional experience of academic failure: Investigating the precursors and consequences of shame. *Educational Psychologist, 37,* 79–89.

Underwood, B. J. (1961). Ten years of massed practice on distributed practice. *Psychological Review, 68,* 229–247.

Urman, H. N. (1982). *Ethnic differences and the effects of test-wiseness training on verbal and math achievement.* Unpublished doctoral dissertation, University of Southern California, Los Angeles.

Van Blerkom, D. L. (1994). *College study skills: Becoming a strategic learner.* Belmont, CA: Wadsworth.

Vasts, R., Haith, M. M., & Miller, S. A. (1992). *Child psychology: The modern science.* New York: Wiley.

Waterman, A. S. (1982). Identity development from adolescence to adulthood: An extension of theory and a review of research. *Developmental Psychology, 18,* 341–358.

Waterman, A. S. (1993). Developmental perspectives on identity formation: From adolescence to adulthood. In J. E. Marcia, A. S. Waterman, D. R. Matteson, S. L. Archer, & J. L. Orlofsky (Eds.), *Ego identity: A handbook for psychosocial research* (pp. 42–68). New York: Springer-Verlag.

Watson, D. L., & Tharp, R. G. (1992). *Self-directed behavior: Self-modification for personal adjustment.* Pacific Grove, CA: Brooks/Cole.

Wegner, D. M., & Wheatley, T. (1999). Apparent mental causation: Sources of the experience of will. *American Psychologist, 54,* 480–492.

Weiner, B. (1986). *An attributional theory of motivation and emotion.* New York: Springer-Verlag.

Weiner, B., & Kukla, A. (1970). An attributional analysis of achievement motivation. *Journal of Personality and Social Psychology, 15,* 1–20.

Weinstein, C. E., Schulte, A. C., & Palmer, D. R. (1987). *LASSI: Learning and Study Strategies Inventory.* Clearwater, FL: H&H.

Weinstein, C. L., & Mayer, R. E. (1986). The teaching of learning strategies. In M. Wittrock (Ed.), *Handbook of research on teaching* (3rd ed., pp. 315–327). New York: Macmillan.

Wolff, F. I., & Marsnik, N. C. (1992). *Perceptive listening* (2nd ed.). Fort Worth, TX: Harcourt Brace.

Wolters, C. A. (1998). Self-regulated learning and college students' regulation of motivation. *Journal of Educational Psychology, 90,* 224–235.

Youngs, B. B. (1985). *Stress in children: How to recognize, avoid, and overcome it.* New York: Arbor House.

Zeidner, M. (1995). Adaptive coping with test situations: A review of literature. *Educational Psychologist, 30,* 123–133.

Zimmerman, B. J. (1989). *Self-regulated learning and academic achievement: Theory, research, and practice.* New York: Springer-Verlag.

Zimmerman, B. J. (1998a). Academic studying and the development of personal skill: A self-regulatory perspective. *Educational Psychologist, 33*(2/3), 73–86.

Zimmerman, B. J. (1998b). Developing self-fulfilling cycles of academic regulation: An analysis of exemplary instructional models. In D. L. Schunk & B. J. Zimmerman (Eds.), *Self-regulated learning. From teaching to self-reflective practice* (pp. 1–19). New York: Guilford.

Zimmerman, B. J., Bonner, S., & Kovach, R. (1996). *Developing self-regulated learners: Beyond achievement to self-efficacy.* Washington, DC: American Psychological Association.

Zimmerman, B. J., & Martinez-Pons, M. (1986). Development of a structured interview for assessing student use of self-regulated learning strategies. *American Educational Research Journal, 23,* 614–628.

Zimmerman, B. J., & Martinez-Pons, M. (1988). Construct validation of a strategy model of student self-regulation. *Journal of Educational Psychology, 80,* 284–290.

Zimmerman, B. J., & Risemberg, R. (1997). Self-regulatory dimensions of academic learning and motivation. In G. D. Phye (Ed.), *Handbook of academic learning: Construction of knowledge* (pp. 105–125). San Diego, CA: Academic Press.

Author Index

Subject Index